Business Unit Strategy

CBI Series in Practical Strategy

Other titles in this Series are:

Hedberg et al./Virtual Organisations and Beyond: Discovering Imaginary Systems

McNamee/Strategic Market Planning: A Blueprint for Success

Hussey & Jenster/Competitor Analysis: Turning Intelligence into Success

Mockler/Multinational Strategic Alliances

Hussey/Strategy and Planning: A Manager's Guide

Business Unit Strategy

Eli Segev

JOHN WILEY & SONS, LTD
Chichester • New York • Weinheim • Brisbane • Singapore • Toronto

National 01243 779777
International (+44) 1243 779777
e-mail (for orders and customer service enquiries): cs-books@wiley.co.uk
Visit our Home Page on http://www.wiley.co.uk
or http://www.wiley.com

Other Wiley Editorial Offices

John Wiley & Sons, Inc., 605 Third Avenue,
New York, NY 10158-0012, USA

WILEY-VCH GmbH, Pappelallee 3,
D-69469 Weinheim, Germany

Jacaranda Wiley Ltd, 33 Park Road, Milton,
Queensland 4064, Australia

John Wiley & Sons (Asia) Pte Ltd, 2 Clementi Loop #02-01,
Jin Xing Distripark, Singapore 129809

John Wiley & Sons (Canada) Ltd, 22 Worcester Road,
Rexdale, Ontario M9W 1L1, Canada

Library of Congress Cataloging-in-Publication Data

A catalogue record for this book is available from the Library of Congress

British Library Cataloguing in Publication Data

A catalogue record for this book is available from the British Library

ISBN 0-471-49993-5

Typeset in 11/13pt Times by Laser Words, Madras, India.
Printed and bound in Great Britain by Biddles Ltd, Guildford and King's Lynn.
This book is printed on acid-free paper responsibly manufactured from sustainable forestry, in which at least two trees are planted for each one used for paper production.

Contents

Series Foreword

The aim of this series is to provide managers with books on strategy, strategic management and strategic change, which are helpful, practical, and provide guidance for the practical application of sound concepts in real situations. It is thus very welcome that a number of the books in the series should be selected for publication under the logo of the CBI, whose member organisations are very much concerned with the topics covered in the series.

In the mid 1960s when the subject of planning began to emerge, the whole literature could have been listed on one or two sheets of paper. It was easy to decide which books to read, because so few were available. This state of affairs changed rapidly, and the scope of the subject has moved from a focus on formal planning to a broader view which merges with the literature of leadership, change management, strategic analysis, and organisation. Modern writing sees the organisation and its strategies in an integrated way, and there are many, often conflicting, theories about the "right" way to formulate strategies and practice strategic management.

Management usually does not take an academic interest in theories, but is concerned about what works best in the situation in which it operates. Hence this series. Each book is conceptually sound, and gives proper acknowledgement to the originators of concepts and ideas, but the emphasis is on using the concepts or methods, rather than academic argument. Hence, too, the choice of the six subjects initially offered under the auspices of the CBI.

There are two books which offer complementary overviews of strategic management. McNamee's *Strategic Market Planning* follows the author's belief that enduringly successful firms are those that understand most clearly, and then serve most effectively, the markets they address, and offers a blue print for this. Hussey (*Strategy & Planning*) provides essential, up to date, information for managers and practitioners of strategic management who require a practical view of the whole subject.

Segev writes on business unit strategy, and its emphasis is on analytical method for businesses that focus on one industry or product/market grouping. The remaining three books deal with specific aspects of strategy which are topical concerns for many organisations. They cover the subjects of virtual organisations (Hedberg et al), the related but different subject of multinational strategic alliances (Mockler), and competitor analysis, (Hussey & Jenster).

The emphasis of all the books is on practical application. The aim is to give the reader clear guidance on how to make the subject of the book work in his or her own situation, while at the same time taking care to ensure that the books do not over-simplify situations. Check lists and questionnaires are included when they aid the aims of the book, and examples are given. The experience of the author in actually applying the concepts, rather than just knowing about them, is intended to show through the writing.

The books are written by authors from Denmark, Israel, Sweden, the UK and the USA, which brings an international flavour, as well as helping to make complex matters understandable. We hope that it will become a catalyst that helps managers make a difference to the strategic performance of their organisations.

David Hussey, Series Editor
Visiting Professor in Strategic Management
Nottingham Trent University
Managing Director, David Hussey & Associates

August 2000

Preface

WHAT IS IN THIS BOOK

Over the last two decades, during which the subject of business policy and strategy has been studied extensively, a number of experts have devised interesting and important ways of categorizing strategies so that every business unit falls into one strategic category. The strategies have received specific names, some of them quite colorful, such as defender, stuck-in-the-middle, and umbrella. I have taken nine of the more important categories, which I have called approaches, and analyzed them in detail. These approaches involve 53 different strategies. From this analysis I found that I could define and evaluate all the strategies in terms of 28 strategic variables. This book shows the professional and the student how to make strategy of strategic business units by:

- Offering a comprehensive way of examining business strategies.
- Having an underlying knowledge base which was obtained from experts.
- Supporting strategy making.

The first chapter provides an overview of the book, and the second chapter introduces the underlying conceptual foundations, mainly of strategic profiles and approaches. The next eight chapters follow a standard format: each chapter introduces an approach, the approach and its strategies are then defined, and its uses and misuses discussed. Relevant strategic variables are introduced, defined, examples are given, and operational measures (indicators) are suggested. In Chapter 11, adding new approaches into the framework is discussed. The conclusions are presented in Chapter 12. The core chapters are highly focused and concise. Two appendices present in-depth discussions of the framework, methodology, comparisons between approaches, and suggested synthesis among the approaches.

WHO THIS BOOK IS FOR

This book is aimed at three audiences:

1. Business managers and planners to help them understand their current strategy, the strategy of their competitors, and the implications of any changes in strategy which they are contemplating.
2. MBA students in a course on business policy and strategy to teach them about strategy systematically. The book is profusely illustrated with case examples that describe the strategic variables. This book would supplement the classic case books.
3. Executive MBA students—mid-career people returning to school for their MBA's—to help them gain a deeper insight into strategy at a time when they are already in a position of influence in their firm. To them, the strategy of the firm is not an abstract matter but a serious day-to-day concern. I believe few texts exist that are aimed at this level of student.

This book was written for managers rather than for their staff assistants. It is my firm opinion that strategy making cannot be subcontracted or delegated downward.

ACKNOWLEDGMENTS

First and foremost I would like to thank my friend and colleague Dr Paul Gray, of the Claremont Graduate School. Paul has been involved with this project since 1986, leading the development of an expert support system based on this book's framework. His insights have been extensively incorporated. Without his good advice and continuous support, this book would never have been written.

A book project such as this which is so heavily dependent on research cannot be accomplished in a reasonable time without the valuable support of graduate students. At the Faculty of Management of Tel Aviv University I am indebted to Dr Tamar Almor Ellemers, Clifford Rosenberg, Dr Gabriel Szulanski, Adi Bildner, Dr Shlomo Noy, Beth Pfeffer, and at the Claremont Graduate School to Victoria Goodrich, James E. Rhodes and Richard D'Souza. Each of them added to my intellectual capital.

I am grateful for the advice and insight provided by many practicing managers and MBA students who were exposed to earlier drafts of this book. Special thanks are due to Gerda Kessler for her painstaking copy-editing. Finally, I am indebted to Shy Segev for his meticulous proofreading.

Eli Segev
Tel Aviv

ABOUT THE AUTHOR

Eli Segev received his D.B.A from Harvard Business School where he specialized in environmental analysis and corporate planning. He is the incumbent of the Haimovich Chair for Business Policy, Faculty of Management, Tel Aviv University, and has taught at the University of Texas, Dallas; New York University; China Europe International Business School, Shanghai, P.R.C; the University of California at Los Angeles; the University of British Columbia, Vancouver; and the Claremont Graduate School, California. His consulting, teaching and research have been in the fields of business policy and of top management information systems. He has written eight books and over forty journal articles.

1

Introduction

THE IMPORTANCE OF BUSINESS STRATEGY

Strategy defined

Any ongoing business has a strategy, whether it thinks so or not. Even if the strategy is undocumented, informal, or unplanned and the business is unaware of, unconscious of, or flatly denies it, a strategy exists. A strategy is created because a working organization can neither be totally flexible nor turn around constantly. Location, premises, facilities, technology, employees, product lines, target markets, supply and distribution channels, reputation, standards, and procedures, to name just a few, are chosen, created, and adhered to for various lengths of time. The decisions and investments made in the past create organizational inertia and momentum.

Organizational inertia and momentum change over time. Few business organizations are totally rigid from startup to divestment. Most organizations modify and change; some are even revolutionized. However, these are not daily changes. Over time, organizational inertia and momentum create a unique business pattern of investments and activities. The essence of this pattern may be identified, analyzed, and modified. This pattern has a name: strategy. Thus, even though it may be unplanned, unintentional, nondeliberate, or even misdirected, strategy exists. It exists because most managerial decisions are consistent and logical. When defined and adopted consciously, a formal strategy can become a set of guidelines for future activities.

Example. The 1979 annual report of Mary Kay Cosmetics, Inc., stated: "Our corporate goal is to be the finest skin care organization in the world," and "growth in sales and net income should follow achievement of our goal" ("Mary Kay Cosmetics, Inc.," 1981).

Example. "The strategy of our company, in very simple terms, is to supply low-volume forming machinery for the small plastic fabricators" ("Hamlin Machinery Company, Inc.," 1982).

Example. In 1985, Apple Computer, Inc., announced that it was launching an attack on IBM's position in the personal computer business (*Business Week*, 1984). The intent was to promote the Macintosh as the foremost office machine. As announced, Apple's strategy included the following:

1. Introducing the Macintosh Office, including an inexpensive local-area communications network, a high-speed laser printer, and linkups with IBM computers.
2. Speeding up software development for the Macintosh.
3. Signing up large customers, especially high-visibility corporate buyers.
4. Improving dealer relations by replacing its entire network of manufacturer's representatives with its own sales force.
5. Forming strategic alliances with such companies as Wang, AT&T, and Xerox.

Example. Heileman, the fourth-largest brewer in the United States, decided to try to tap new markets as a way of overcoming a production slump (*Business Week*, 1987c). In 1987, R.G. Cleary, chairman and CEO of Heileman, probed for ways to challenge the top two brewers. His working strategy was "growth through acquisition." Since 1971, when Cleary took over the $104 million company from his father-in-law, he had acquired eight unsound regional brewers or their brands. Cleary either sold an acquisition's assets and kept its brands or turned it around with new cash and aggressive marketing. Although Cleary predicted that nonbeer products might account for half of the company's revenues by 1997, for the short term he remained on the alert for brewing properties.

The concept of strategy has evolved over time, although the basic concept has not changed. For example, a 1962 definition stated that strategy is "the determination of the basic long-term goals and objectives of an enterprise, and the adoption of courses of action and the allocation of resources necessary for carrying out these goals" (Chandler, 1962). That is, strategy is the alignment of goals and courses of action of an organization.

Strategy is created at the topmost level of an organization. This level sets the organization's goals and decides on its investments and the deployment of its resources. Although, as we discuss later in this book, many other forces have an impact on strategy, it is the mandate of top management to make strategy. Successful or not, strategy is defined by top management.

As strategy was studied further over the years and the important role of the organization's external environment was better understood, the focus of its definition shifted to "the basic characteristics of the match an organization achieves with its environment" (Hofer and Schendel, 1978). Some people began using the term policy, with the result that these two terms are now used interchangeably. Although the term strategy was borrowed from the military and the term policy from government, their use in business is the same.

In the literature, some authors divide an orderly, formal corporate-planning process into hierarchies of aims, goals, objectives, policies, strategies, and programs. In this book, strategy is treated as a single concept, undivided into phases or stages. However, we will operationalize strategy by considering the variables that compose it.

The hierarchy of strategies

Although strategy is a comprehensive concept, it is sometimes applied to different kinds and levels of organizations, organizational activities, or geographic regions. Thus, people talk about divisional strategy, export strategy, West Coast strategy, or departmental strategy. One categorization, used in this book and illustrated in Figure 1.1, follows the way businesses organize and separate strategy into:

- Corporate strategy (which includes many business units)
- Business-level strategy (one business unit)
- Functional strategy (functions such as finance, information systems, marketing)

The definitions of a business unit and business strategy are intertwined. A business unit is "the level in the organization at which the responsibility for the formulation of a multifunctional strategy for a single industry or product-market arena is determined" (Hofer, 1975), whereas a business strategy is a set of competitive weapons used to

Figure 1.1 Hierarchy of strategies.

give a business unit its distinctive competence within its industry (Bourgeois, 1980). Thus, business strategy is one level above functional strategies. In a well-run firm, functional strategies are included in the business unit strategy. Conversely, the functional strategies are guided, coordinated, and directed by the individual business unit strategies. Ideally, functional strategies combine to form a consistent and comprehensive strategy.

Many organizations are single business units, and thus their business unit strategy is their highest level of strategy. This book is aimed directly at the top management of these organizations. On the other hand, many large organizations are corporations composed of multi-industry or multi-product-market units. For these firms, corporate-level strategy involves the selection of product-markets or industries and allocation of resources among them. This book does not deal with corporate strategy, which deserves special attention and a different approach. However, since each business unit within a corporation has its own business strategy, this book is also intended for the top managements of business units within large corporations.

Finally, this book is directed at students, most of whom will spend a significant portion of their career, particularly their early career, working in business units and will contribute actively to their business unit's strategy formulation and implementation.

Example. In 1981, the Coca-Cola Company issued a pamphlet called "Strategy for the 80s" ("Coca Cola Company," 1986). In it, Coca-Cola stated that, as a corporate-level strategy, packaged consumer goods and consumer services were the businesses that Coca-Cola preferred. The corporate aim was to maintain or improve its position in current businesses, thereby increasing earnings per share annually. In addition, Coca-Cola aimed at increasing return on assets while entering new businesses that it felt had growth potential. Strategies were also defined for each business unit. For example, in soft drinks, Coca-Cola would follow a stability strategy, working to maintain its leadership position. In foods, the strategy was also stability, working to maintain market share in frozen fruit juices, coffee, etc. In wine, on the other hand, the company would try to match its growth to the growth of the wine industry. A typical functional-level strategy involved the decision to use aseptic packaging for preservatives or refrigeration for its HiC fruit drink.

Success and failure of a business strategy

The success of a business unit's strategy is indicated by the unit's profitability. Any performance measure (e.g., return on equity, return on sales, cash flow) applied to a group of competing business units will rank them according to their degree of success. Although different measures, and different time spans (e.g., two, three, or five years), will yield variations in ranking, it is possible to divide business units into two nonoverlapping groups: those whose performance is above the industry average, and those whose performance is below the industry average (Porter, 1980). Strategies applied by the first group of business units have proved successful, whereas those used by the second group are defined as failures.

The success of a business strategy is not directly related to whether the business unit is in a specific industry or product-market, but to its relative performance in this industry. Because we are interested in a consistent pattern of activities for an observable period of time, strategic success does not relate to accidental windfalls (property sale, investment in a rising security, a competitor's sudden crisis), "hit-and-run" operations (a one-time invasion into the product-market as the result of an opportunity), or unsuccessful attempts to enter an industry. Although this last type of failure is highly relevant in analyzing success and failure strategies in a particular industry, these are short-term, "grand" failures. The available post-mortem information that exists on such failures is often of dubious accuracy and usually meager. The failure is usually attributed to a single factor or mistake, whether or not that was the case.

> *Example.* Blakeston and Wilson, a manufacturer of medium- and high-priced chocolate candy, was organized in 1938 when it purchased the assets of the bankrupt Sidwell Wilson company ("Blakeston and Wilson," 1947). Wilson, with a 52% ownership of the Blakeston and Wilson company, noted that the Sidwell Wilson company failed primarily because selling expenses were too high. Further, they were selling to wholesalers who played one manufacturer off against another to force prices down. As Wilson put it, "We worked and sweated to make a few dollars manufacturing candy while the wholesalers and retailers took large margins for distributing and selling our products."

The essential strategic role of top management

Strategy does not happen, it is made. It is the result of the interplay of power within the business unit's dominant coalition. In a very few business units, because of past decisions, inertia is so great and momentum so strong that current management has no control over the unit's strategy and has to continue implementing the existing strategy, whether it is correct or not. In most business units, strategy is constantly evaluated, modified, and sometimes even changed radically. Those involved in strategy making are called the business unit's strategy-making team. In most cases (except in highly centralized corporations), they are the top managers of the business unit. Many external and internal factors, discussed in the following chapters, affect the business unit strategy, but it is made—by commission or omission—by the strategy-making team. Be it a formal planning effort, an ad hoc disjointed decision, or an ignored opportunity, the result is a strategy formulated and implemented by the business unit's top management. Thus, a strategy of a business unit is highly dependent on the strategy-making team and its composition.

Managers assess the business unit's performance, gather information, apply their expertise, and make decisions. Thus, top managers perform their essential role in strategy making based on their knowledge, skills, experience, formal education, perceived information, values, and relative power in the strategy-making team. One way of changing a business unit's strategy is to change its strategy-making team. In crises, when a turnaround strategy is required, the entire top management is sometimes replaced.

Example. In 1987, the proud, 118-year-old Mellon Bank Corp. was confronted with the possibility of being a takeover target (*Business Week*, 1987f). The stock had dropped so low that the holding company, with $34 billion in assets, could have been snapped up for $1 billion. The new CEO of Mellon took action to deter the threat. On taking office in June 1987, F.V. Cahouet froze salaries, ordered the 19,500 staff reduced by about 10% by year-end, and decided to take a $566 million second-quarter loss. The greatest change was in the executive suite, where only one of the previous seven-member team remained (Vice-Chairman G.T. Farrell, valued for his rapport with customers). In assembling the new team, Cahouet hired two former colleagues from San Francisco's Crocker National Bank and installed Chase Manhattan's vice-president, A.P. Terracciano, as chief operating officer.

Example. Midway through 1970, it became clear that Blow-Mold Packers, Inc., would not continue to enjoy the growth in sales and profits that had, in the past, made financing acquisitions through exchange of stock both easy and profitable ("Blow-Mold Packers, Inc.," 1976). As fiscal 1970 grew worse, the organizational structure was changed. The post of executive vice-president to coordinate manufacturing policies was created. The corporate staff was disbanded, with five of 12 members leaving the company. The company's treasurer was reassigned to another division, and a recent MBA graduate took his place.

THE UNDERLYING CONCEPTS OF THIS BOOK

We now outline briefly the structure of this book and how it can be used. We will elaborate on each of these points throughout this book.

A comprehensive integrative approach to business strategy

Atomistic vs. holistic approaches

Two basically different approaches to business strategy exist:

- atomistic
- holistic

This book uses the holistic approach.

An atomistic approach focuses in depth on a critical strategic variable (or a small set of variables) and its contribution to the organization's strategy; for example, the effects of environmental uncertainty, innovation, or low market share. This approach is very useful for building theories, since it is anchored in previously accumulated knowledge, which makes it easy to draw extensively on previously found relationships. The atomistic approach lends itself to step-by-step refinement and accumulation of knowledge on the phenomenon studied. On the other hand, it provides the manager with a very limited view, since it deals with strategic variables serially and lacks overview.

A holistic approach entails a search for simultaneous relationships (profiles) for a large number of variables, identifying classification of organizational strategies (Hambrick, 1984; Miller, 1981). Thus, it enables understanding, analysis, and manipulation of the strategy as a whole, rather than in an incremental fashion. In the approach presented in this book it is a simple matter to consider many variables simultaneously and thereby identify classes of organizational strategies.

Internal consistency of strategic variables

This book is based on internal consistency of strategic variables. A business unit is a complex system that is composed of various subsystems (technical, economic, social) and conducts multiple transactions with its environment. The functioning of a system is not defined by the properties of one of its components (e.g., the size of the speakers in a compact disk system), but on the internal consistency of all components. A business unit's strategy is the composite pattern in which the unit conducts its multifunctional activities. Thus, the success of such a strategy is not dependent on one strategic variable (e.g., aggressive advertising campaigns) but on the variable's internal consistency with the strategic profile (such as the unit's ability to produce the advertised product on time). Thus, increasing product quality results in a successful strategy only if it is consistent with such factors as the product price, the business unit's quality control system, employee competence, available facilities, customer needs, and the business unit's reputation.

Compatibility of strategies

This book is based on the compatibility of strategies. Compatibility is defined as the way variables are joined together in a particular configuration to achieve higher performance. The importance of completeness has long been recognized in strategic business planning. It is termed synergy: a combination that is more than its components. The notion that strategies can be expressed in terms of a limited number of compatible combinations has been a fundamental approach in the business strategy field since the field's inception. These combinations have been inferred by examining the large number of cases and looking for similarities.

"Gestalts," modes, archetypes, and typologies

This book is based on well-researched classifications of business strategies. These classifications of strategies are variously termed:

- Typologies (Galbraith and Schendel, 1983)
- Gestalts (Miller, 1981)
- Modes (Mintzberg, 1973b)
- Archetypes (Miller and Friesen, 1978)
- Taxonomies (Hambrick, 1984)

Whichever term is used, the classifications assume that clusters of organizations share a common strategy. The common strategy is identified and defined based on an extensive list of strategic characteristics. Thus, a population of organizations, in our case strategic businesses' units in an industry, could be subdivided into a manageable number of subpopulations each pursuing a similar archetype or generic strategy. In what follows we will describe how we used nine such classifications. We will use the term 'approach' to define a classification.

Manager choice of strategic approach

A large number of approaches have emerged, and are emerging, in the study of business strategy. The approaches do not substitute for, but rather enhance, one another. Each approach is based on different assumptions, populations of businesses, databases, research methods, and researcher expertise.

Each approach can be relevant for examining business unit strategy. However, the degree of relevance of an approach to a specific business situation is highly dependent on the business unit's characteristics:

- The nature, size, and life-cycle stage of the business unit's industry.
- The size and position of the unit within the industry.
- The nature of the product or service.
- The way strategy is made.

All of these impact on the usefulness of the approach for the business unit's managers.

This book allows managers to choose one or more strategic approaches as a basis for analyzing their business unit. Based on their judgment, managers initially choose an approach and analyze the business situation. If not satisfied, it is a simple matter to choose different approaches until a satisfying synthesis is achieved. A detailed understanding of each approach's assumptions, uses, and limitations facilitates this process. The approaches are presented in Chapter 2.

Expert knowledge base

This book is based on expert knowledge. Each approach included in this book was developed by one or more leading experts in the area. Some of these approaches initiated schools of thought and practice that have been followed by other scholars and practitioners. To obtain the comprehensive expert knowledge base used by this book, we operationalized this knowledge for managers.

Basically, we asked a panel of evaluators/judges to study each approach and to assign values to the strategic variables. A structured form of maximum-minimum seven-point scales was used in a formal questionnaire. The mean values of the evaluations by the judges were used as representing the value for the variable to be included in the strategy's profile. The evaluations on the seven-point scale were transformed into a percentages base: the value used is $100 \times$ (mean minus 1)/6. For example, if the mean value observed was 3.58, then $100 \times (3.58 - 1)/6 = 43$. It is these percentage values that are used in this book.

Using this book to identify strategy

One of the most important concepts underlying this book is the manager's personal identification of the business unit strategy. Even experienced managers with long tenure are not completely acquainted with the fine details of their business unit's strategy; some managers have a totally distorted perception of the business unit's strategy in the past. Experience in working with the approach presented in this book showed that by applying it over and over and by using a variety of levels of aggregation, managers gained a very deep and thorough understanding of their current business unit strategy. Fine details became clear, as did the relationships among details. This is possible because our framework for business strategy is based on four levels:

1. *Strategy*. The highest level in our approach hierarchy is a concise verbal description of the strategy. This description captures the essence of the unit's business approach at a specific point in time. The strategy statement generalizes the business unit's competitive strategy based on its investments, decisions, and activities.
2. *Metavariable*. Six related groups of strategic variables.
3. *Strategic variable*. Definition of the six metavariables in terms of 28 strategic variables.
4. *Indicator*. Operational measures that help you define the value of a strategic variable. Up to ten indicators can be used for each variable.

These four levels are used to determine the strategy being followed by a particular business unit.

Using this book to search for strategic alternatives

Choosing among alternatives is much less complicated than the search for alternatives. Experience with both seasoned managers and MBA students has consistently demonstrated that sophisticated people who can master complex methods of decision making are lost when asked to formulate alternatives. Our approach contains two important concepts:

1. Presenting a basic inventory of strategic alternatives to the manager.
2. Supporting the manager's ability to search for additional alternatives.

THE CONTRIBUTIONS OF THIS BOOK

Identifying and evaluating the current strategy of the business unit

Like the title character in Molière's play *Le Bourgeois Gentilhomme* who found out that all his life he had been talking prose but was not aware of it, many business units consistently pursue an identifiable strategy, although their managers are not aware of it.

> *Example.* Hudepohl Brewing Company served Cincinnati and nearby urban areas ("Hudepohl Brewing Company," 1980). Its management saw its strategy in 1979 as focused on selling popular-priced products (such as draft beer in barrels) in bars to sports-minded, blue-collar workers. Analysis of their operations, however, showed that the major financial contribution was being obtained from the efficient route sales of case-packaged beer by its truck drivers. This implicit strategy had evolved naturally from the bottom up in the organization.

The first contribution of this book is to help you identify your own business unit's strategy. You will be able to decompose your strategy systematically into identifiable components and then reconstruct a recognizable comprehensive strategic profile. Once you have identified your profile, you will be better able to evaluate it. This is the second contribution of this book. This book is based on what is known about state-of-the-art business strategies.

Identifying and analyzing

A good strategy is based on external opportunities and the business unit's abilities to build on these opportunities.

> *Example.* To fulfill the sales forecasts for the next several years, Vlasic Foods Inc. needed to create considerable additional capacity ("Vlasic Foods Inc.," 1977). For a number of reasons it was considered best to locate new plants in different parts of the US. The cost of the first proposed plant was estimated at $3.5 to $4.0 million. It would take

> two years to bring it on line at full capacity, during which time the company would probably sustain losses from this plant. Financing the coming expansion created a number of difficulties. First, the company was drained financially. The tentative plan to finance the new plant called for a bond issue with the possibility at some point in the future of a public offering of Vlasic stock. Second, the organizational consequences of expansion were of concern to the management group. Additional operating managers and possibly a new organizational structure would be needed.

Defining the business unit's strategy in terms of its components, and then further delineating these components in terms of operational measures, facilitates the third contribution of this book: analysis of opportunities and limitations. By building a model of the business unit's inventory of strategic resources and limitations, a manager can investigate the feasibility of potential strategic changes.

Once a business unit's strategic profile is evaluated systematically, a manager can examine the effects of proposed changes to determine if they result in better strategic profiles. For example, changes in costs, competences, availability, and the length of time required for making these changes can be explored in these "what if" scenarios. The results are hypothetical strategic profiles, in which existing resources are increased or economies are introduced. The results point toward the business unit's capacity for growth, change, and strategic success.

Finding viable strategic alternatives for the business unit

The fourth contribution of the book is to help managers find viable strategic alternatives for the business unit. Any business unit's manager should evaluate its strategy periodically to determine if internal and external conditions have changed and if these changes make it necessary to change strategy. This approach is contrary to the way many managers act. They assume this responsibility only when problems are already evident and the current strategy is failing.

A recurrent mistake in these cases is the focus on a single aspect of the business unit strategy (such as product price, production facilities, organization structure) in an effort to counter negative trends and solve growing business problems. This piecemeal approach is a mistake, since strategy is a whole and should be treated as such.

In creating alternatives, a manager will find that some of the suggested strategic profiles are not feasible for the business unit and some are failure strategies. In each business situation, there are a few viable alternative strategies the managers of a business unit may consider.

Example. Throughout most of the mid-twentieth century, the Joseph Schlitz Brewing Company had been the leading brewer in the US. ("Joseph Schlitz Brewing Company," 1984). By 1980, it had fallen to fourth place. From 1976 to 1980, Schlitz's sales had dropped 14% to $1.03 billion, representing only 58% of its 1980 capacity. Under new leadership Schlitz had the following strategic alternatives:

1. Attempt to turn around its beer business through improved quality control and increased advertising.
2. Increase total sales and total income through the acquisition of smaller breweries.
3. Maintain its beer business at current levels, stopping the continuing decline.
4. "Retrench" by reducing its beer business to selected regions, attempting to gain market share in those regions.
5. "Retrench" to specific regions, then try to maintain current levels in those regions.
6. "Harvest" its beer business by minimizing expenses on R&D, advertising, etc.
7. Sell off its beer business to a competitor.

Example. In 1977, the manager of the Methocel Product Team identified seven major alternatives for the production of the Methocel product line ("Methocel Product Division at the Dow Chemical Company," 1982):

1. No additional capacity. Allow the plants to run out gradually.
2. Add additional capacity at plant A, using a batch process, in a single increment of five million pounds.
3. Add additional capacity at plant A, using a continuous process, in a single increment of 25 million pounds.
4. Add additional capacity at plant A, using a continuous process, in a single increment of 40 million pounds.
5. Add additional capacity at plant A, using a continuous process, in a single increment of 50 million pounds.
6. Build a new process in Texas with a 20-million-pound capacity.
7. Build a new process in Plaquemine, Louisiana with a four-million-pound capacity.

2

The Underlying Conceptual Foundation

This chapter focuses on the underlying conceptual foundations of our approach, and is basically divided into two parts:

1. The systematic identification of the strategic unit profile.
2. The concept of the integrative approach.

SYSTEMATIC IDENTIFICATION OF THE STRATEGIC UNIT PROFILE

First we describe a framework for identifying business strategy and introduce the following four levels:

- Strategy
- Metavariable
- Variable
- Indicator

that are used to determine the strategy being followed by a particular business unit.

A FRAMEWORK FOR STRATEGIC VARIABLES

A generally accepted framework for strategic variables does not yet exist. The area is relatively new and is evolving very quickly. Business texts emphasize the complex nature of the strategy area, the multiplicity of variables, the network of interrelationships, and the contingent nature of the area (Christensen et al, 1982; Glueck and Jauch, 1984; Hofer et al, 1984). Comparison among the available textbooks shows inconsistencies, even conflicts, in concepts, in measures, and in the attempts to operationalize the concepts and the measures.

Appendix 2.1 presents a framework for a grounded theory of corporate policy, which has been slightly modified and is used here (Segev, 1988a). In this book, we basically adopted the hierarchical framework presented in Appendix 2.1. Some modifications were needed to make this approach applicable to strategy at the business unit level. In essence, we created a hierarchy that has four levels:

- Strategic business unit strategy
- Strategic metavariables
- Strategic variables
- Indicators for strategic variables

THE LEVELS OF A BUSINESS UNIT STRATEGY

A comprehensive strategy

The highest level in our approach hierarchy is a concise verbal description of the strategy. This description captures the essence of the unit's business approach at a specific point in time. This statement generalizes the business unit's competitive strategy based on its investments, decisions, and activities. The strategy statement may be used as a concrete guideline for top management of the business unit if management decides it wants to continue pursuing the same strategy. Many different structures for describing strategy exist.

Example. Personal style can be adapted by an organization to instill a visible strategy throughout the organization without depending on implementation through structure. Al Davis of the Raiders has long been regarded as a renegade manager in the professional football business (*Newsweek*, 1984; *Time*, 1984). In the early 1980s, he infuriated the league with a unilateral move from Oakland to Los Angeles. His strategy of tough intimidation reached throughout the Raiders organization. It included both the players and the fans, who reveled in the "bad guy" image of a team of malcontents and castoffs who dominated their opposition. The Raiders enjoyed financial success, and in 1984 the "bad guy" won Super Bowl XVII.

This is an example of an emergent strategy. Although never formally written or decided upon, the Raiders followed this strategy strictly. Other business units formulate and implement their strategy in an orderly, formal process.

Example. John Scully was hired by Apple Computer as CEO in 1983 to improve the company's marketing effectiveness (*Fortune*, 1985). However, the strategic focus over the next two years was on structural reorganization. The first reorganization moved Apple from nine decentralized divisions into a much more centralized structure. As friction developed between its Apple II and Macintosh product groups (and between Scully and Steven Jobs, the chairman and cofounder), a second reorganization took place, with Jobs departing. The strategic objective of the structure changes was to present a more unified marketing position to Apple's dealers and customers.

Strategy statements cover a wide range and lack standards. Some strategies, like the Raider example, may relate to the process by which the content of the strategy is decided upon. Others, like Apple, may relate to the structure of the organization. This book includes descriptions of 53 comprehensive business unit strategies. These descriptions are all based on six metavariables:

- The business unit's environment
- The content of the strategy
- The strategy-making process
- The unit's organizational structure
- The unit's performance
- The unit's basic characteristics

Don't be put off by the term "metavariable." It simply means a collection of variables that is conveniently described by a general term. We now describe these six metavariables.

Six strategic metavariables

More than two decades of research on organizational strategy produced four metavariables on which theory in the area rests. These metavariables are the first four listed above. References for these variables are:

- Environment (Anderson and Paine, 1975; Duncan, 1972; Emery and Trist, 1965; Lawrence and Lorsch, 1967)

- Strategy (Andrews, 1971; Boston Consulting Group Staff, 1968; Chandler, 1962; Glueck, 1976; Rumelt, 1974)
- Strategy making (Aharoni, 1966; Allison, 1971; Ansoff, 1965; Bower, 1970; Cyert and March, 1963; Mintzberg, 1973b)
- Structure (Chandler, 1962; Channon, 1973; Child, 1972; Galbraith and Nathanson, 1978; Lawrence and Lorsch, 1967; Perrow, 1970; Woodward, 1965)

The fifth, and usually the dependent metavariable in strategic studies, is performance. We added a sixth metavariable, basic characteristics of the business unit.

Environment

The environment includes all factors outside the organization that affect or are affected by the strategic business unit. The environment includes both the unit's industry, which is its immediate environment, and the general, wider environment (international and national policies, the economy, other industries). The environment will be operationalized by considering four variables that best describe its nature (uncertainty, dynamism, hostility, and complexity). To measure these variables we will use indicators (which are the next level down from variables in our framework).

> *Example.* Aerosol Techniques, Inc. (ATI) manufactured over 200 aerosol products for nearly 150 customers ("Aerosol Techniques, Inc.", 1984). However, in 1965, because of environmental factors, ATI was not certain that it would be able to attain its objectives of $100 million in sales and 7% profit after taxes by 1969 unless it made strategic changes. The environmental factors included maturation of both the structure of the entire industry and of aerosol technology. In addition, ATI was faced with heavier competition by job shops that threatened its markup levels and by the increasing power of marketing companies.

Strategy content

The strategy content is the output of the strategy-making process. It is what most people refer to as the strategy. It is the multifunctional posture of the business unit. At the next level of our framework, strategy content is operationalized by variables related to the unit's posture in functional areas such as engineering, production, and marketing.

Example. Crown Cork and Seal was on the verge of bankruptcy in 1957 when John Connelly was named president ("Crown Cork and Seal Company and the Metal Container Industry," 1972). He examined the internal situation and made a series of strategic changes over a three-year period:

- Extensive simplification of the corporate structure.
- Plant modernization and increased geographic dispersion of the company.
- Reduced scope and risk of product specialization.
- Emphasis on customer service.

Crown's crisis with its bankers was solved. The company had examined the marketplace and set logical product-market goals. It had also set a clear financial goal. With the company healthy, Crown was able to establish a program of building overseas plants. By 1963, Crown enjoyed the highest profit margins among the four industry leaders.

Strategy-making process

Strategy-making is an ongoing process whereby, intentionally or not, the business unit's objectives and means for achieving them are determined, that is, the strategy formulation and implementation. In operationalizing the strategy-making process in this book, strategic variables were chosen to cover its formal aspects (such as analysis) as well as its informal aspects (such as risk and initiative).

Example. Texas Instruments developed its Objectives-Strategies-Tactics (OST) system for facilitating the management of innovation ("Texas Instruments Incorporated Management Systems," 1972). Through a matrix of strategic and operating modes, the OST system expressed and implemented:

- Corporate objectives
- Business objectives
- Strategies
- Tactical action programs (TAP)

in 77 product-customer centers (PCC). Each PCC had a short-term operating profit responsibility. More than 50 strategies cross-linked the TAPs with the work packages of the functional areas in each PCC. Reporting systems focused on the managers of both the TAPs and the PCCs.

Structure

Structure is the deployment of management resources within the business unit. It is both an important tool used in strategy implementation and a critical factor affecting strategy formulation, in other words, an integral part of the unit's strategy.

Example. In late November 1981, Club Mediterranee (Club Med) instituted a new structure based on the following objectives ("Club Mediterranee (A)," 1984).

- To continue its growth and double its capacity every five years.
- To be innovative and to be responsive to both its French and non-French customers.
- To cut costs.
- To maintain the essential philosophy of Club Med.

The new structure was based on three world zones rather than the functional structure used previously. Marketing and operations would be handled by regional directors reporting to the head office.

Performance

Performance is the ultimate dependent variable in our framework: the result of the major decisions taken to match the unit with its environment. Strategic variables operationalizing this metavariable in our approach relate to the effectiveness of the unit's competitive posture: the rate of success of the business unit's strategy.

Example. Digital Equipment Corp. (DEC) went on a winning streak (*Business Week*, 1987e). DEC's 1988 revenues were forecast to be double those of 1984 and pretax income five times as high. Its momentum made the company a star on Wall Street. In 1986, DEC's shares split and then doubled to $173. In the year ended June 30, 1987, net income jumped about 80% to $1.1 billion on a 24% increase in revenues, to $9.4 billion. Furthermore, DEC kept costs under control, propelling net margins from 5.7% in 1985 to 12% in 1987. In 1986, the company introduced a major new product about every four weeks to try to capitalize on its flourishing reputation among customers as a viable full-line competitor to IBM. Continuing to introduce new products was DEC's primary strategy for growth and for smoothing out swings caused by product cycles.

Basic characteristics

Basic characteristics are the inherent outcomes of the unit's establishment, history, and past strategy. They affect and constrain strategy change and are difficult, if not impossible, to modify in the short run. Here, in this book, they include two strategic variables: size and age of the business unit.

Table 2.1 Strategy types.

Subject studied	Year	Authors
Compatibility of strategy and organizational structure	1962	Chandler (Chandler, 1962)
	1972	Child (Child, 1972)
	1973	Channon (Channon, 1973)
	1978	Galbraith and Nathanson (Galbraith and Nathanson, 1978)
Viable environment-structure combinations	1962	Burns and Stalker (Burns and Stalker, 1961)
		Hambrick (Hambrick, 1981)
	1967	Lawrence and Lorsch (Lawrence and Lorsch, 1967)
Compatibility of strategy-making modes and the environment	1972	Mintzberg (Mintzberg, 1973b)
Compatibility of strategic types with environment	1978	Miles and Snow (Miles and Snow, 1978)
	1981	Hambrick (Hambrick, 1981)
Relationships between strategy making and strategy content and effect on performance	1987	Segev (Segev, 1987)

Relations among metavariables

Many studies point to relationships among two or more of these metavariables and the effects of these relationships on the dependent variable: performance. Table 2.1 lists these studies and the relationships involved.

The intertwined maze of relationships in Table 2.1 points out that strategy is a whole, a gestalt if you like, rather than a collection of variables. Thus, although we define strategy in terms of six metavariables and although we will divide it further into more and more refined components, the point of departure in this book is always *the strategy*, viewed as a comprehensive whole.

Strategic variables

The next lower level of our framework is the division of the six metavariables into 28 strategic variables. Table 2.2 lists the 28 variables used in this book together with a short definition of each. The short definitions in Table 2.2 may leave too much to the

Table 2.2 The 28 variables.

Variable	Definition
	Metavariable: environment
1. Environmental uncertainty	The amount of information available to decision makers for predicting the occurrence and nature of environmental factors and external changes, and their impact on the strategic business unit's performance.
2. Environmental dynamism	The rapidity and amount of change in the environment of the business unit (e.g., changes in customer tastes, in production, in service technologies, or in the rate of inflation).
3. Environmental hostility	The prevalence in the environment of factors that have a negative impact on the strategic business unit and its interests (e.g., price, product, technological and distribution competition, regulatory restrictions, antagonistic community).
4. Environmental complexity	The number and diversity of external elements with which the business unit has to contend.
	Metavariable: strategy content
5. Technological progress	The relative innovativeness of the business unit compared with its competitors, in terms of the number and novelty of new techniques that are employed in the production of existing services and products.
6. Product-market breadth	The relative number and diversity of the business unit's products and customers.
7. Product innovation	The strategic business unit's innovativeness relative to the industry in terms of the number and novelty of new products and services introduced.
8. Quality	Customers' perception of the superiority of the business unit's products or services compared with those of competitors.
9. Price level	The customers' perception of the amount of money they have to pay for the business unit's products and services, in comparison to similar products in the market.
10. Active marketing	The amount of resources allocated by the business unit to marketing and management's general awareness of the marketing concept.
11. Control system level	The degree of use of mechanisms to standardize behavior and to assess performance.
12. Resource level	The state and availability of the business unit's human and material resources.
13. Investment in production	The relative amount and frequency of investment in production equipment and facilities.
14. Number of technologies	The relative number of different core technologies employed in production processes.

Table 2.2 *(continued).*

	Variable	Definition
15.	Professionalization	The level of formal education and training of employees.
		Metavariable: strategy-making process
16.	Internal analysis level	The ability of the business unit to assess its performance, based on internal data, trends, and developments.
17.	External analysis and forecasting level	The ability of the business unit to systematically track opportunities and threats in the environment in order to design long-term strategies.
18.	Level of risk	The extent to which strategy makers have made, and are willing to make, commitments that involve high proportions of the business unit's resources to risky (business risk, marketing risk, financial risk, political risk) projects.
19.	Proactiveness of decision style	The extent to which the business unit tries to shape its environment as opposed to merely reacting to trends in the environment in, for example, lobbying, advertising, introducing new products, changing customers' habits.
		Metavariable: structure
20.	Size of the strategy-making team	The number of main strategic actors in the business unit.
21.	Centralization	The hierarchical levels that have authority to make or participate in a strategic decision.
22.	Mechanistic structure of the organization	The extent to which the internal organization of the formalized management structure is characterized by rules, procedures, and a clear hierarchy of authority.
		Metavariable: performance
23.	Profitability	Return on equity.
24.	Market share	The percent of the relevant market share held by the business unit.
25.	Rate of growth	The average increase in total sales of the business unit over a relevant period in the industry (e.g., one, three, or five years).
26.	Operational efficiency	The degree of utilization of resources to produce output, measured as a ratio of input to output.
		Metavariable: basic characteristics
27.	Business unit size	The relative total sales, total assets, and number of people in the business unit.
28.	Business unit age	Number of years in business.

imagination. These definitions are elaborated upon in Chapters 3 through 7, where measures for scoring each variable are also presented. Because it may be difficult to determine directly the appropriate value to assign to each variable, we introduce the notion of indicators.

Strategic indicators

Strategic indicators are quantities that help you define the value of a variable. Although you can talk in general terms about a variable such as, say, environmental uncertainty, quantifying the variable can be difficult. However, it is possible to examine the factors that make up the environment (e.g., government, competitors, customers, lenders, unions, etc.) and estimate the uncertainty of each. The idea then is to take a weighted average of these uncertainties to come up with a single number that represents the variable "environmental uncertainty." The average is weighted because some of the indicators are more important to you than others.

The first three levels of our approach—strategy, metavariable, and variable—are quite universal. That is, these categorizations do not depend on specific business situations. At the fourth level, strategic indicators, our framework gives up universality for preciseness. The indicators used and their relative importance depend on the specific business situation. In Chapters 3 through 7, where we discuss each strategic variable in detail, you will also find a list of suggested indicators. You are not limited to using the suggested indicators. You can use some or none of them. You can also add indicators of your own if you believe them appropriate to your situation.

It is our firm opinion that strategy making cannot be subcontracted or delegated downward. Strategy is a process (strategy making) as well as content (the strategy itself). It is the responsibility of top management, and it should be performed by them.

THE CONCEPT OF THE INTEGRATIVE APPROACH

The four strategic levels used to determine the detailed strategy being followed by a particular business unit were described above. In this book, we have 53 such detailed strategies, forming nine groups of three to ten strategies each. These groups of strategies are termed approaches and are described below.

As we discussed in Chapter 1, our integrative approach is built around eight different approaches. The fragmented and sometimes marginal or conflicting findings, and the lack of significant progress in strategy research, prompted Danny Miller to propose and initiate a holistic approach: classification of organizational strategies (Miller, 1981). These classifications are called gestalts, modes, taxonomies, or approaches. We will use the term approaches in this book. The idea is that if we start with the universe of all firms, we can subdivide it into categories that contain clusters of firms following similar strategies. You might think of the universe as a box containing strategic business units. We have drawn this as a box containing points that represent the firms (see Figure 2.1). The approaches are divisions of the universe (the box) into categories or, if you like, pigeon-holes. Each firm in the universe fits into one of the categories. Figure 2.2 shows such a categorization. Thus, each approach tries to categorize strategic business units in terms of typical strategies that the business units follow. Each approach has a different set of strategies associated with it. Furthermore, each approach defines these strategies in terms of a subset of the 28 variables we presented above.

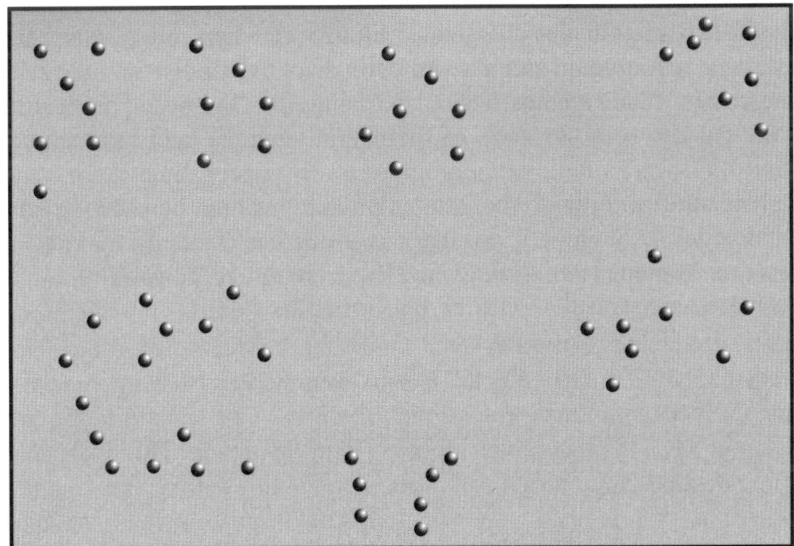

Figure 2.1 The universe of strategic business units.

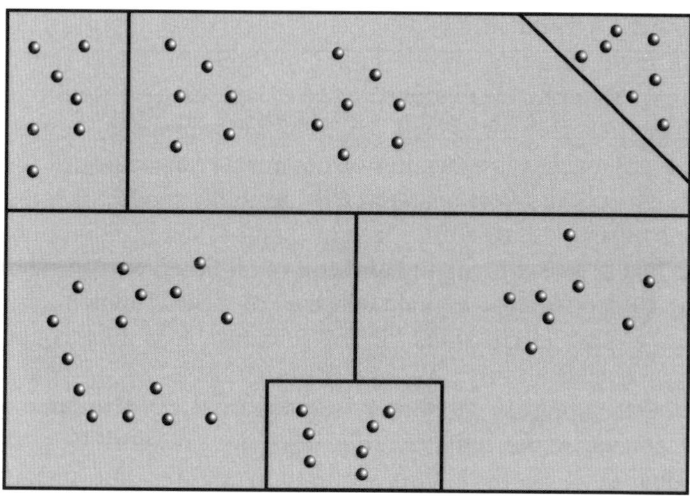

Figure 2.2 Division of the universe of strategic business units into strategy categories.

NINE PLUS ONE APPROACHES

The approaches chosen for this book are listed in Table 2.3. For each approach we give its name, its author or authors, a brief discussion, and the names of the strategies that make up the approach. Where possible, the strategies are divided into success and failure types.

These approaches were chosen because of their universality, their inclusion of the metavariables, their industry life-cycle coverage, their capture of both static and dynamic strategic postures, source discipline, and the methodology used in developing them. By universality we mean that the approach may be applied to all industries, although with varying degrees of relevance. An exception to the universality criterion is the Empiric Strategy Types (Galbraith and Schendel, 1983), which has separate criteria for business units producing consumer and industrial products. We chose to treat Empiric Strategy Types as two approaches. Nine approaches are derived from the professional literature. We also discuss, in Chapter 11, a tenth approach, termed Your Approach. This approach can be other approaches not discussed in this book, and unique situations that relate to specific industrial segments (e.g., mature capital goods industries (Hambrick, 1983b)) or to specific industries (e.g., banking (Jemison, 1987)).

Table 2.3 The approaches.

Approach	Authors	Description	Strategies
Deliberate and Emergent Strategies (Chapter 3)	Mintzberg and Waters	Deliberate and Emergent Strategies can be conceived of as two ends of a continuum describing the different ways in which strategy is made. It may range from completely realized as intended to order in the absence of intention.	• Planned • Entrepreneurial • Ideological • Umbrella • Process • Unconnected • Consensus • Imposed
Seven Survival Strategies (Chapter 4)	Vesper	These strategies describe the optimal behavior for a spectrum of strategic postures, based on the business unit's superiority and flexibility in adapting to its environment.	• Multiplication • Monopolizing • Specialization • Diversification • Cooperation • Capitulation • Liquidation
Ten Strategic Archetypes (Chapter 5)	Miller and Friesen	This is a set of ten strategic types with different environmental, organizational, and strategy-making characteristics: six of the types provide for organizational success and four lead to failure.	*The success types are:* • The adaptive firm under moderate challenge • The adaptive firm in a very challenging environment • The dominant firm • The giant under fire • The entrepreneurial conglomerate • The innovator *The failure types are:* • The impulsive firm running blind • The stagnant bureaucracy • The headless giant • Swimming upstream — the aftermath
Strategy-making Modes (Chapter 6)	Mintzberg	Three distinctive modes of decision making are described. Each mode represents a different linkage among important decisions on which a strategy is built.	• Entrepreneurial • Adaptive • Planning

(*continued overleaf*)

Table 2.3 *(continued).*

Approach	Authors	Description	Strategies
Competing Generic (Chapter 7)	Porter	There are three internally consistent generic strategies for taking offensive or defensive action to cope successfully with competitive forces and thereby yield a superior return on investment for the business unit. One of these strategies, focus, is further divided into focus-costs and focus-differentiation.	*Success strategies:* • Cost leadership • Differentiation • Focus-costs • Focus-differentiation *Failure strategy:* • Stuck-in-the-middle
Empiric Strategy Types — Consumer products (Chapter 8)	Galbraith and Schendel	Based on a cluster analysis of different strategy posture and strategy direction components.	• Harvest • Builder • Cashout • Consumer niche • Climber • Continuity
Empiric Strategy Types — Industrial products (Chapter 8)	Galbraith and Schendel	Based on a cluster analysis of different strategy posture and strategy direction components.	• Low commitment • Growth • Maintenance • Industrial niche
An Adaptation approach (Chapter 9)	Miles and Snow	Every business unit has to make strategic choices based on three broad problems: the entrepreneurial, the engineering, and the administrative. Together, these strategic choices form an adaptive cycle.	*Three successful types:* • Defenders • Analyzers • Prospectors *One unsuccessful type:* • Reactors
Product-market Strategies (Chapter 10)	Wissema, Van der Pol, and Messer	A product-market combination is defined as one of the six routes from the current to the desired strategic position.	• Explosion • Expansion • Continuous growth • Slip • Consolidation • Contraction

Each approach emphasizes the metavariables in a different way. For example, the Competing Generic (Porter, 1980) and the two Empiric Strategy Types approaches stress the environment and the strategy-making process less and the content of strategy more. The Strategy-making Modes (Mintzberg, 1973b) and the Deliberate and

Emergent Strategies (Mintzberg and Waters, 1985) approaches focus more on the process by which strategies are made and less on their content. The Ten Archetypes Strategies (Miller and Friesen, 1978) approach has the best coverage of metavariables even though it sometimes crosses the border between business unit strategy and corporate strategy.

While most approaches do not refer directly to the business unit's industry life-cycle (for example, the Competing Generic approach applies to industries in any stage of their life-cycle), the Seven Survival Strategies (Vesper, 1979) and the Product-market Strategies (Wissema, Van der Pol, and Messer, 1980) approaches do. These two approaches, and the Empiric Strategy Types, also stress the time dimension of strategy. They identify where the business unit is heading as well as describing its current static strategic posture. Some approaches included in here originated in industrial economics (e.g., the Competing Generic approach) and organizational behavior (e.g., the Adaptation (Miles and Snow, 1978) approach). The two Empiric Strategies approaches are derived from the marketing school of thought, and their databases are oriented accordingly. Together, the three disciplines of industrial economics, organizational behavior, and marketing are the major contributors to the strategy/policy area (Jemison, 1981a). All three schools of thought are integrated into our approach.

The last, but not the least important, criterion was the databases on which the approaches were developed and the methodologies used. Because every database (for example, PIMS) and methodology (for example, factor analysis) has its limitations, to avoid cumulative distortions, we included approaches that use different databases, and many methodologies. The nine approaches define 53 strategies. All are built on the six metavariables. The metavariables, in turn, are divided into 28 strategic variables, each of which can be evaluated by using up to ten indicators.

CHOOSING AN APPROACH FOR COMPARISON

How should a manager select the approach to be used? One approach is to simply try all the approaches. As discussed above, universality was an important criterion for including an approach in this book. However, the relevance of the approach to your business unit is highly dependent on your specific situation. In the chapters that follow, we not only describe each approach but also discuss the assumptions that went into creating it and its limitations. Read these chapters carefully before you decide which approaches to use and how to use them. We return to the issue of choosing an approach again in the last section of Chapter 12.

APPENDIX 2.1

A FRAMEWORK FOR A GROUNDED THEORY OF CORPORATE POLICY[1]

Introduction

The set of cases used in capstone policy and strategy courses in the AACSB accredited graduate schools of business administration can serve as the basis for developing a grounded theory in corporate policy. The term "grounded" is used because the method employed is a systematic discovery of theory from data by use of comparative analysis (Glaser and Strauss, 1967). The framework for developing the theory does not yet exist. Business school texts emphasize the complex nature of corporate policy, the multiplicity of variables, the network of interrelationships, and its contingent nature (Christensen et al, 1982; Glueck and Jauch, 1984; Hofer et al, 1984), but provide no directions for research. At the same time, the empirical literature is partial, pragmatic and segmented; concepts and measures are not used consistently and can conflict. Even the most complex empirical studies investigating a large number of variables are narrow in focus (Galbraith and Schendel, 1983; Miller and Friesen, 1980; Zeithaml and Fry, 1984). To make a meaningful contribution, a good empirical study should define a limited topic, feasible to research, for which data are available. For this reason, most empirical studies focus on a small number of variables, not necessarily at the heart of the strategic process. The variables often seem to have been chosen for their availability rather than their importance to understanding the strategic process.

The fragmented, sometimes marginal or conflicting findings and the lack of significant progress in strategy research prompted Miller (1981) to propose and initiate a holistic approach: classification of organizational strategies (such as those of Galbraith and Schendel, 1983; Hambrick, 1983a; Miles and Snow, 1978; Miller and Friesen, 1978; and Porter, 1980). These *gestalts*, typologies, or taxonomies

[1] Reprinted by permission, "A Framework for a Grounded Theory of Corporate Policy" by Eli Segev, *Interfaces*, Vol. 18, No. 5, Sept.—Oct. 1988. Copyright © 1988, The Institute of Management Sciences (currently INFORMS), 2 Charles Street, Suite 300, Providence, Rhode Island 02904, USA.

suggest different clusters of organizations based on a higher but still limited number of variables. Even in this type of research, a most important question is what exactly should be classified (Hambrick, 1984). Though some metavariables are used in most studies, each research effort is initiated with a unique set of variables and results in different archetypes or generic strategies.

Most empirical research in the strategy and policy area has been conducted since the mid-1970s. The current empirical investigations suffer from the lack of an accepted framework for research in the policy and strategy area.

Both traditional hypotheses—testing studies and classification studies—deal with partial lists of variables and the relationships among them. Such studies can make a meaningful contribution only if they are based on a defined framework that delineates the strategy and policy area and identifies the relevant variables. The framework could then be used to file existing research findings and to facilitate the orderly and systematic accumulation of new findings. It could also be used as a conceptual scheme for researchers to help assure that research focuses on the most important topics, and that the most important findings are highlighted (Kuhn, 1972).

Theoretical background

Several conceptual schemes for strategic research have been used to categorize strategy and policy studies (Beard and Dess, 1981; Bourgeois, 1980; Camillus, 1981; Jauch and Osborn, 1981; Jemison, 1981a, 1981b; Lenz, 1981; White and Hamermesh, 1981). These studies point to only four important concepts in strategic management: *strategy* (Andrews, 1971; Boston Consulting Group, 1968; Chandler, 1962; Glueck, 1976; Rumelt, 1974), *strategy-making* (Aharoni, 1966; Allison, 1971; Ansoff, 1965; Bower, 1970; Cyert and March, 1963; Mintzberg, 1973b), *structure* (Chandler, 1962; Channon, 1973; Child, 1972; Galbraith and Nathanson, 1978; Lawrence and Lorsch, 1967; Perrow, 1970; Woodward, 1965), and *environment* (Anderson and Paine, 1975; Duncan, 1972; Emery and Trist, 1965; Lawrence and Lorsch, 1967). I will review the conceptual schemes and their treatment of these four concepts.

Camillus (1981) focused on the translation of corporate strategy into operating decisions. In a matrix categorization of previous works, he distinguished between corporate and business strategy and posed three dimensions linking strategies and actions: structure, process, and content.

Lenz (1981) focused mainly on the interdependencies of environment, strategy, and structure over time and included process by introducing an administration factor encompassing the quality of management, managerial discretion, strategic group structure, and coalignment of decisions.

Bourgeois (1980) integrated business policy and organizational theory literature, and distinguished between primary and secondary strategies. Primary or corporate strategy is the selection of product markets or industries and the allocation of resources among them. Secondary or business strategy refers to the competitive weapons used to give an organization its "distinctive competence," and depends on task environment characteristics. Bourgeois also differentiated between strategy content and the strategy-making process, although he saw this distinction as a "disciplinary and methodological artifact."

In the empirical study of corporate- and business-level strategies, Beard and Dess (1981) discussed strategy formulation versus strategy on each level. Jemison (1981b) discussed the contribution of administrative behavior to strategic management, citing works in the following areas: organizations and environments, process in organizations, and organizational design. Jemison (1981a) compared the industrial organization, marketing, and administrative behavior concepts of strategic management in relation to unit of analysis, type of problem addressed, predominant inference patterns, and usefulness in strategy formulation and implementation.

White and Hamermesh (1981) also integrated industrial organization economics, organizational theory, and business policy, suggesting a model composed of environment, strategy, and structure and the characteristics or position of the firm (its strategy type). A more elaborate strategy framework is suggested by Jauch and Osborn (1981). In addition to environment and structure, they included context (size and technology) in their strategic profiles and pointed out the role of strategic actions in strategy making.

Thus the literature suggests building blocks for a research framework, the most important being the concepts of strategy, strategy making, structure and environment.

Toward a grounded theory

A model for corporate policy is embodied in the set of cases used in the integrating course of policy usually given at the end of MBA programs in graduate schools of business administration. These courses are referred to as the *capstone* policy and strategy courses. Case studies capture, albeit in a very unstructured way, all the factors affecting or affected by a specific business situation. Written by researchers, they encompass a wide array of business situations and organizations. Unlike the pragmatic, partial, and segmented empirical literature, case studies encompass all the variables affecting strategy, and give examples and descriptions of how these variables interrelate and produce "good" and "bad" outcomes.

In addition to using textbooks, papers and articles, lectures, seminars, and projects, teachers in capstone business policy courses use cases extensively. Most believe that the study of cases is the best method by which students can acquire knowledge. They think that, after analyzing many real-life situations, the student will gain a basic understanding of business policy and its concepts, and will acquire keener analytical skills and the ability to apply them.

Several thousand cases have been written and collected. In any one university, only a small number of cases are used each semester, and one can compile a set of the cases used. Instructors include particular cases because they view them as compatible with the theoretical basis of the course and contributing to it. The inventory of existing written cases in general, and the specific cases included in the syllabus of a business policy course in particular, indicate a certain perception of the existing body of knowledge in the field.

Thus an analysis of the cases used in policy courses and the topics they concern (based on the instructors' notes, the topics studied in the courses, and the case questions) indicate the underlying theory of corporate policy today. Although universities and instructors probably differ in their perceptions of the core of corporate policy, the set of cases currently taught in the capstone policy and strategy courses in the graduate schools of business administration defines the area. A comparative analysis of these cases and the theory covered in these courses will map the area and identify the relevant concepts and variables. In this way, we can identify a grounded theory in corporate policy. Such a theory of corporate policy already exists implicitly; strategy teachers implicitly subscribe to a framework or a set of frameworks when developing course outlines, and case writers use vocabulary guided by these frameworks and attempt to frame the central problem around an implicit overarching framework. Since this implicit theory is precisely what I am attempting to develop in the present research by analyzing the data generated, I use the term *grounded theory*.

Discussing theory building and testing in strategic management, Duncan (1979) pointed out that:

> A particularly useful approach to theory-building for policy is the grounded theory approach of Glaser and Strauss (1967). This approach is particularly relevant to policy because it starts with the data. In the grounded theory approach, conceptual categories are developed from the data, then developed into hypotheses, and tested through comparative analysis to see if they are empirically verifiable in different settings (p. 432).

Generating a theory from data means that most of the hypotheses and concepts not only come from the data, but are systematically worked out in relation to the data during the course of the research. "In discovering theory, one generates conceptual categories or their properties from evidence; then the evidence from which the category emerged is used to illustrate the concept" (Glaser and Strauss, 1967, p. 23). Lyles and Mitroff (1980) stress that "the theory is grounded on the data but is not rigidly bound to it, and the researcher can go beyond the original research plan and original theory" (p. 104). Burgelman (1983a) comments, "Data must be collected until patterns have clearly emerged and additional data no longer add to the refinement of the concept" (pp. 224–225). The initial and critical steps in theory-building using this approach are concept identification and suggestion of a framework.

Development of the framework

My main assumption at the outset of this study was that it would be possible to classify the tremendous number of concepts discussed in the policy and strategy literature into four metavariables: strategy content, strategy process, organizational structure, and business environment. The fifth, and usually dependent, variable was taken to be organizational performance. Each of the first four metavariables is a defined subsystem which affects and is affected by the others, and the performance of an organization pursuing a specific policy is affected by the interrelationships among them. I also assumed that, within each subsystem, a clear hierarchy of variables elaborates and operatively defines the main concepts.

In February and March 1984, requests for syllabi of their courses were sent to policy and strategy professors at 189 US universities with accredited master's programs in business administration. In universities with large policy faculties, several professors were approached. I received 147 syllabi, of which 142 from 107 different universities were relevant (five were either for an undergraduate course or a noncapstone policy course).

Most of the 670 different cases appearing in the syllabi were collected along with instructors' notes when available. For a few widely used cases, more than one set of notes existed. A multi-step classification procedure was used to determine the match between cases and course topics. An initial list of key words (strategic variables) was constructed from 889 course topics extracted from the syllabi. Additional key words emerged from content analysis of the instructors' notes. A special effort was made to study as many instructors' notes as possible, in order to ascertain the use of cases according to university, topic, and professor. The flood of strategic concepts identified in the instructors' notes decreased exponentially as I proceeded, the last half of the notes yielding very few additional concepts and only peripheral variables. I even included concepts only remotely connected with strategy in the list.

The raw list of strategic variables extracted from the course syllabi and instructors' notes was categorized according to the five metavariables (for a "mental factor analysis", see, for example, Keys and Miller (1984)). Inconsistencies and leftovers made it necessary to further review the definitions of strategy and the variables in two related areas: decision making and organizational theory. This suggested the following changes in the *a priori* variables:

1. Dividing *strategy content* into *strategy* and *strategic actions.*
2. Extracting *strategic actors* from *process.*
3. Introducing *organizational design* and breaking it down to include *organizational structure* and *systems and processes.*
4. Recognizing *organizational characteristics* as contingent strategic variables (see Figure A2.1).

STRATEGY

- Mission, goals, objectives
- CORPORATE STRATEGY
  - Business portfolio
- BUSINESS STRATEGY
  - Product market scope
  - Type of innovation
  - Pace of product-market change
- FUNCTIONAL STRATEGY
  - Accounting strategy
  - Environmental strategy
  - Distribution strategy

STRATEGIC ACTIONS

- ACQUISITION
  - Takeover
  - Tender
- INVESTMENT
  - Foreign
- DIVESTMENT
  - Liquidation

ORGANIZATIONAL CHARACTERISTICS

- OWNERSHIP
- SIZE
- RESOURCES
- TYPE

ENVIRONMENT

- Environmental changes
- GENERAL ENVIRONMENT
  - Economic environment
  - Political/legal environment
  - Social environment
  - Technological environment

STRATEGIC PROCESS

- VALUE SYSTEM
  - Risk
  - Ideology
  - Management style
  - Ethics
- POWER
- ANALYSIS
  - Analysis of strategy
  - Environmental analysis
  - Forecasting

Figure A2.1 Delineation of strategic metavariables. (*continued overleaf*).

ORGANIZATIONAL DESIGN

- ORGANIZATIONAL STRUCTURE
  - Type of structure
  - Formalization
  - Hierarchy
  - Professionalization
  - Centralization
  - Span of control
  - Authority
  - Integration
  - Units

STRATEGIC ACTORS

- BOARD OF DIRECTORS
- CHIEF EXECUTIVE OFFICER
- EXECUTIVE TEAM
- MIDDLE-LEVEL MANAGEMENT
- CORPORATE STAFF

ORGANIZATIONAL PERFORMANCE

- SURVIVAL
  - Success
  - Fit
  - Effectiveness
- GROWTH
- MARKET SHARE
- PROFITABILITY
  - Net return on equity
- STOCK PRICE
  - Earning per share

Figure A2.1 *(continued).*

These changes resolved the inconsistencies and made possible an eight-metavariable framework: a *strategy* is the *actions* taken to match an *organization* with its *environment*. The strategy is formulated and implemented by a *process* and an *organizational design* in which various *actors* take part. Strategic match results in high *performance*.

Eleven residual variables that were still oddities were omitted from the new framework. This framework covers the main strategic variables included in the cases used in strategy and policy capstone courses, and captures the main relationships among them as well. I do not claim that the raw variable list is exhaustive. Nevertheless, I have identified the metavariables and their major properties and structure. Additional variables may refine, add to, or elaborate upon the lower-level variables but will not alter the framework.

Definitions of metavariables

The framework consists of eight metavariables: strategy, strategic actions, organizational characteristics, environment, strategic process, organizational design, strategic actors, and organizational performance.

- *Strategy* is the organization's long-term goals and the means to achieve them. The framework follows the accepted hierarchical division: corporate strategy, business strategy, and functional strategy. All refer to long-term organizational goals and the means to achieve them. Corporate strategy focuses on the mix of industries and product markets and the allocation of resources among them. Business strategy focuses on the distinctive competence of a business unit within its industry. Functional strategy is the consistent implementation in the functional areas of the upper-level strategies. It is also possible to distinguish among stated (official, written, and verbal communications), intended (pursued), and resultant strategy. The three may be identical; for example, if management discloses its real strategy and succeeds in implementing it. Or, differences may exist among the three because of competitive tactics or unforeseen opportunities, constraints, and failures in implementation. Resultant strategy can always be identified afterwards, even when it was not intentionally pursued. A strategy is planned, implemented, identified, and depicted by strategic actions.
- *Strategic actions* are the acquisition, development, allocation, and application of a significant portion of the organization's resources to achieve or affect its long-term goals. These actions affect the organization for long periods and are difficult to undo. Examples may include acquisitions, divestiture, joint ventures, expansion and mergers. The choice and nature of these actions are heavily dependent on organizational characteristics.
- *Organizational characteristics* are the inherent outcomes of the organization's establishment, history, and past strategy. They

affect and constrain organizational actions and are difficult, if not impossible, to modify in the short run. Thus, mode of ownership, size, and resources, for example, should be considered in the effort to match the organization with its environment.

- *Environment* covers all the factors outside the organization that affect (and may affect) it or are affected (and may be affected) by it. The framework I suggest lends itself to the accepted practice of dividing the environment into general and task environments. The above definition better fits the general environment, which includes all the factors with which the organization may interact in the future (and is composed of the economic, political, legal, social, and technological subenvironments). Task environment refers to those aspects of the environment that impinge on goal attainment activities. The match between the organization and its environment is the focus of the strategic process; one task environment variable of the business unit—the relevant industry—deserves special attention.
- *Strategic process* is the decision-making process whereby, intentionally or unintentionally, the organization's goals and the actions to be taken to achieve them are decided. This subsystem of strategic variables includes organizational ideology, value, and power, as well as formal analysis, planning, and analytical tools. Through this process, organizational strategy is formulated and implemented. The strategic process takes place within an organizational design.
- *Organizational design* includes organizational structure, systems, and processes. Since organizational design variables are usually modified in the strategy implementation stage, they were separated from the category of organizational characteristics that are hard or impossible to manipulate, and classified as a separate metavariable.
- *Strategic actors* are the participants in the strategic process, such as the board of directors, the chief executive officer, the executive team, and the corporate staff.
- *Organizational performance* is the ultimate dependent metavariable in the framework. The variables and measures in this category relate both to the choice of organizational goals and the

degree to which they are achieved. While fit, survival, and effectiveness focus on long-term performance, which is the result of the major decisions taken to match the organization with its environment (such as products, markets, and technology), performance measures, such as profitability, market share, and cash flow, relate to the degree of match in a given domain.

The next research steps

I have described the first steps toward a grounded theory of corporate policy, discussing the need for a framework and reviewing the literature. I have suggested a method for developing a framework. The next steps are theory-building and defining operational measures for the variables. Theory-building may proceed on two very different planes: holistic and atomistic. The holistic approach entails a search for simultaneous relationships or profiles for the vast number of variables. The atomistic approach entails serial but comprehensive attention to relatively small sets of variables. Testing atomistic hypotheses has recently been a target of criticism (Hambrick, 1984; Miller, 1981), and much of the current research in the area is holistic (for example, Miller and Friesen, 1978), or bounded holistic, in which subpopulations are studied (for example, Hambrick's (1983a) typology of mature industrial products). I decided, nevertheless, to pursue a theory-building approach that is basically atomistic.

Certain characteristics of the holistic approach render it unfit for theory-building in the present case. First, it is only partially anchored in the accumulated knowledge. A holistic approach may be *a priori* rooted in the accumulated knowledge by the choice of variables and the definition of the population. There is no place for drawing extensively on previously found relationships or hypothesized strategic types. Thus conceptualizations may not accurately reflect reality (Hambrick, 1984), and empirically found strategic clusters are just that. Second, results are highly dependent on the population, variables, and methods (Hambrick, 1984). The cases in our database focus on a very heterogeneous population of organizations, and any classification of its strategic types will be unique. Moreover, all variables would have to be measured for each organization and the data are just not available. Third, validation by further studies will be highly problematic. A large number of incompatible and noncomparable typologies emerge from the literature (Dess and Davis, 1984; Galbraith and Schendel, 1983; Hambrick, 1983a; Miles and Snow, 1978; Miller and Friesen, 1978; Mintzberg, 1973b; Porter, 1980; Thietart and Vivas, 1984; Vesper, 1979; and Wissema, Van der Pol, and Messer, 1980). Comparative analysis of the different studies is cumbersome and yields only minor contributions, if any. Fourth, the holistic approach does not lend itself to step-by-step refinement and to accumulation of knowledge on the studied phenomenon. Empirical studies using this approach have rarely prompted subsequent research, although conceptual typologies have done so.

In this project I will use a piecemeal but comprehensive approach. I will use subsets of cases that focus on one or two metavariables and analyze them to identify patterns. I will study the emerging patterns in light of the existing literature and report them as propositions. This is a large-scale project, and it will require considerable time to complete. In order to demonstrate the approach chosen, I have selected a few variables: three relate to business strategy (product-market scope; type of innovation; pace of product-market change), and two to the strategic process (power centralization; formal analysis).

Following are some suggested operational measures of these variables. The product-market scope may be measured by some or all of the following measures: SIC (Standard Industry Classification) codes; the number of different products; the number of different markets; the domain coverage relative to industry leader; the relative breadth of product line; the relative number of customers; the relative variety of customer types. Type of innovation could be divided, for example, into innovation in the market (first-in), innovation in the organization (me-too), and product adaptation. The pace of product-market change may be measured by the number of product-market changes made by the organization per time unit or by the relative number of new products.

Of the strategic process variables, power centralization may be measured by the number of decision units, the degree of power distribution for strategic decisions measured in monetary values, and the size and composition of the strategy-making team. Formal analysis measures may include the amount of time invested in analysis, use of formal techniques, the use of staff specialists, and the formal choice among alternatives.

Three propositions emerge from the literature survey that relate to the product-market scope (because space is limited, I will not discuss the relevant literature):

- *Proposition 1*: A narrow product-market scope ("niche strategy") enhances business performance when pursued in a context of extensive power centralized in the hands of the chief executive officer of the business unit.
- *Proposition 2*: Pursuit of a wide product-market domain in a centralized context decreases the performance of the business unit.
- *Proposition 3*: A wide product-market strategy increases business performance in a context of formal analysis.

Two propositions relate to the type of innovation:

- *Proposition 4*: A first-in product-market innovation strategy increases business performance when power in the business-level unit is centralized.
- *Proposition 5*: A first-in product-market innovation business strategy in a context of formal analysis increases business performance.

The last three propositions relate to the pace of product-market change:

- *Proposition 6*: A rapid product-market change strategy in a centralized business decreases its performance.
- *Proposition 7*: Performance is decreased when a centralized business with a low performance record implements a strategy of rapid product-market changes.
- *Proposition 8*: An accelerated product-market change business strategy requires formal analysis procedures to increase the business's performance.

Although each proposition by itself cannot convey the complex system of interrelationships in business policy, a comprehensive set of such propositions will encompass and map all interrelationships in the system of variables. Single propositions of this type lend themselves to empirical research and to further refinement in manageable research projects. Sets of these propositions may be used to identify and study further unique strategic populations and types. Once this enormous project, or meaningful parts of it, are completed, it will serve as a filing system for existing research findings and may facilitate the orderly and systematic accumulation of new findings. My aim is to enable rather than constrain future research efforts. Although the list of variables is defined, no single population, data base, or research method is implied, and specific operational measures will depend on the research method and its context. The only requirement is an identifiable additional contribution to the area.

3

Indicators, Distance Measures and Deliberate vs. Emergent Strategies

The present chapter and Chapters 4 through 10 each focus on an approach and its relevant strategic variables. The strategic variables are defined as they are needed in specific approaches.

This chapter also first introduces indicators. Indicators are the most detailed level at which a business unit's strategy is operationalized in our approach. Indicators serve three purposes:

1. They facilitate better definitions of the strategic variables.
2. They enable better measurement of the variables.
3. They provide a basis for feasibility analysis of strategic change.

As we define each variable, we will also list indicators that we believe are appropriate for that variable. You can use these indicators or you can add or delete from the list. We do recommend, of course, that if you use a variable in different approaches for a given SBU, you keep the same indicators.

At the end of this chapter we present and discuss distance measures between strategic profiles.

APPROACH 1: DELIBERATE VS. EMERGENT STRATEGIES

This approach was chosen as the first one to be presented because it requires the smallest number of strategic variables: 13 out of our 28 variables. The approach focuses on the strategy development process and distinguishes between deliberate and emergent strategies. Deliberate and emergent strategies may be conceived of as two ends of a continuum along which strategies lie. The continuum is based on the different ways in which the strategies are created rather than on their content. At one end are completely planned strategies (called deliberate) while at the other are strategies created with no prior specific intent (called emergent).

The deliberate vs. Emergent Strategies approach is now ten years old, old enough to prove its practicality and to be included in our framework. Of all the approaches discussed in this book it took the longest time to construct. The approach was developed by Professors Henry Mintzberg and James A. Waters on the basis of 11 longitudinal studies of strategy formation processes conducted over a period of more than ten years (Mintzberg and Waters, 1985.) Studying streams of decisions in organizations, Professors Mintzberg and Waters identified patterns or consistencies in these streams. Each pattern was defined to be a different strategy and its origin was studied.

THE STRATEGIES

The names of the eight strategies included in this approach are:

- Planned
- Entrepreneurial
- Ideological
- Umbrella
- Process
- Unconnected
- Consensus
- Imposed

Table 3.1 shows the values of the variables for each of the strategies in this approach. In the description of the strategies that follows we will use the term strategic actors to refer to those individuals involved in the strategy-making process. Since deliberate and emergent are opposite ends of a continuum, we will describe strategies that are in the middle of this continuum as being deliberate-emergent.

Planned strategies

Planned strategies originate in formal plans. Precise intentions exist, formulated and articulated by central leadership and backed up by formal controls to ensure surprise-free implementation if the

Table 3.1 Variable values for the strategies in the Deliberate vs. Emergent approach.

Variable Strategy:	1	2	3	4	5	6	7	8
Metavariable: environment								
1. Environmental uncertainty	4	48	26	81	88	66	56	65
2. Environmental dynamism	8	54	23	75	83	71	55	75
3. Environmental hostility	4	14	21	71	60	28	25	95
4. Environmental complexity	11	26	31	82	88	76	60	76
Metavariable: strategy making								
16. Internal analysis level	95	44	82	61	60	27	46	33
17. External analysis & forecast	86	75	76	67	56	47	41	13
18. Level of risk	8	76	37	49	49	50	47	68
19. Proactive management	65	94	82	47	48	50	30	1
Metavariable: structure								
20. Size of strategy-making team	30	2	65	54	59	56	87	40
21. Degree of centralization	79	82	47	33	32	24	26	45
22. Degree of mechanism	87	45	56	35	52	13	18	45
Metavariable: performance								
23. Profitability	75	33	42	63	58	63	50	13
26. Operational efficiency	93	31	42	64	52	19	36	13

Strategies:
1 = Planned, 2 = Entrepreneurial, 3 = Ideological
4 = Umbrella, 5 = Process, 6 = Unconnected
7 = Consensus, 8 = Imposed

environment is benign, controllable, and predictable. Strategies are for the most part deliberate.

Entrepreneurial strategies

Entrepreneurial strategies originate as the personal, unarticulated vision of a single leader and are adaptable, therefore, to new opportunities. The organization is under the personal control of the leader and is located in a protected niche in the environment. Strategies are for the most part deliberate but can be emergent.

Ideological strategies

Ideological strategies originate in shared beliefs. Intentions exist as the collective vision of all strategic actors, in an inspirational form. They are generally immutable and are controlled normatively through indoctrination and/or socialization. The organization is often proactive with respect to its environment. Strategies are for the most part deliberate.

Umbrella strategies

Umbrella strategies originate in constraints. Leadership, in partial control of organizational actions, defines strategic boundaries or targets, and other strategic actors respond within the constraints of their own forces or those of the complex, perhaps unpredictable, environment.

Process strategies

Process strategies originate in processes. Leadership controls the process aspects of strategy (hiring, structure, etc.), leaving content aspects, in complex environments, to other strategic actors. Strategies may be deliberate, emergent, or, again, deliberate-emergent.

Unconnected strategies

Unconnected strategies originate in enclaves. Strategic actors, or professional experts, loosely coupled to the rest of the organization, produce patterns of actions in the absence of, or in direct contradiction to, central or common intentions. Strategies are organizationally emergent, whether or not they were initiated deliberately.

Consensus strategies

Consensus strategies originate in general agreement among top management. Through mutual adjustment, strategic actors converge on patterns that become pervasive in the absence of central or common intentions. Strategies tend to be emergent.

Imposed strategies

Imposed strategies originate in the environment. The environment dictates patterns of actions either by imposing them directly, or implicitly by pre-empting or bounding organizational choice. Strategies are for the most part emergent. However, once established, they may be internalized by the organization and made deliberate.

USES AND MISUSES OF THE DELIBERATE VS. EMERGENT APPROACH

The Deliberate vs. Emergent approach is the "thinnest" in our framework. Only 13 variables are used to define its eight strategies. Thus, when using this approach to identify your business unit's strategy, remember that only a very partial, albeit important, classification can be obtained. For a comprehensive identification of your strategy, other approaches (presented in later chapters) should be used in conjunction with this one.

This approach emphasizes the relations between the business unit and its environment, mainly the degree of environmental turbulence (uncertainty, dynamism, hostility, and complexity) and the organization's ability to control and forecast environmental conditions. Thus, it is a good starting point for an analysis that starts outside the organization and works its way inside.

You should use the Deliberate vs. Emergent approach before you begin an in-depth analysis of your business unit's strategy. The analysis itself is an indication of deliberate intentions that, we hope, will result in proposals for a better strategy for your business unit. Will the current strategy process allow for the adoption of such proposals?

Use of this approach immediately places the business unit's strategy on the deliberate—emergent continuum. It points out which of the eight benchmark strategies is best matched with the way strategies are currently created in your organization. Thus, this approach is a starting point from which the content of the strategy may be analyzed. Since the eight strategies form a continuum, it may sometimes be difficult to pinpoint a single strategy that your SBU matches. You may fall between two adjacent benchmark strategies, indicating a hybrid strategy. For example, the distance from your strategy to the process strategy may be nearly equal to the distance to the umbrella strategy.

The major shortcoming of this approach is its complete lack of consideration of variables that describe strategy content. You are probably anxious to deal with strategic variables such as product-market breadth, technological progress, product innovation, and investment in production. Sorry, but you will have to wait until these variables are introduced in the next chapter. The Deliberate vs. Emergent Strategies approach tells you only how important strategic decisions were made previously in your SBU. The approach may indicate possible changes required in the strategy process before the strategy content is modified.

The approach is universal and may be applied to any size or kind of organization. It is applicable not only to the business unit but even to non-profit organizations or government agencies. This universality inhibits the use of the approach for evaluating and analyzing business success. Any strategy may be associated with both success and failure. Although profitability and operational efficiency are variables evaluated and used in this approach, and although some initial conclusions may be made about performance (for example, low relative profitability for the unconnected strategy), no operational decisions should be made on the basis of this approach alone. Parallel use of at least the Ten Archetypes approach (Chapter 5), the Competing Generic Strategies approach (Chapter 7), and the Adaptation approach (Chapter 9) is required before an SBU's strategy can be defined as a success or a failure strategy, and before you can make a decision on how to change it.

THE 13 VARIABLES USED IN THIS APPROACH AND THEIR INDICATORS

Use of this approach in our framework for identifying a business unit's strategy, requires a strategic profile composed of the following 13 variables. These variables have been organized into four metavariables or groups as shown.

Environmental variables:

1. Environmental uncertainty
2. Environmental dynamism
3. Environmental hostility
4. Environmental complexity

Strategy-making process variables:

16. Internal analysis level
17. External analysis and forecasting level
18. Level of risk
19. Proactiveness of decisions
20. Size of strategy-making team

Organizational structure variables:

21. Centralization
22. Mechanism

Performance variables:

23. Profitability
28. Operational Efficiency

As we noted at the beginning of this chapter, the strategic variables that define the strategy are evaluated by using up to ten indicators for each variable. For each strategic variable used in the Deliberate vs. Emergent Strategies approach, we present

1. The definition of the strategic variable.
2. The scale for measuring the variable.
3. One or more examples based on real-life situations.
4. A short discussion of the place of the strategic variable in the business unit's strategy.
5. Recommended indicators for the variable.

ENVIRONMENTAL VARIABLES

Environmental uncertainty

Definition. The environment is a source of information used by top management as one of the bases in determining strategy. Environmental uncertainty reflects the lack of information available to decision makers for predicting environmental events and external changes and for determining the impact of these events and changes on the strategic business unit's performance.

Measurement. Complete uncertainty about the environment is evaluated as 100. Average uncertainty is evaluated as 50. If there is no uncertainty about the environment (a rare situation), assign a value of zero.

Example. The management team of Methocel Product Division of the Dow Chemical Company was faced with both internal and external uncertainties ("Methocel Product Division at the Dow Chemical Company," 1982). The internal uncertainties involved productive capacity and cost of production. The major uncertainties were external:

1. Forecast demand. A two-year sales decline that had started three years ago had been ascribed to a general business recession. However, sales forecasting was now more difficult because previous sales could no longer be extrapolated.
2. Average revenue per pound of product.
3. Competitive action. Large, well-financed major competitors exist who could buy market share if they so chose.

4. New product development by competitors.
5. New process development.

Based on these considerations, Methocel's environmental uncertainty would have to be judged as 75.

Discussion. Environmental uncertainty has long been widely accepted as an important strategic variable. Its impact on organizational activities and performance has been studied in depth (Lawrence and Lorsch, 1967; Duncan, 1972; Tosi, Aldag, and Storey, 1973; Downey, Hellreigel, and Slocum, 1975; Aldrich, 1979). The level of environmental uncertainty is largely dependent on the beholder. True, environments may be unstable, volatile, complex, turbulent, and, speaking objectively, highly uncertain. In strategy making, however, the relevant factor is the information about the environment as perceived by the strategy-making team, and the impact of uncertainty on the team's ability to make decisions.

Indicators. Since environmental uncertainty is measured by the amount of information decision makers have about external factors, the best way of further delineating this strategic variable is to divide the environment into its components and evaluate the uncertainty posed by each: i.e., the amount of information available to the decision makers on each relevant component of the environment.

Several approaches for subdividing the total environment into comprehensible and manageable components exist, including division into its economic, political and legal, social and demographic, and technological subsystems. For a business unit, however, the stakeholder approach is the most useful one. In this approach, the environment is subdivided into external categories that affect or may affect decisions. The stakeholders include the business unit's owners, suppliers of machinery and raw materials, subcontractors, customers, competitors, lenders (banks), workers, labor unions, government (both bureaucracy and legislative bodies), and community (local authorities, residents). Business units in industries with special structures (such as the insurance industry, pharmaceutical industry, or record industry) should also take into account the industry's unique stakeholders (such as reinsurance companies, pharmacists, physicians, or disk jockeys).

The indicators recommended for measuring environmental uncertainty are:

1. Owners
2. Suppliers
3. Subcontractors
4. Customers
5. Competitors
6. Lenders
7. Workers
8. Labor unions
9. Government
10. Community

We will use the same indicators for each of the environmental variables.

Environmental dynamism

Definition. Environmental dynamism is the rapidity and amount of change in the environment of the business unit. It reflects the rate of change in the number and size of the competitors and competitive practices; the rate of obsolescence of products and services; the predictability of demand and consumer tastes; the rate, direction, and amount in which the production or service technology changes; the changes in the relevant regulation; and the changes in the economy at large (rate of inflation, foreign exchange rates).

Measurement. A score of 100 indicates quick and total change in the wider environment as well as in the business unit industry, while 50 indicates the long-term average environmental dynamism across all industries.

Example. After a long stretch of relative stability, the US chainsaw industry went through a period of rapid growth in the early 1970s ("The Chain Saw Industry 1978," 1981). This growth was stimulated by increased consumer interest caused by the energy crisis and the trends of returning to nature and of self-sufficiency. Homelite, a division of Textron, Inc., was the dominant company in a relatively calm mass market. Homelite suddenly encountered an extremely dynamic environment in which it was faced with increased competition from two other major companies that had been acquired by large parent organizations, as well as from many other participants who were taking a renewed interest in this fast-growth market. Homelite's problem was how to respond to these changing conditions.

Homelite's environmental dynamism is estimated to be 80.

Example. Montedison S.p.A was formed in 1966 by a merger between two Italian business groups, Montecatini and Edison Company ("Montedison, S.p.A.," 1985). In its early stages of development, the company was faced with a multitude of crises. Labor conflicts in 1969 led to wage increases three times larger than those negotiated in previous years and to a host of new labor laws. Montedison's labor costs rose from 29% of sales in 1969 to 34% in 1972, and moderate profits turned into heavy losses. The company's debt-to-equity ratio rose from 0.4 in 1969 to 1.8 in 1972. The oil crisis of 1973–74 did not help matters. The price of oil quadrupled, and the lire devalued 25% against the dollar. Prior to the oil shock, the petrochemical industry had a ratio of variable to fixed costs of 30:70. By the end of the 1970s, the variable costs had reached 70%.

Environmental dynamism for Montedison is estimated to be 75.

Discussion. When the interdependence between the business unit and its environment first became a focus for study, the degree of dynamism in the environment was recognized as one of its important dimensions (Emery and Trist, 1965; Miller and Friesen, 1978). The four environmental variables chosen here (uncertainty, dynamism, hostility, and complexity) are not totally independent (Pfeffer and Salancik, 1978). It is clear that high dynamism, for example, contributes to uncertainty. However, environments do not lend themselves to definition by a single variable. Creating an environmental profile in terms of the four variables is sufficient and not excessive.

Indicators. Environmental dynamism, like environmental uncertainty, is best evaluated by adopting the stakeholder approach. The same indicators apply:

1. Owners
2. Suppliers
3. Subcontractors
4. Customers
5. Competitors
6. Lenders
7. Workers
8. Labor unions
9. Government
10. Community

Environmental hostility

Definition. Environmental hostility reflects the prevalence in the environment of factors that pose threats to the strategic business unit and its interests. These factors may include tough price competition, dwindling markets, technological and distribution competition, regulatory restrictions, and an antagonistic community. A benevolent environment, on the other hand, has munificent raw materials and other resources, positive and supportive attitudes by national and local leaders, and secure and protected markets.

Measurement. A score of 100 indicates a completely hostile environment. Zero indicates a highly benevolent environment, and 50 a neutral one.

Example. In 1975, Albertson's Inc. recorded consolidated sales of $1.27 billion ("Albertson's Inc.," 1984). It had been ranked by both *Fortune* and *Forbes* magazines as one of the leading supermarket chains in the United States. The previous two years had been times of high price inflation and high unemployment. By early 1975, the economy was in the worst recession since World War II. Economic recovery began in mid-1975, and by mid-1976 the economy had improved to the same level as in the fall of 1974. Food price increases during 1973–74 were attributed to such forces as the following:

- Economic activity had increased.
- Foreign countries had purchased more US farm products, decreasing the domestic supply levels.
- US livestock production was down.

- People had bid up the price of meat in 1973, causing a rapid rise with the small cutback in meat production.
- Food marketing margins had increased more sharply in recent years.
- US food stamps and food distribution programs were helping 15 million lower-income people (more than twice as many as in 1969); they were spending more on food, thereby adding to demand.

The food-retailing industry had been subjected to customer boycotts during the times of the highest inflation in 1973 and 1974. These reactions were especially intense during times of shortages and high prices of specific items, such as beef. Food processors and retailers were accused of raising prices more than the increase in costs. Farmers complained that they were being hurt by inflation and that middlemen were taking the profits.

In 1975, the Joint Economic Committee of Congress had subpoenaed the records and documents of the 17 largest US food chains, including Albertson's. The committee was interested in the structure of the food-retailing industry and the resulting impact on prices. By mid-1976 the committee had not yet released any of its findings. At that point in time, the vice-chairman of Albertson's recognized that several changes in the business environment could affect his firm's way of doing business:

- Concern over food prices and food expenditures as a percent of disposable income would put pressure on improving productivity, store design, and merchandising concepts.
- The need to reduce time and distance necessary to shop would require more "one-stop" stores.
- "Eating out" would have an effect on grocery sales.
- More convenience foods.
- Larger quantity sales, such as case lots.

Environmental hostility for Albertson's is estimated as 80.

Example. In 1969, BASF, the German petrochemical giant, expanded operations in the US by acquiring land to build a $100 million petrochemical plant in Beaufort County, South Carolina ("BASF Corporation versus the Hilton Head Island Developers," 1983). State officials wanted BASF to locate in this county because of the extreme poverty and economic imbalances in the area. In late 1969, the developers of a nearby multimillion-dollar resort area claimed that the plant would pollute the Colleton River, one of the few remaining unspoiled estuaries, thereby destroying the wildlife, the fishing industry, and, of course, their resort development. Charges of ecological damage were made by conservationist groups as well. After a series of legal battles, the Secretary of the Interior and the state legislature stopped construction of the plant.

BASF's experience in South Carolina is an example of total environmental hostility. This variable is therefore set at 100.

Example. KIS, a French company with 10,000 photo outlets worldwide, earned about $4 million in 1986 (*Business Week*, 1986f). A *Business Week* investigation revealed that KIS might have engaged in questionable business practices, including false advertising and misrepresentation to prospective investors. Worldwide reaction against the company included the following:

- Angry customers sued KIS for fraud. They complained that KIS provided low-quality equipment and service, that its sales tactics were coercive, and that its equipment and supplies were overpriced.
- Former KIS executives and employees sued the company for questionable business practices.
- Several governments, including the French, Canadian, and US governments, were inundated with complaints from KIS customers and started investigations into KIS's business practices.
- Sizable anti-KIS groups sprung up in France and West Germany.

KIS was facing environmental hostility at a nearly but not quite total level. An appropriate value would be 95.

Example. In 1987, the Food and Drug Administration attacked the new anti-aging creams that purported to eliminate wrinkles from the skin (*Business Month*, 1987c). The FDA's reasoning was that if the creams really did what they claimed to do, they were drugs and not cosmetics. This interpretation would subject the creams to testing and regulation. Major targets were Alvin Fragrance's Glycel and Avon Products' Bioadvance Beauty Recovery System. According to the FDA, if the manufacturers did not submit the creams for testing, a seizure order might follow. As of June 1987, the target companies had filed for postponements while they decided what to do to counter the threat to their new products.

The FDA action made the government regulation indicator more important for these firms. In evaluating government regulation, both the weighting allocated to this indicator and its value had to be increased. Under these conditions, environmental hostility had risen to 80.

Example. In 1975, the Environmental Protection Agency (EPA) instituted fuel-efficiency requirements (*Business Month*, 1987b). While Chrysler Corp. complied with the regulations from the beginning, Ford Motor Co. and General Motors Corp. ignored them. In 1986, the Environmental Protection Agency relaxed its fuel-efficiency requirements. This revision got Ford and GM off the hook. However, the companies did not consider the possibility of consumer groups bringing lawsuits against the government's policy on fuel economy. When the consumer groups went into action, Ford and GM were faced with approximately $300 million in fines. In December 1986, the US Court of Appeals for the District of Columbia ruled that the EPA must rescind its action of relaxing the fuel-efficiency requirements, effectively placing Ford and GM in contravention of the regulations.

These events increased the environmental hostility for Ford and GM into the 60 to 70 range but decreased it for Chrysler to under 50. This example illustrates the fact that the same environmental conditions can result in different values of the environmental variables for different firms.

Example. Although R.J. Reynolds Industries was cleared by a Santa Barbara jury of all responsibility for the death of a long-time cigarette smoker, Wall Street analysts spoke of increasingly critical attitudes toward the industry and concluded that the outcome of future suits was unpredictable (*Business Month*, 1986c). As of February 1986, there were four product liability suits pending against cigarette producers. In December 1985, the American Medical Association called for a total ban on cigarette advertising, and in 1987, the Surgeon General of the United States declared cigarettes addictive.

Cigarette SBUs operate in a climate of hostility toward their product. For them, the environmental hostility variable is rated at 75 despite support from smokers, tobacco farmers, and state legislatures eager for additional tax revenue.

Example. In the mid-1980s, the bureaucracy and red ink in Brazil and Argentina was reportedly driving Ford Motor Co. and Volkswagen into each other's arms (*Business Week*, 1986e). By joining forces, the two companies planned to reap greater profits. In both countries, they were up against government-imposed price controls. In 1986, Brazil's anti-inflationary Cruzado Plan restricted the flow of imported auto parts and disrupted production. Since they were unable to influence government policy, Ford and VW could at least, by combining forces, achieve greater efficiency and economies of scale in their 15 plants in the two countries.

The major threat to the venture, scheduled for mid-1987, came from the auto workers' unions. These strong unions wielded a lot of power among the companies' combined workforce of 75,000. In strike-prone Argentina, where Ford has faced many bitter struggles, intense union opposition was expected.

Environmental hostility had moved to 80 and was heading up.

Discussion. A hostile environment creates a threat to the survival of the business unit. High environmental hostility may severely affect the business unit's innovative capacity, strategy making, and structure (Khadwalla, 1972; Miller and Friesen, 1982a).

Indicators. Stakeholder indicators are again recommended:

1. Owners
2. Suppliers
3. Subcontractors
4. Customers

5. Competitors
6. Lenders
7. Workers
8. Labor unions
9. Government
10. Community

Environmental complexity

Definition. Environmental complexity is the number and diversity of external elements relevant to the business unit's operations. In a complex environment, a large number of diverse stakeholders interact and influence the business unit. In a simple environment, few and highly homogeneous external elements have an impact on the organization.

Measurement. A score of 100 indicates the most complex environment, 50 an average environment, and zero a very simple one.

Example. In 1984, the telecommunications market was in a state of turmoil. The courts had ordered the breakup of American Telephone and Telegraph (AT&T) (''AT&T Longlines Department National Account Selling,'' 1980). The legal environment changed with the institution of deregulation and the changes in the remaining regulatory requirements. The mid-1980s became a time of price wars and cut-throat competition in the industry. Many new products and services were introduced, including accounting codes, cellular mobile phones, videotext, and facsimile, with varying degrees of success. In the midst of this complex and diverse environment, MCI Communications tried to apply its philosophy of being a market responsive, full-service telecommunications company and to generate increased market share.

For AT&T, the environment that had once been relatively placid (value 35) had suddenly changed to being highly complex (value 90).

Discussion. The complex—noncomplex spectrum relates to the number of critically important information categories necessary for decision making (Child, 1972; Duncan, 1972; Jurkovitch, 1974). It contains within it the homogeneity—heterogeneity spectrum sometimes used as a stand-alone environmental variable by other authors (Aldrich, 1979; Miller and Friesen, 1978). As in the case of the other three environmental variables, it is the decision makers' perception of the complexity of the environment, or its components, that counts. Practice has shown that managers have a definite evaluation of the degree of complexity in their business unit's environment. This evaluation may be refined by using the indicators to evaluate each stakeholder in the unit's environment.

Indicators. Stakeholder indicators are recommended:

1. Owners
2. Suppliers
3. Subcontractors
4. Customers

5. Competitors
6. Lenders
7. Workers
8. Labor unions
9. Government
10. Community

STRATEGY-MAKING PROCESS VARIABLES

Since the Deliberate vs. Emergent Strategies approach focuses on the process by which strategies are formulated and implemented and not on their content, using this approach in our framework requires no strategy content variables. The next four variables relate to the strategy-making process.

Internal analysis level

Definition. Internal analysis level is the ability of the business unit to assess its performance, based on internal data, trends, and developments.

Measurement. A score of 50 indicates the average capability across all industries, and the use of some formal qualitative analysis techniques. A score of 100 indicates the existence and use of a thorough and very detailed simulation of the unit's activities based on long-term accumulated data.

Example. In 1980, the General Electric Company (GE) was the tenth-largest industrial corporation in the United States (''G.E.,'' 1970). GE's management system, and particularly its system of strategic planning, were highly regarded. GE was divided into SBUs, each of which employed specialists in strategic planning. Both managers and planners were required to attend corporate strategy-planning seminars. SBU managers were required to use a formal technique (called the 9-block summary) to help them define and report their business plans. Among the subjects to be covered were environmental assumptions, competitors, and strategy alternatives. Each SBU was required to prepare a five-year strategic plan and a one-year operating plan.

General Electric, as one of the leaders in internal analysis, is scored at 95.

Discussion. The level of internal analysis is measured by the systematic and formal effort of data gathering, criteria definition, and evaluation of alternatives using management science techniques. For these purposes, the business unit employs staff specialists who involve senior management in identifying, evaluating, and choosing strategic alternatives.

Internal analysis focuses on the business unit's strengths and weaknesses by careful managerial audit of all major systems, including finance, production, and marketing management.

Indicators. The recommended indicators of internal analysis level are:

1. Data availability
2. Time invested
3. Formal techniques
4. Staff specialists
5. Choice among alternatives
6. Human resources analysis
7. Production capacity analysis
8. Marketing efforts analysis
9. Transportation analysis
10. R&D efforts analysis

External analysis and forecasting level

Definition. The external analysis and forecasting level is the extent to which the business unit employs formal scanning to gather, analyze, and forecast information about its environment.

Measurement. A business unit with highly developed formal environmental scanning and forecasting abilities is scored 100. The all industries' average is 50.

Example. In the early 1970s, Borden Inc., the large food product manufacturer, began a program of public involvement ("Borden Inc.," 1974). In response to difficulties with the Food and Drug Administration regarding its dry milk and a $6 million product recall, Borden set up a Public Affairs Office to monitor government regulations and their possible effect on Borden. Meetings and newsletters were instituted to help in the exchange of opinions with outside experts. A special department was formed within the Public Affairs Office to monitor the environmental impact of various actions.

Through its new public affairs activities, Borden had become above average in external analysis and is assigned a value of 65.

Example. Rubbermaid, a company that doubled sales and tripled earnings between 1981 and 1987, claims a success rate of 90% on new products (*Fortune*, 1987c). It maintains that record by going to great lengths to keep in touch with customers. For example, it runs year-round tests for color preferences among customers, consumer focus groups, and person-to-person interviews with potential consumers. Rubbermaid generates reams of consumer research through user panels, brand awareness studies, and diaries that consumers fill with new ideas about product use.

Rubbermaid's external analysis level is estimated at 75.

Example. In August 1969, W.C. Koepf, national sales manager of the Graphics Division of Gould, Inc., was instructed by headquarters to investigate the marketing possibilities for a new printer ("Gould, Inc.," 1977). Koepf explained:

> We are a very small division . . . we don't have the time and the money to do much research. There is no planning group, no research group like in some of the larger divisions of Gould. Electrostatic printing is entirely new. Ours is not a 'me-too' product. So it's very difficult to say anything really firm about the market. But everybody knows that existing printers are much too slow.

Even after the prototype was ready, very little market information was gathered before the printer was introduced in 1969.

Gould's Graphics Division external analysis level is estimated at 15.

Discussion. Environmental scanning, analysis, and forecasting are performed by firms by various methods, through different channels, and with different intensity (Aguilar, 1970). Elements include routine gathering of opinions from clients, explicit tracking of the policies and tactics of competitors, forecasting sales, customer preferences, technology, demographic trends, and frequent market research studies. These activities enhance the ability of the business unit to systematically track opportunities and threats in the environment in order to design long-term strategies. Methods may include informal social conversations (e.g., on the golf course or at social events); participation in professional conferences; reading professional literature; focused studies of specific environmental factors; maintaining large and updated databases on external elements (competitors, customers, suppliers); environmental model building; and formal forecasting activities.

Indicators. Recommended indicators for external analysis and forecasting level are:

1. Formal scanning
2. Data gathering
3. Database availability
4. Time invested
5. Staff specialists
6. Formal forecasting activity
7. Forecasting computerized
8. Demographic forecasting
9. Sales forecasting
10. Environmental model

Level of risk

Definition. Level of risk is the extent to which strategy makers make, and are willing to make, commitments that involve high proportions of the business unit in risky projects. The risk may be technological, marketing, financial, or political.

Measurement. A low score indicates a highly conservative approach; 50 is the cross-industries' average; 100 indicates a strictly risk preferring approach.

Example. In 1986, Cincinnati Milacron Inc. surrendered its dominance in the machine tools industry to Cross and Trecker Corp (*Business Week*, 1986c). Milacron was trying hard to maintain its lead as a supplier to the aerospace industry. However, the company lost a large order to Ingersoll Milling Machine Co., being less than aggressive in trying to win the job. Jerry Ennis, an executive at McDonnell Aircraft Co., was quoted as saying that "if they [Milacron] have a weakness, I'd have to say it's their cautiousness." Milacron's cautiousness also shows through its unwillingness to cooperate with other companies in developing machines.

Milacron's level of risk is evaluated at 20.

Example. After a heated three-month standoff during which Donald Trump held 9.9% of Bally's stock and continually threatened a takeover, Bally agreed to buy out the New York real estate developer in a deal estimated at $83.7 million (*Business Week*, 1987b). The transaction assured Trump a $24 million profit and freed Bally to proceed with its $439 million purchase of the Golden Nugget Hotel & Casino in Atlantic City. Together with the acquisition of MGM Grand hotels in Las Vegas and Nevada a year earlier, the deal made Chicago-based Bally one of the gaming industry's biggest firms, with four major casinos and more than 5,900 hotel rooms. However, the deals also represented a big gamble. Its acquisitions increased Bally's debt to 75% of capitalization. After a year of operating the hotels in Nevada, Bally was still losing money on them. Absorbing the MGM properties had slashed 1986 earnings by 41%. R. E. Mullane, chairman and CEO of Bally Mfg. Corp., told the press that "everything you do in business is a gamble, but I think the odds are greatly in our favor."

The level of risk is estimated to be 70.

Example. Harry E. Sloan and Lawrence L. Kuppin used junk bonds and brashness to form one of the most rapidly growing companies in Hollywood (*Business Week*, 1987d). They acquired New World, a rundown B-movie producer, in 1983 with $2 million of their own money and $10 million in loans. By 1987, revenues had increased from $8 million to $400 million as the company moved into TV programs, comic books, and videocassettes. However, the company paid monthly interest charges of more than $3 million. Sloan and Kuppin are known for boldness and audacity, once suing MGM for increased royalty rights to CHIPS star Erik Estrada. In 1986, they agreed to finance the TV series "Crime Story" and "Rags to Riches" after other studios refused the low fees being offered by the networks. Through deals like these, New World jostled its way into four networks in 1987. Sloan and Kuppin were gambling that the shows they were financing would last three years, giving them enough episodes to allow syndication. A $430 million offer for Kenner Co. was New World's biggest risk. The offer would nearly double the company's debt. If successful in its bid, New World would be able to distribute Marvel comic books' 900 characters and rely on stable revenues from board games such as Monopoly. However, winning Kenner would not be easy as the toymaker considered numerous defenses, including a leveraged buyout and a cash dividend to shareholders.

The level of risk at this point in time was estimated to be 85.

Example. For over a century, Cable and Wireless PLC had designed, managed, or owned telecommunications systems all over the world (*Business Week*, 1986d). In the mid-1980s, Sir Eric Sharp, the company's chairman, began creating a telecommunications network to link the world's major financial centers, mainly New York, Hong Kong, and Tokyo. The plan was a huge gamble. Many pieces to Sir Sharp's puzzle would only come together when key governments, some of which were potential competitors, approved his plans. Sharp was gambling that the new company, having recently purchased a majority stake in Hong Kong Telephone, would receive the regulatory approvals it needed to build its empire.

Cable and Wireless PLC is estimated to have a level of risk of 85.

Example. Gary Stibel of the New England Consulting Group, noted that "PepsiCo's stress on risk taking is what sets its managers apart, it simply doesn't allow them to not take risks" (*Business Month*, 1987f). In evaluating the company's senior executives, Chairman Calloway of PepsiCo analyzes each executive on the basis of ten criteria, including team management, strategic skills, executive maturity, idea leadership, and the drive for results. The two yardsticks he is most interested in are the executive's risk-management profile and his or her impact and influence on the rest of the company. Roger King, senior vice-president of human resources at PepsiCo, stated that "you can't grow into a leader here without knowing how to take risks or being able to affect other segments of our business with your decisions and performance."

PepsiCo prefers risk takers and hence has a higher level of risk than its competitors. We evaluate it to be 65.

Discussion. Some business units have a strong proclivity to low-risk projects with normal and certain rates of return. This low risk-taking behavior prefers timid, incremental decisions. On the other hand, bold and wide-ranging acts indicate a business unit with high risk preference for chances at high returns (or losses). One way of evaluating the level of risk taking is to evaluate the last ten major projects the unit undertook and to assess the level of risk of each project. Another way is to divide risk by type. For example, in a small country, political risk is created by political volatility engendering difficult to anticipate discontinuities in the business environment. The political change may lead to risky events such as instability of the government, military unrest, labor unrest, instability of the country's external relations, or factional troubles. Market or competitive risk relates to the tendency of the business unit to compete against strong competitors, challenging their reactions and responses. Technological risks usually involve embarking on long-term projects that rely on technological breakthroughs that are anticipated but not yet made. Financial risk is usually indicated by high financial leverage.

Indicators. We recommend an analysis based on the last ten major projects the business unit undertook. Alternatively, use the four types of risk:

1. Financial risk	6.
2. Technological risk	7.
3. Market risk	8.
4. Political risk	9.
5.	10.

Proactiveness of decisions

Definition. Proactiveness of decisions refers to the constant search for new decision situations, for new opportunities, rather than just trying to solve problems as they crop up.

Measurement. A proactive business unit continually trying to shape its environment should receive a score of 100, while a business unit that merely reacts to trends in the environment should receive a score of zero.

Example. Richardson-Merrell's original business, started in 1905, was built around Vick's VapoRub and subsequently other proprietary cold remedies ("Tom McGuire," 1978). To increase stability and achieve growth, the company began to diversify in the 1930s. A number of other products were added to RMI's lines, but the Vick division continued to be the core of the business. When Tom McGuire became division general manager in 1969, Vick International, Latin America/Far East, was experiencing difficulty maintaining adequate growth and profitability. In November 1971, Tom McGuire assembled a division management conference to look at the organizational problems.

The 1971–72 situation, as defined by managers, can be summarized as follows:

- Managers were influenced too much by immediate circumstances or events. Managing consisted of disposing of one crisis quickly enough to be ready for the next.
- Managers were overly concerned with "making this year's budget." They expected their budgets to be revised in detail arbitrarily at headquarters.
- Corporate and division objectives were known to have been stated for sales and profit growth. However, this was not the starting point for planning or budgeting within the markets.
- The overall feeling was that immediate problems did not allow much time to worry to any great extent about the long-term future.

- Managers believed that as long as everyone carried on as he or she had been doing, there was no reason for serious doubts about the short-term future.
- Headquarters staff (division and corporate) was essentially "reaching over the shoulder" of both line management and functional counterparts in markets.
- Emphasis was on audit ("police") and problem-solving ("intervention") activities, self-generated, or on behalf of corporate or division management.

This situation is estimated to represent a proactiveness of 35. The objective of McGuire's meeting was to move his division of Vick so that it would become above average in proactiveness of decision making.

Discussion. Two basic methods can be used to evaluate the proactiveness of decisions. The first is to list the last ten major decisions made by the business unit and evaluate the relative proactiveness in each. The second and better method is to evaluate the proactiveness in each of the following areas which can be used as indicators: lobbying, advertising, introducing new products, changing customers' habits, creating new distribution channels, establishing sources of supply, becoming involved in local or national education and training programs, investing in research and development, and conducting activity in industry and employer organizations.

Indicators. The recommended indicators for proactiveness of decisions are:

1. Lobbying
2. Advertising
3. New products introduction
4. Changing customers habits
5. Distribution channels
6. New supply sources
7. Education and training
8. Research and development
9. Industry activity
10.

ORGANIZATIONAL STRUCTURE VARIABLES

Size of the strategy-making team

Definition. Size of the strategy-making team is measured by the number of main strategic actors in the business unit.

Measurement. An exclusively one-person show is scored 0; three to five strategic actors is scored 50; a highly dispersed decision-making team (about 30 persons, or in smaller units 30% of the staff) is scored 100.

Example. As described in Chapter 1, the Mellon Bank Corporation executive team, which consisted of seven members, was reduced to four when a new chief executive officer took over. Thus, the value in our framework for the size of the strategy-making team became 50 after having been 70 previously.

Discussion. The emergence of a strategy in a business unit is the result of power interplay within the dominant coalition that manages the business unit. This internal power play constantly questions the status quo. Individual executives motivated by their own values and interests as well as by functional or subsystem affiliation may exert influence to modify strategy. In defining the strategy-making team, you must distinguish between internal and external coalitions. The former is composed of members of the business unit (usually top management); the latter consists of "outsiders," such as corporate officials, board members, large stockholders, customers, suppliers, regulatory agencies, or community and public pressure groups (Mintzberg, 1983). Here we include only the internal coalition in the strategy-making team.

Indicators. A useful way of measuring the average size of the strategy-making team is to recall up to ten of the last major strategic decisions made in the business unit, and to evaluate the number of participants in each decision. These numbers should be weighted by the importance of the decision.

To illustrate how the weighting is done, consider the numerically simpler case of three decisions. Suppose that the following is agreed upon:

Decision	Size of Team	Relative importance
1	4	30
2	14	20
3	6	50

Note that the relative importance numbers add to 100. This is in keeping with our practice of allocating the weights so that they add to 100%. Multiplying the size of the team by its relative importance and then dividing by 100, we have

$$(4 \times 30 + 14 \times 20 + 6 \times 50)/100 = 7$$

as the weighted average size of the strategy-making team. We would therefore assign a score of 60 to this variable.

Centralization

Definition. Centralization is the degree to which the strategic decision-making process tends to remain at the top levels of the organization. In a centralized organization, decision-making power and resource allocation are completely in the hands of the highest level of top management.

Measurement. When the decision-making authority is kept strictly at the top level (score 100), the business unit is very centralized; when decisions are delegated to the lowest managerial level (score 0), the business unit is decentralized. A score of 50 indicates an average level of centralization.

Example. Until organizational restructuring began in 1975, the management of the Hewlett-Packard Company (H-P) was almost totally under the control of its founders, Bill Hewlett and David Packard ("Hewlett-Packard Company (A): Problems of Rapid Growth," 1983). They ran both the board of directors and the company. H-P experienced a period of financial difficulty in the early 1970s when prices were too low and products were entering the market too early. Short-term debt rose dramatically as a result. The founders were forced to step in personally to rectify the situation. They imposed an "asset-management discipline" in each of the divisions and increased prices and R&D expenditures. Both founders were reported dismayed that they had been forced to intervene personally, and they proceeded to restructure the company in preparation for their impending retirement.

Here was a company that made a conscious decision to move from a degree of centralization that would be scored in the 90s to one that would be scored much lower.

Example. The Lincoln Electric Company has never had a formal organization chart, the objective being to ensure maximum flexibility (Sharplin, 1984). An open-door policy is practiced, and personnel are encouraged to take problems to whoever is most capable of resolving them. Routine supervision is almost nonexistent, and a production foreman may supervise as many as one hundred workers. There is, however, some organizational structure, established through position titles and traditional flows of authority. For example, the vice-president of sales reports to the president, as do various staff assistants such as the personnel director. With such an existing relationship, production workers have no more than three levels of supervision between themselves and the president. At Lincoln, formal authority is quite strong. Protecting management's authority is stressed. While management must be obeyed, employees are given a lot of responsibility and employees do participate in managerial decisions concerning those areas about which they are most knowledgeable.

Given the strong management authority levels, Lincoln is scored 80 on centralization despite its propensity to delegate.

Example. Lavalle Steel Company, Ltd. practiced highly centralized decision making (Olson, 1983). The Financial, Planning, and Legal functions reported to the chief executive officer (CEO), while all other functions reported directly to the chief operating officer (COO). By necessity, these two officers worked together very closely to ensure consistency of action. In simple terms, the COO dealt with internal matters while the CEO dealt with external forces. Both men became involved in the daily operations. Few decisions were made without their knowledge and consent. Matters of consequence were generally settled by them after they had reached a consensus. Because of this highly centralized decision-making style, each of the functions was oriented internally toward vertical communications. Lateral communications mainly occurred at or near the vice-presidential level.

With almost total control at the top, Lavalle Steel's centralization is given a value of 95.

Discussion. Centralization is measured by the hierarchical levels that have authority to make or participate in strategic decision making. Strategic decisions are those that relate to capital budgeting, introduction of new technology or production facilities, large acquisitions including mergers, pricing of major product lines, entry into new markets, and hiring and firing of senior personnel. Centralization, in contrast to decentralization, provides less flexibility in decision making and is more suitable for static situations.

In many industries, wide product-market breadth is accompanied by a low degree of centralization, while niche markets are accompanied by a high degree of centralization (Grinyer and Yasai-Ardekani, 1981; Miles and Snow, 1978; Mansfield, Todd, and Wheeler, 1978; Horovitz and Thitart, 1982). An example is a study of the strategic moves made by Steinberg, Canada (a large retail organization), over a sixty-year period (Mintzberg and Waters, 1982). The firm had to relax centralization when it was adding new product lines. On the other hand, consolidation of product lines is often accompanied by centralization (Miller and Friesen, 1980).

Indicators. To evaluate the degree of centralization in a business unit, major decision areas should be identified and the degree of centralization of each evaluated. The indicators recommended for centralization are:

1. Capital budgeting
2. Technology
3. Production facilities
4. Acquisitions
5. Pricing
6. Market entry
7. R&D efforts
8. Manager hiring and firing
9.
10.

Mechanism

Definition. Mechanism is the extent to which the internal organization of the formalized management structure is characterized by rules, procedures, and clear hierarchy of authority.

Measurement. A highly mechanistic business unit is given a score of 100, while a completely nonmechanistic business unit receives a score of zero.

Example. In the early 1980s, Steve Jobs and many of Apple's leaders were not so much managers as they were impresarios who dealt with creative artists (Scully, with Byrne, 1987). Apple's creativity thrived on instinct, uncertainty, and freedom and was not stifled by structure, process, or specifically defined goals. John Scully, the CEO, aptly described Apple's work environment as follows:

The work environment needs to be informal and relaxed; it needs to remove the symbols of management, which in the traditional company means the uniform of the business suit, the closed-in offices, the overabundance of titles, the executive perks. We try to remove all those symbols, creating an egalitarian environment, because we don't believe there is a difference between the contribution of a single artist or an orchestrator.

We don't give creative people traditional responsibilities, like being at the office every day from eight to five, or check on them for efficiency and punctuality. Instead, they are made accountable for the results of their work. People are given the flexibility to perform a lot of work at home.

Despite Scully's statement, even in the early 1980s, Apple did have some rules and regulations. However, compared with IBM (see below), it was a laid-back place. On mechanism, Apple would rate at 10.

Example. (This example differs from previous ones in that it focuses on an indicator, loyalty and obedience, rather than the variable itself. The point to recognize is that indicators follow the same estimation techniques as the variables.) IBM has a reputation for strict concern with employee behavior, appearance, and attitude (*Wall Street Journal*, 1982). What this means to employees is a lot of rules. These rules, written or unwritten, draw their force from a founding legacy of value placed on loyalty. Thomas J. Watson, Sr. believed that joining IBM called for absolute fidelity to the company in matters big and small. IBM tries to inspire positive feelings for the company by following Watson's formula: systematic goading toward excellence, constant supervision, and frequent rewards.

A manager neatly lays out the employee's responsibility. Every year an employee is given a written performance plan containing a set of specific goals. Meeting or exceeding the goals leads to promotions and raises. Tight discipline is enforced by near-constant observation and grading. Extensions to deadlines for handing in reports are given only for good reasons (a broken leg may do). A former IBMer described the way the atmosphere affected him: "In my fifteen years there," he said, "I never lost the feeling that I was breaking a rule. But I never knew what the rule was."

Given IBM's extreme passion for loyalty and obedience, this indicator would be rated, say, 98.

Discussion. In a mechanistic system of management, such as the military, the structure is formalized. Operations and working behavior are governed by instructions and decisions issued by superiors. The command hierarchy is maintained by the implicit assumption that all knowledge about the business situation of the unit and its task is, and should be, available only at the top (Burns and Stalker, 1961). Conversely, in a nonmechanistic, organic business unit, the internal organization is loose, free flowing, and adaptive. Rules and regulations are flexible. Usually no written criteria exist, and people are expected to find their own way through the system.

Indicators. Level of mechanism can be measured by the degree to which a business unit's tasks are differentiated and broken down; emphasis on technical improvements of means; preciseness in defining tasks, methods, and obligations; strictness of hierarchy, control, authority, and communications; location of knowledge; activities governed by vertical interactions (i.e., superior–subordinate); instructions and decisions issued by superiors; loyalty and obedience to superiors as a condition of employment; and rate of importance attached to "the way we do it" compared with knowledge, experience, and skill. These indicators can be described by the following short titles:

1. Degree of differentiation of tasks
2. Preciseness in job
3. Strictness of hierarchy
4. Strictness of control
5. Strictness of authority
6. Strictness of communications
7. Knowledge at top
8. Vertical interactions
9. Loyalty and obedience
10. Tradition-based operations

PERFORMANCE VARIABLES

Profitability

Definition. Profitability of an SBU is measured relative to its industry.

Measurement. The industry's average return on equity is scored 50. The industry's most profitable business unit is scored 100.

Example. After going public in 1965, quarterly earnings for McDonald's, the fast-food chain, have always been higher than those reported in the comparable quarter of the previous year ("McDonald's Corporation," 1987). The annual average return on stockholders' equity was over 20% in the l972–81 decade. Profits before taxes in 1983 were $342.6 million, an 11.1% return on sales.

As profit leader in its industry, McDonald's scores 100 on profitability.

Example. Consolidated sales of Albertson's Inc. (discussed under environmental hostility earlier in this chapter) reached $1.27 billion in fiscal 1975, with net profit after taxes of $15.8 million ("Albertson's

Inc.," 1984). In January 1976, total assets were nearly $222 million, with stockholders equity of more than $91 million. In July 1976, *Fortune* magazine ranked Albertson's as the twenty-ninth largest retailer in the United States (in terms of sales), with the eighth highest return on equity capital of all US retailers. In January 1976, *Forbes* magazine ranked Albertson's as number 83 in American industry in terms of five-year average return on equity. *Forbes* also rated the company as number four out of 25 regional chain stores in five-year average return on equity, number four in five-year average return on total capital, and number four in five-year average earnings per share growth.

While not as strong as McDonald's, Albertson's still scores 80 on profitability.

Example. In 1985, General Foods experienced one of the lowest profit margins in the food industry (*Business Month*, 1987e). The company's operating profit on $9 billion in sales was 3.6% compared with an average of 4.8% for the seven other leading food processors. Thus, it was not surprising that on August 18, 1987, the chairman of General Foods, Philip L. Smith, announced a major reorganization. A large percentage of the corporate staff was to be eliminated in an effort to streamline operations and boost profit margins.

General Foods scores low on profitability in its industry and is assigned a value of 10. The management's restructuring is an effort to move the profitability variable closer to the industry average.

Discussion. One useful approach to conceptualizing profitability is to view it as a combination of productivity and price recovery (Miller, 1984). Thus, profitability results from two contributions:

- Productivity performance
- Net price recovery (the difference between the sales prices and direct costs such as labor, raw materials, and energy)

An alternative, recommended for use as indicators, is evaluation of profitability ratios.

Indicators. Profitability ratios include:

- Gross profit margin = (sales minus costs of goods sold) divided by sales
- Net profit margin = net profit after taxes divided by sales
- Rate of return or common stock equity = (net profit after tax minus preferred stock dividend) divided by (net worth minus par value of preferred stock)
- Return on assets = net profit after taxes divided by total tangible assets

- Return on capital (equity) = net profits after taxes divided by net worth
- Earnings per common stock share = (net profit after taxes minus preferred dividends) divided by number of shares of common stock outstanding

The indicators recommended for profitability are described by the following short titles:

1. Gross profit margin
2. Net profit margin
3. Return on common stock
4. Return on assets
5. Return on capital
6. Earnings/common stock share
7.
8.
9.
10.

Operational Efficiency

Definition. Operational efficiency is the degree of utilization of resources by the management of the business unit to produce output. It is measured as the ratio of input to output.

Measurement. The industry's average efficiency is evaluated as 50. If the business unit can achieve a given production level with fewer resources than the industry's average, its score is higher. The most efficient competitor is scored 100.

Example. At the beginning of World War II, Dr Earle Shouldice developed a surgical technique for repairing hernias that was superior to all other known treatments ("Shouldice Hospital," 1983). By the war's end, two hundred civilians had contacted the doctor and were awaiting surgery upon his being discharged from the army. Because of the scarcity of hospital beds, he started his own hospital. Initially, a 36-bed capacity was created in Thornhill, a suburb of Toronto. After some years of planning, a large wing was added to increase capacity to 89 beds. Dr Shouldice died in 1965. Under the leadership of Dr Nicholas Obney, the volume of activity continued to rise, reaching a total of 6,850 operations in 1982.

All the patients' rooms at the hospital were semiprivate, containing two beds. Patients with similar jobs, backgrounds, or interests were assigned to the same room wherever possible. During their stay, patients were encouraged to explore the premises and make new friends. Every square foot of the hospital was carpeted to reduce the hospital feeling and the possibility of a fall. Carpeting also gave the place a smell other than that of disinfectant. Parents accompanying children for an operation stayed free of charge because the hospital saved more in nursing costs than it spent for the parent's room and board. The nursing staff consisted of 22 full-time and 19 part-time members. Minimal patient needs for physical assistance allowed Shouldice to operate with a much lower nurse-to-patient ratio than the typical hospital. The hospital employed 12 full-time surgeons, seven part-time assistant surgeons, and one anesthetist. The operating load typically varied from 30 to 36 operations per day, resulting in each surgeon performing three or four operations per day.

Unless a patient asked for a specific doctor, cases were assigned to give doctors a nonroutine operation several times a week. More complex procedures were assigned to more senior and experienced members of the staff. Dr Obney commented that experience was most important and that the surgeons at Shouldice each performed 600 or more hernia operations per year, compared with 20 to 25 for the typical general surgeon. Training in the Shouldice technique was important because the procedure could not be changed. It was done through direct supervision by one or more of the senior surgeons. The rotation of teams and frequent consultations enabled an ongoing opportunity to evaluate performance and take corrective action.

Shouldice Hospital is much more efficient than its industry and understands the nature of its business. Its operational efficiency is evaluated as 100.

Discussion. Efficiency is usually contrasted to effectiveness. Efficiency is a more limited concept than effectiveness, since it is concerned with internal processes. It is the amount of resources (capital, human time, material, information) required to produce a unit of output. Operational efficiency is the use of resources in the production and managerial processes. Operational efficiency is not directly related to the business unit's goals but to its output: the product and its handling. Operational efficiency increases as output increases per unit cost of the resources used in operational activities.

Indicators. Basic indicators of operational efficiency include capacity utilization; employee productivity; inventory turnover, sales divided by inventory; fixed assets turnover, sales divided by fixed assets; total assets turnover, sales divided by total assets; operating assets turnover, sales divided by operating assets; average collection period, accounts receivable divided by daily credit sales; accounts receivable turnover; and credit sales divided by accounts receivable. Specific measures may include relative costs per unit (direct labor, material, and overhead divided by number of units); indirect labor cost index (indirect labor cost divided by total direct costs); units produced per work-hour; cost of raw materials; labor costs; and inventory costs. The following is a recommended short list of indicators:

1. Capacity utilization
2. Employee productivity
3. Inventory turnover
4. Sales/inventory
5. Accounting efficiency
6. Direct labor efficiency
7. Material efficiency
8. Indirect cost efficiency
9.
10.

DISTANCE MEASURES

Normally the strategy in an approach selected by you as being representative of the business unit you are evaluating is the one with the smallest average distance from all the variables (according to our approach you have to compute the distance to every strategy in the approach).

The values of the strategic variables for a business unit never match all the values of the variables in a given strategy exactly, nor should they be expected to. Every business unit is unique and a perfect match is highly unlikely. Our approach recognizes this phenomenon and finds the strategy within an approach that is "closest." You have, in fact, computed the "distance" to every strategy in an approach. This section describes how the calculations according to three different criteria may be made and how to interpret their meaning.

We use the term measure to refer to the way the distances between the business unit's profile and the nominal strategies in the approach are measured. Three measures, each with slightly different characteristics, are suggested: average distance, RMS distance, and SMR distance:

1. *Average distance*: For each variable, you compute the difference between the value of the variable for the business unit you are evaluating and the nominal value in a strategy. You then compute the average of the absolute value of these differences. For example, if the SBU's and the strategy's values are as follows:

	SBU value	Strategy value	Difference	Absolute difference
Variable 1	20	30	−10	10
Variable 2	40	20	20	20

then you compute the average distance as $(10 + 20)/2$, or 15. Note that this approach says that whether the difference is positive or negative does not matter, only the amount of the difference is important. In mathematical terms, the average distance is:

$$\sum_{i=1}^{n}(|\text{SBU value of variable i} - \text{strategy value of variable i}|)/n$$

where n is the number of variables in the approach.

2. *The RMS distance*: This measure is somewhat more sophisticated than average distance. It starts from the assumption that really large differences in some variables between the nominal value in a strategy and the value for the unit you are evaluating are more important to you than small differences among all the other variables. If we use the same values as for the average distance, then the RMS value is computed as follows:

	SBU value	Strategy value	Difference	Square of difference
Variable 1	20	30	−10	100
Variable 2	40	20	20	400

In an RMS calculation you compute what is called the root mean square. Actually, you compute it backwards. That is, you first compute the square of the difference (as shown above), then you find the mean (or average) of the squares, and then you compute the square root of the mean. Thus, in our example, the mean of the squares is $(100 + 400)/2 = 250$ and the RMS value is the square root of 250, or slightly under 16. As you can see from this calculation, RMS values are close to average values, but unless all the differences are the same, they will be larger than the average values. The reason for the increase is that the largest differences dominate the calculations.

The use of RMS distances can change the relative closeness of strategies in an approach from that observed in the case of average distances. Because you are averaging the square of the distance from each variable, if your strategy contains a few variables whose values are outliers (i.e., significantly different from the nominal value of a strategy), they can create large contributions to the RMS distances and, as a result, reduce the fit of the strategies in the approach. In mathematical terms, the RMS distance is:

$$\sqrt{\sum_{i=1}^{n} (\text{SBU value of variable i} - \text{strategy value of variable})^2/n}$$

where n is the number of variables in the approach.

3. *The SMR distance*: The SMR distance has the opposite view from the RMS distance. It starts from the assumption that the largest differences should not dominate the results. For example, if you have 11 variables in your approach and ten of them differ by one unit from the value that variable has in the strategy norm while the eleventh differs by 34 units from the variable value in the norm, your average distance will be four units (check this!). The SMR approach recognizes that one or two very large values can distort the average significantly. Thus, it reduces the differences by taking their square root first. The SMR value is computed as follows:

	SBU value	Strategy value	Difference	Square root of absolute difference
Variable 1	20	30	−10	3.162
Variable 2	40	20	20	4.472

In the SMR calculation you first compute the square root of each absolute difference. In our case, the differences are −10 and 20, so you take the square roots of 10 and 20 as shown above. You then take the average (mean) of the square root values. In our case, $(3.162 + 4.472)/2 = 3.817$. Finally you square the result to obtain a value of 14.57. Unless the absolute differences are all equal (an unlikely case!), the SMR distance will always be less than the average distance or the RMS distance. In mathematical terms, the SMR distance is:

$$\left(\sum_{i=1}^{n} \sqrt{(|\text{SBU value of variable i} - \text{strategy value of variable i}|)}/n\right)^2$$

where n is the number of variables in the approach.

The distance measure you should use depends upon your view of the world. Most people will work with the average distance. It is simple, direct, easy to understand, and easy to explain to others. If you believe that the outlier values (those farthest away) are more important, then the RMS average is for you. If you believe outliers distort the picture, then use the SMR value.

For an example, assume an evaluated strategic profile of a business unit (called here SBU Inc.) composed of all 28 strategic variables:

An example: strategic profile for SBU Inc.

Strategic variable	Value	Strategic variable	Value
1. Enviro. uncer.	71	15. Profession.	64
2. Enviro. dyn.	48	16. Inter. analysis	63
3. Enviro. host.	34	17. Exter. analysis	62
4. Enviro. comp.	59	18. Level of risk	43
5. Tech. prog.	55	19. Proactiveness	60
6. Prod./market	16	20. Strat. making	58
7. Innovation	53	21. Centralization	39
8. Quality	80	22. Mechanism	46
9. Price level	50	23. Profitability	68
10. Marketing	54	24. Market share	50
11. Control	48	25. Growth	26
12. Resources	59	26. Efficiency	27
13. Invest. prod.	51	27. Size	29
14. No. tech.	45	28. Age	40

The distances for this strategy, based only on the 13 strategic variables discussed above, from the eight strategies which comprise the Deliberate vs. Emergent approach are:

An example: distances* of SBU Inc. from the Deliberate vs. Emergent Strategies

Strategy name	Average distance	RMS distance	SMR distance
Planned	36	40	34
Entrepreneurial	25	30	22
Ideological	19	22	17
Umbrella	13	18	11
Process	13	17	11
Unconnected	13	17	11
Consensus	15	17	13
Imposed	28	34	24

*Distances were rounded to the nearest integer.

This example, not very different from many real-life situations, suggests that the current strategy of SBU Inc. is close to three strategies included in the Deliberate vs. Emergent approach—umbrella, process, and unconnected, and is not too far from a forth strategy—consensus. The strategic profile of the planned strategy is the farthest, or the least similar, to SBU Inc. strategic profile.

Note, that the RMS distance measure, unlike the two other measures, includes the consensus strategy among the closest strategies with a little higher distance to the umbrella strategy. This is the result of the structure of the variances, or differences, between the values for the strategic variables allocated to SBU Inc. and the strategic profiles of the eight strategies of the approach. Strategy variance analysis is discussed in the next chapter.

4

Strategy Variance Analysis and the Seven Survival Strategies

In the preceding chapter the strategic profile of a chosen business unit was compared with eight strategies that make up the Deliberate vs. Emergent Strategies approach. The closest strategies were found. In this chapter, we discuss how you can compare the strategic profile of the business unit you are evaluating with the strategic profile of the strategy you match most closely. In fact, you can compare the profile of the business unit with that of any strategy included in the approach. You can choose to make this comparison in either table or graph form.

To analyze a business unit's strategic profile, the variances (i.e., the differences) between the values of the variables in the business unit's strategy and those of the strategy being matched should be reviewed and understood. This chapter focuses on the analysis of a business unit's strategic profile. For this purpose, the second approach, Seven Survival Strategies, and some additional strategic variables are presented first (Vesper, 1979).

APPROACH 2: SEVEN SURVIVAL STRATEGIES

The concept of this approach comes from cybernetics. The idea is to apply Ashby's law to the survival of a firm within its environment (Ashby, 1961). A firm survives only if its strategic variables are kept within limits that result in superiority within its environment. Furthermore, the firm must adapt to environmental changes when the firm (and its industry) move forward along a life-cycle of innovation, introduction, growth, maturity, and decline.

The Seven Survival Strategies approach was developed by Dr Volker D. Vesper of Dusseldorf, Germany. Dr Vesper, a researcher and consultant in business policy, based his seven "standard strategies" for survival on an analysis of 200 published strategic business cases and on 12 in-depth case studies in the Netherlands.

The Seven Survival Strategies approach describes the optimal behavior of an SBU for a spectrum of strategic postures. The strategies are based on the firm's superiority and flexibility in adapting to its environment. The strategies are:

- Multiplication
- Monopolizing
- Specialization
- Diversification
- Cooperation
- Capitulation
- Liquidation

The values of the strategic variables for this approach are shown in Table 4.1.

Multiplication strategy

The multiplication strategy is based on quantitative expansion, which is achieved by multiplying simple structures as fast as possible. It only works in markets that have high purchasing power and comparatively weak competition.

Monopolizing strategy

The monopolizing strategy involves erecting strong boundaries around existing market territories that were gained by expansion. In keeping competition at bay, resources are monopolized and exploited exclusively. In a lesser version of this strategy, a market position is consolidated and may be used as a strong base when competition emerges in a hitherto expanding environment.

Table 4.1 Variable values in the Seven Survival Strategies approach.

Variable	Strategy: 9	10	11	12	13	14	15
Metavariable: environment							
1. Environmental uncertainty	11	15	43	89	68	44	28
2. Environmental dynamism	21	23	39	72	76	68	63
3. Environmental hostility	3	42	44	56	75	68	59
Metavariable: content							
5. Technological progress	61	53	71	63	31	10	1
6. Product-market breadth	81	82	23	63	52	8	1
7. Product innovation	65	65	67	68	32	6	1
12. Resources level	83	85	67	46	32	6	1
13. Investment in production	86	83	78	44	30	10	1
Metavariable: strategy making							
16. Internal analysis level	76	77	80	51	21	10	4
17. External analysis & forecast	81	83	80	69	31	10	4
18. Level of risk	16	25	54	82	57	63	62
19. Proactive management style	86	65	64	76	33	10	1
Metavariable: performance							
23. Profitability	93	95	81	46	34	12	1
24. Market share	90	95	38	36	40	11	1
25. Rate of growth	94	75	56	47	28	8	1
26. Operational efficiency	70	60	87	40	33	5	1
Metavariable: characteristics							
27. Size	84	94	37	58	48	13	1

Strategies:

9 = Multiplication 10 = Monopolizing 11 = Specialization
12 = Diversification 13 = Cooperation 14 = Capitulation
15 = Liquidation

Specialization strategy

This strategy is based on specializing the product or the production process. Specialization leads to economies of scale and efficiency under increased competition. Increased efficiency leads to improved quality and may even lead to a technological monopoly and increased sales appeal of the product.

Diversification strategy

The diversification strategy is based on migration to a different environment. It is used when the existing environment is no longer profitable and the firm is locked in by competitors. Since the firm is forced to leave its traditional area of know-how, it incurs a high element of risk.

Cooperation strategy

This strategy involves cooperation with other entities. On the one hand, this implies participation in large-scale benefits, but, on the other, it entails a partial loss of autonomy. This strategy may involve joint ventures or long-term contracts, or special organizations such as co-ops and franchise buyers.

Capitulation strategy

The capitulation strategy involves selling the firm's autonomy and becoming a "servant" of another firm. When applying this strategy, the firm usually merges with another so that at least some parts of the organization can survive.

Liquidation strategy

The life-cycle of the firm is finished and liquidation is the only action left.

USES AND MISUSES OF THE SEVEN SURVIVAL STRATEGIES APPROACH

This approach focuses only on survival. It is not concerned with achieving maximum performance once survival is ensured. Liquidation is a clear failure strategy. Many managers may view the capitulation and cooperation strategies as failures. Some may even view diversification as an admission of failure, even though diversification into additional markets (e.g., exports) and related products is widely pursued by successful firms.

Use of this approach by a business unit crudely places it on a success–failure scale. We will introduce other approaches later in this book that will allow refinement of this initial placement. Thus, this approach is recommended for the initial stages of business unit analysis.

Although this approach uses only 17 of the 28 variables in our framework, it introduces us to several important strategy content variables as well as to the concept of industry life-cycle. (Industry life-cycle will be discussed further in Chapter 10.) As a business unit moves along the life-cycle, it moves from one environment to another. Its strategy should change accordingly.

This approach is applicable to different types of industries, from monopolies, through oligopolies, to unconcentrated industries composed of many business units. Thus, it may be used by any business unit, as long as it focuses on one product-market. The approach is not appropriate for a multiproduct corporation operating in a dynamic environment.

ADDITIONAL VARIABLES

Use of this approach for identifying and analyzing a business unit's strategy requires a strategic profile composed of 17 variables. Nine of these variables were discussed in the previous chapter:

1. Environmental uncertainty
2. Environmental dynamism
3. Environmental hostility
16. Internal analysis level
17. External analysis and forecast level
18. Level of risk
19. Proactive management style
23. Profitability
26. Operational efficiency

However, eight additional variables are introduced in this approach:

- Strategy content
  5. Technological progress
  6. Product-market breadth
  7. Product innovation
  12. Resource level
  13. Investment in production
- Performance
  24. Market share
  25. Rate of growth
- Organizational characteristics
  27. Business unit size

We now present a detailed discussion of these additional variables. For each strategic variable, we present:

1. The definition of the strategic variable.
2. The scale for measuring the variable.
3. Example(s) based on a real-life situation.
4. A short discussion of the place of the strategic variable in the business unit's strategy.
5. Recommended indicators for the variable.

STRATEGY CONTENT VARIABLES

Technological progress

Definition. Technological progress is the number and novelty of new techniques that are used by an SBU to produce existing services and products relative to its competitors.

Measurement. The industry leader in technological progress is scored 100. The industry average is 50.

Example. In early 1987, the president of Canon USA Inc. introduced the long-awaited single-lens reflex camera with an automatic focusing system (*Business Week*, 1987a). The camera was Canon's attempt to regain its lead position in the 35 mm SLR market. Although Canon's EOS (electronic optical system) technology might seem evolutionary, industry experts concurred that Canon's new system had produced the most advanced SLR camera yet. Canon packed the entire focusing system inside the lens. To do so, it had to build ultraminiature motors that were major technological accomplishments in themselves. Other innovations resulted in a camera that typically took one-third of a second to focus, the quickest autofocus camera on the market. Canon bet that its new technology would once again spur SLR growth. Company engineers began working on such visionary products as "gyroscopic" lenses, which would enable the camera to produce sharp pictures even if the camera moved partially while the shutter was open.

Canon's technological progress is estimated to be 90.

Example. In 1969 the Graphics Division of Gould, Inc. developed a printer that was innovative in design and was said to have incredible sales potential ("Gould Inc.," 1977). According to W.C. Koepf, national sales manager of its Graphics Division: "Our feelings ranged from the belief that customers would break our door to take the device from our hands to the opinion of the engineers that the product was almost too good to be put on the market."

The Gould 4800 was a nonimpact printer using electrostatic printing technology. With a printing speed of 4,800 lines per minute, the Gould 4800 was at least four times faster than conventional line printers. In contrast to conventional line printers, the Gould 4800 could also print any kind of graphic output. Since there were few moving parts and no printing hammers as in conventional line printers, the Gould 4800 operated noiselessly and presented relatively few maintenance problems. The Gould 4800 thus offered major benefits over the traditionally slower, noisier, and less reliable line printers.

The Gould Graphics Division is estimated to score 80 on technological progress. (See also Chapter 3 for Gould's External Analysis Level.)

Example. In October 1986, two IBM scientists were awarded the Nobel Prize in physics (*Business Week*, 1986a). The award came five years after these two scientists built the first STM (scanning tunneling microscope), a device that enables scientists to view previously unseen pictures of the atomic structure of matter. For the first time pictures were seen of the electron bonds that hold atoms together. STMs are used for research in biology, chemistry, physics, bioengineering, metallurgy, and micro-electronics. The STM spawned a whole range of lensless tools for researching microscopic problems.

For IBM's research laboratories, technological progress is rated at 95.

Example. FileNet Corporation, a California-based company, sells systems that can turn printed material into electronic information rapidly and economically (*Business Week*, 1986j). Many companies, such as Hitachi, Toshiba, and Philips, offer similar systems. However, what makes FileNet unique is its technology. It is the only company supplying a range of off-the-shelf systems with sophisticated software and networking. As D.A. Stadler of Arthur Andersen and Co. put it, "This technology is just incredible in allowing you to give better service at lower cost."

FileNet is estimated to be at 90 in technological progress.

Discussion. Technological innovativeness is an integral part of the business unit's competitive profile and affects the relative advantages of actual and potential competitors. However, what may be a startling breakthrough to the engineer, and a revolution to the production worker, may be unremarkable to the user of the product (Abernathy and Clark, 1985). Technological innovations may disrupt established technical and production methods or even make them obsolete. Innovativeness can change the basic configuration of the production process and sometimes create a new industry. It may have invisible yet dramatic effects on product cost and performance, or it may result in a trivial change with incremental impact on productive systems and technical knowledge.

Indicators. The rate of technological progress is indicated by innovation in product or process technology; ownership of state-of-the-art technology; investment in new types of equipment; production organization and procedures; technical, production management, and labor expertise; and material substitution.

The indicators recommended for operationalizing technological progress are:

1. Technology design
2. New/total equipment
3. Production organization
4. Production procedures
5. Technical management
6. Production management
7. Labor expertise
8. Material sophistication
9. Advanced technical knowledge
10. Experience

Product-market breadth

Definition. Product-market breadth is evaluated by the relative number and heterogeneity of the business unit's products and customers.

Measurement. Product-market breadth is measured relative to the industry leader, which is given a score of 100.

Example. Kalo Laboratories, Inc., a subsidiary of Marion Laboratories, Inc., was involved in the specialty agricultural market in the late 1970s ("Marion Laboratories, Inc.," 1984). The total US and Canadian agricultural market was about $3.2 billion in 1978. This market was dominated by such large manufacturers as Dow Chemical and DuPont. Kalo was quite successful in identifying specialty chemical needs in the agricultural segment of the market. Its product line consisted of four major groups: seed treatments, adjuvants (additives to other agricultural products), bactericides, and herbicides. Each product was designed for a narrow market.

Its score on product-market breadth, relative to the industry leaders, was judged to be 15.

Example. Artisan Industries was a $9-million-a-year family-run manufacturer of wooden decorative products (Barnes, 1977). Its 1,400-item product line was carried by 13,000 retail outlets. The largest product was a tea cart, and the smallest was a clothespin-type desk paper clip. About 100 new products a year were added to the line, with practically no items ever being dropped.

Clearly, this firm was the market leader in product-market breadth and scores 100.

Example. The Westinghouse Electric Corporation has long been one of the largest and most diversified corporations in the United States ("The Westinghouse Electric Corporation," 1976). It is the manufacturer of a wide range of industrial and consumer equipment for the generation, transmission, distribution, control, and utilization of electric power. In 1964, Westinghouse made 8,000 different products in 300,000 variations. The company's 59 different divisions, with their 64 plants spread throughout 20 states, daily confront almost every US citizen with some Westinghouse product, ranging from 6,000 types of light bulbs to the output of five TV stations and seven radio stations. In 1964, the company employed about 115,000 people and had investments in about 35 foreign countries, with over 150 foreign licensees.

Westinghouse would be scored as 90 on product-market breadth.

Discussion. By definition, strategic business units are related to product-market combinations. The product-market breadth may range from narrow and limited, usually defined as a niche, to a wide and less related product-market. A niche is the sale of a limited number of products to a small market of clients with special requirements, needs, or tastes. At the other end of the spectrum, when organizations diversify into additional, less related product-markets, they are no longer strategic business units but corporations.

In analyzing the PIMS database, Galbraith and Schendel identified a factor later defined as a breadth posture (Galbraith and Schendel, 1983). This factor includes product breadth, breadth of customer type, and number of customers. Note that product-market breadth relates to the scope and nature of the product-market, rather than to the process by which it is formulated or the rate of product innovation. For example, some tend to relate niche strategy to the absence of changes and adherence to established product-markets. However, a niche strategy may be highly proactive, involving considerable changes in the product-market mix when adapting to new demands or when a new niche is selected. On the other hand, stagnant but successful niche strategies are observed in stable environments.

Indicators. In addition to breadth in product, customer type, and number of customers, product-market breadth may be measured by the number of Standard Industry Classification (SIC) codes of the business unit relative to the industry average, and by the number of different products, number of different markets, domain coverage relative to industry leader, customer fragmentation, relative backward integration, and relative forward integration.

The indicators recommended for operationalizing product-market breadth are:

1. Relative breadth of product line
2. Relative no. of customers
3. Relative variety of customers
4. Customer fragmentation
5. Relative no. of SIC codes
6. Domain relative to leader
7. Consumer heterogeneity
8. Relative forward integration
9.
10.

Product innovation

Definition. Product innovation is the number and novelty of new products and services introduced by an SBU relative to its industry.

Measurement. Product innovation is measured in terms of the number and novelty of new products and services introduced over a given time period. The industry average is scored as 50.

Example. Until 1974, the Hershey Chocolate Company was number one in the sales of candy bars in the United States ("Hershey Foods Corporation," 1983). In the mid-1970s, Hershey dropped to second place when many candy manufacturers started producing chocolate-coated rather than solid bars. After the introduction of Hershey Milk and Almond Bars in the early 1900s, Hershey's R&D did not produce any significant product innovations. Over the years since then, the emphasis in Hershey's R&D was on the improvement of production efficiency and raw material quality and not on product innovation. Other best-selling Hershey lines, such as Reese's Cup, were acquired through licensing agreements and not developed internally. While the competition was busy churning out new products to adapt to the changing market, Hershey clung to its proven winners.

Hershey is rated as being 15 in product innovation.

Example. Merck, a leader in the pharmaceutical industry, was acclaimed by *Fortune* magazine in 1987 as America's most admired company (*Fortune*, 1987b). Although drug manufacturers are traditionally very slow to launch new products, the flood of innovative prescription drugs from Merck was the talk of the drug industry. In calendar year 1986, Merck had introduced five new drugs in the US and had a host of experimental drugs in the pipeline.

In contrast to Hershey, Merck is the leader in its industry and is evaluated at 100 in product innovation.

Example. In the mid-1980s Polaroid introduced the Spectra camera (*Business Week*, 1986g). Even though the camera was priced at more than twice Polaroid's previous entry in the field, it was the first real hit in instant photography since the company introduced the SX-70 in 1972. Spectra's success has been attributed to technical innovation, canny salesmanship, and lucky timing. The advertising campaign emphasizes the quality of Spectra's pictures as well as the state-of-the-art electronic accessories, such as automatic focus.

Polaroid's camera business is estimated to score 70 on innovation.

Example. Joseph R. Canion founded Compaq Computer Corporation in 1981 (*Business Month*, 1987a). His strategy, which has proved itself again and again, is "to make products that people would prefer over

IBM's because of their higher quality and additional features." When Compaq introduced the DeskPro 386 personal computer in September 1986, the company again beat IBM to market with the latest in personal computer technology. Based on the new Intel 386 chip, the new Compaq computer ran some programs three times faster than any other personal computer on the market. By the time IBM offered a competitive product, nine months later, Compaq was well on its way to introducing a portable version of the computer, called the Portable 386.

Compaq's strategy relies on product innovation, and it is estimated to rate 85 on this variable.

Discussion. Product-market innovations may be new to the market and to the business unit (first-in product-market innovations—for example, Post-It Notes from 3M Corporation); new to the business unit but not to the market (me-too innovations—for example, a similar product from Avery); or, at the extreme, innovations that are neither new to the market nor to the organization but are modifications of old products (product adaptation). Thus, a business unit may strongly emphasize the marketing of true and tried products or services, or may strongly emphasize the introduction of new products. High product innovation is indicated by the number of new products and services introduced over the relevant (one, three, or five years) past period, and the nature of change in the new product (minor or dramatic).

The tendency to innovate is probably a personal, rather than an organizational, characteristic. Managers who perceive themselves as the locus of control over events ("internals") tend to innovate, while those who believe that the events in life are beyond their control and should be attributed to fate, luck, or destiny ("externals") do not (Miller, Kets de Vries, and Toulouse, 1982). However, the nature of innovation and the context in which it is pursued will surely affect its success. Two models of product innovation are (Miller and Friesen, 1982b):

- Conservative innovation, when the innovation is performed reluctantly, mainly in response to serious challenges.
- Entrepreneurial innovation, which is pursued aggressively.

Indicators. The indicators recommended for operationalizing product innovation are:

1.	No. of new products/services	6.	Product adaptation
2.	New/total SBU products	7.	
3.	SBU/industry new products	8.	
4.	Products new to the market	9.	
5.	Products new only to the SBU	10.	

Note that indicators 2 and 3 are ratios, one comparing the new products introduced with the total products in the line, and the other comparing the number of new products introduced with the number of new products in the industry.

Resource level

Definition. Resource level is the amount of existing and potential resources available to the firm.

Measurement. A business unit with abundant resources is scored 100. A business unit with depleted resources is scored 0. An average resource level is 50.

Example. In January 1981, Exxon Corp. created a subsidiary, Exxon Office Systems (EOS), which consisted of Exxon's information systems businesses (McGlashan and Singleton, 1978). This action was part of an effort to develop fields of activity outside the company's core energy business. This business unit enjoyed the support of abundant resources from its parent company. EOS had the backing to develop or buy any technology it might need. By the time it was formed, Exxon had already poured almost $800 million into information systems ventures. In addition, because EOS was formed with the combined resources and products of acquired companies, management talent was abundant. The combined marketing and sales staff of the three original companies was retained, and the people were cross-trained to handle all product lines. (Although resources were abundant, EOS eventually failed for other reasons.)

EOS is rated 90 on resource level, since it had the backing of Exxon but was not as large as IBM.

Example. Merck's research group is reputed to be one of the finest in the biotechnology industry (*Fortune*, 1987b). The company spent $460 million on research in 1986. Merck maintains its lead by consistently attracting and keeping young PhDs. Staffers publish some 450 papers a year in scientific journals. While hundreds of young biotechnology companies also promise exciting new research projects aimed at important medical discoveries, few startups have the $100 million that it costs to develop, test, and produce a new drug. Merck has nearly unlimited cash by comparison, long experience in getting drugs approved by the Food and Drug Administration, and highly efficient manufacturing plants.

Merck's strong resource base gives it a rating of 95.

Discussion. Resources are critical to the business unit, since its technology is dependent on its available resource level. The resource level is determined by the state and availability of the business unit's physical resources, which include capital, raw material, components and parts, and its human resources: skilled labor and management talent, management experience, skills, know-how, and competence. It also includes the ability of the business unit to raise relatively large amounts of financial resources for long-term investments, either through reserves, debt, or owners' equity, at a minimum price.

Business units are in competition for resources externally or, in a large firm, internally. SBUs can be ranked in terms of their efficacy in obtaining resources. Thus, resources are competitive weapons and a basis for the business unit's strategy. Resources are used to establish the relation between the business unit and its environment (Aldrich, 1979; Christensen et al, 1982; Yuchtman and Seashore, 1967). Liquid resources, like capital, may be converted to other resources, depending on their availability in the environment. However, even when available, such conversion requires a period of time—e.g., in training new employees or delivering raw materials. Thus, money or credit cannot substitute, in the short term, for other resources.

Indicators. Important categories of resources include money (in all forms), labor, raw materials, energy, management talent, machinery, buildings, and land.

The indicators recommended for resource level are:

1. Financial resources
2. Potential financial resources
3. Raw material
4. Components and parts
5. Energy
6. Skilled labor
7. Know-how
8. Management talent
9. Machinery
10. Building and land

Investment in production

Definition. Investment in production is the relative amount and frequency of investment in production equipment and facilities.

Measurement. A score of 100 is given to the business unit with the highest investment in production in the industry.

Example. In December 1986, Deere and Co. was expected to report a loss as high as $150 million, its first loss since the Great Depression (*Business Week*, 1986h). This turnaround in Deere's fortunes was largely the result of a costly ultramodern factory. The factory was idled by a dispute with the United Auto Workers, who wanted new contracts that would protect them against sizable job cutbacks. The labor dispute was the most visible of the many problems facing Deere. Worldwide sales in 1986 were 11% below the depressed levels of 1985. The company's dilemma was that no easy way existed to scale down its farm equipment manufacturing operations. The heavily robotized production process was so closely integrated that it was almost impossible to shut down one part of the operation without shutting everything down. Running the factory at a fraction of capacity meant that Deere had to absorb heavy overhead costs from capital, labor, lighting, and heating. For Deere, bold long-term strategies turned out to be perilous. Costly investments were drowning any hope of an enjoyable 150th anniversary in 1987.

Thus, Deere scores extremely high, say 95, on investment in production.

Discussion. Investment in production relates to management activities in improving the manufacturing system. It includes automation, introduction of computerized systems such as CAM (computer-aided manufacturing) and CIM (computer-integrated manufacturing), robotics, recruitment of highly qualified workers, and purchase of modern equipment. Robots and automatic handling equipment transform individual pieces of equipment into automated work cells which are integrated into manufacturing systems. Business units that choose not to invest in production tend to use subcontractors for all or part of their operations.

Indicators. The indicators recommended for investment in production are:

1. Capacity
2. Locations
3. Fixed assets
4. Work in process
5. Maintenance level
6. New/all facility
7. 1/subcontracting
8. Machinery
9. Auxiliary equipment
10. Added value

PERFORMANCE VARIABLES

Market share

Definition. Market share is the sales of the business as a percentage of the total dollar sales in the market served by the business (Phillips, Chang, and Bussel, 1983).

Measurement. Industry leader is scored 100. Other business units' scores are their sales as a percentage of the leader's sales.

Example. The Kroehler Manufacturing Company produces upholstered furniture (Slovacek, 1978). In 1977, it was the second-largest producer in the United States and the third largest in Canada, with approximately 6% market share in each country. The company employed about 5,600 people, and its products were distributed through 4,175 retail furniture and department stores with a total of 8,950 outlets. The company had reported consolidated revenues of $167 million in 1976, an increase of 24% over the recession level of 1975. Total assets were $80 million.

Kroehler's market share scores 80 because it is a very large, but not the largest, player in the furniture business.

Example. When George Freidenrich, grandson of the founder of Black Hills Bottling Company, decided to investigate the probable causes of his company's declining profits, he found that his market had declined from 50.2% in 1960 to 27.6% in 1977 ("Black Hills Bottling Company," 1982).

Thus, rather than being the industry leader and receiving a score of 100 on market share, Black Hills Bottling now rated 80.

Discussion. Market share is a measure of the business unit's performance (Buzzel and Gale, 1987). For many business units in a mature market, their market share is more or less constant over time. In these cases, a representative average should be inserted as the value of this strategic variable. In cases where market share of the unit has changed dramatically, some caution should be exercised. If the gain or loss is due to short-term pricing activities or dealer promotions, then the average market share should be used, because these changes are easily countered and the SBU is vulnerable. However, if the change is a result of inherent change (such as creation of new distribution channels), then the new market share should be considered. In making your evaluation, try not to kid yourself about what is going on. If the new contender is serious, you have to be serious too in defending your market share.

You must distinguish between market share and gain in market share (discussed later). Here the focus is on current market share relative to competitors. Usually it is easier to gain market share in growth markets than in stable or declining markets. More opportunities exist from yet uncommitted new users. When total sales are growing, competitors tend to react less aggressively to erosion in market share (Aaker and Day, 1986). Conversely, in flat or declining markets, you must guard against your competitors who will be as aggressive as you are in trying to protect their existing market share and in gaining new market share.

Indicators. Sometimes markets are composed of a few product lines. In some cases, a business unit may also produce and market peripheral products and product lines. To measure market share using this framework, you should use only the business unit's main product lines. In doing so you may choose among three kinds of indicators:

- Use up to ten of the unit's main products or product lines as indicators.
- Evaluate the relative weight of each product/product line in the business unit's total product basket.
- Evaluate the SBU's market share relative to the major competitor in the market.

Divide the SBU's markets into distinct submarkets such as consumer, institutional (government, defense), contractual, and export. Evaluate its market share in each market. Weight the results according to the relative weight of the submarket in the SBU's operations.

Use industry accepted indicators for market share,such as:

1. Relative $ sales	6.
2. Relative volume sales	7.
3. Relative no. of customers	8.
4. Relative no. of orders	9.
5. Relative raw material consumption	10.

Rate of growth

Definition. Rate of growth is the average increase of total sales of the business unit over a relevant period in the industry (e.g., one, three, or five years).

Measurement. A high-growth business unit in a high-growth industry is scored 100. A business unit in a mature industry growing at the industry average is scored 50.

Example. The Kroehler Manufacturing Company reported consolidated revenues of $167 million in 1976, an increase of 24% over the recession level of 1975 (Slovacek, 1978). Total assets for 1976 were $80 million.

Kroehler's rate of growth was estimated to range from 60 to 70.

Example. In 1978, the President of Federal Express, A. Bass, stated: "In 5 years we have gone through phases of growth which other companies normally experience over a period of 12 to 15 years. From June 1977 to June 1978 alone our revenues have jumped from $108 million to $160 million" ("Federal Express Corporation (A)," 1984).

Federal Express's growth rate score is set at 90.

Example. In just eight years Reebok International Ltd. leaped to a position of industry dominance (*Business Month*, 1987g). In 1987, it was the top-selling athletic shoemaker in the US and number two worldwide behind Adidas. The company also topped the $1 billion sales mark. In 1986, foreign revenues accounted for only 10% of the company's $923 million total sales. In 1987, Reebok's international chief, Joseph Foster, expected foreign revenues to increase substantially and to eventually reach 50% of the total. Chairman and cofounder Paul Fireman does not intend to rest on his laurels. He intends to diversify Reebok into a $2 billion multi-national by 1990.

Reebok is growth oriented and hence rates 100.

Example. Ronald O. Perelman, a daring and well-known Wall Street investor, has had an impeccable record as a manager (*Business Week*, 1986i). In 1980, he took control of MacAndrews and Forbes. Within two years profits rose 400%, to $90 million. At the same time, sales grew more than 360%, to $750 million. In 1986, the MacAndrews licorice extract business was five times larger than it was in 1980.

Growth rate for MacAndrews and Forbes is evaluated as 95.

Example. In 1986, Lectra Systems, a French manufacturer of CAD computer-aided design and cutting equipment for the clothing industry, emerged as one of the hottest growth companies in France (*Business Week*, 1986b). Lectra, launched in 1973, was growing at an annual rate of 67%, earning $643,000 on sales of $38 million in 1985. By 1986, the company had risen to No. 2 in the worldwide industry behind Gerber Scientific Inc. The company predicted a 50% growth rate until well into the late 1980s.

Lectra's rate of growth was far above average for its industry and is rated 90.

Discussion. Some people define high-growth industries as those that grow more than 10% per year. However, not all business units within a high-growth industry keep pace with the industry average. Some grow faster by internal growth or external acquisition while others fall behind. Mature industries tend to grow at the same rate as the total population. Declining industries may actually experience contraction (negative growth rate). Even in mature or declining industries, some business units may successfully pursue high-growth strategies.

Indicators. The approaches used for market share indicators also apply to rate of growth indicators. You should look only at the SBU's main product lines and choose one of the following three approaches:

- Use up to ten of the unit's main products or product lines as indicators.
- Evaluate the relative weight of each product-product line in the business unit's total product basket.
- Evaluate the SBU's rate of growth relative to the major competitor in the market over a relevant period in the industry (e.g., one, three, or five years).

Divide the SBU's markets into distinct submarkets such as consumer, institutional (government, defense), contractual, and export. Evaluate its rate of growth in each market. Weight the results according to the relative weight of the submarket in the SBU's operations.

Use industry accepted indicators for growth rate, such as:

1. Increase in $ sales
2. Increase in sales volume
3. Increase in no. of customers
4. Increase in no. of orders
5. Increase in raw material consumption
6. Labor increase
7. Market share rate of growth
8.
9.
10.

ORGANIZATIONAL CHARACTERISTICS VARIABLE

Business unit size

Definition. Business unit size is the relative total sales, total assets, and the number of people in the business unit.

Measurement. Take the industry's largest firm as 100.

Discussion. Size is a most important variable in organizational contingency theory. Most, if not all, strategic variables are affected by size, including the environmental variables (uncertainty, complexity, hostility), product-market breadth, market share, resource level, and centralization.

Indicators. The indicators recommended for business unit size are:

1. Relative sales in $	6.
2. Relative sales in units	7.
3. Relative no. of employees	8.
4. Relative balance sheet value	9.
5.	10.

STRATEGY VARIANCE ANALYSIS

In addition to measuring the distances between strategic profiles you can also compare the strategic profile of the business unit you are evaluating with the strategic profile of any strategy in any approach. For example, SBU Inc., whose strategic profile was introduced at the end of the previous chapter, was compared with the specialization strategy of the Seven Survival Strategies approach, whose strategic profile matches SBU's strategy most closely.

An example: variances (var.) between the strategic profiles of SBU Inc. and the specialization strategy (spec.)

Strategic variable*	SBU	spec.	var.
1. Environmental uncertainty	71	43	28
2. Environmental dynamism	48	39	9
3. Environmental hostility	34	44	−10**
5. Technological progress	55	71	−16
6. Product-market breadth	16	23	−7
7. Product innovation	53	67	−14
12. Resources level	59	67	−8
13. Investment in production	51	78	−27
16. Internal analysis level	63	80	−17
17. External analysis & forecasting	62	80	−18
18. Level of risk	43	54	−11
19. Proactive management style	52	64	−12
23. Profitability	68	81	−13

24. Market share	50	38	12
25. Rate of growth	26	56	–30
26. Operational efficiency	27	87	–60
27. Size	29	37	–8

* Only the 17 strategic variables included in the Seven Survival Strategies approach.

** A negative value indicates the value of the strategic variable for the analyzed business unit is smaller than its value for the strategy being compared.

This example points out that although the strategic profile for SBU Inc. is closer to the specialization strategy than to other strategies included in this approach, there are variances between the two profiles. Current operational efficiency (strategic variable number 26) of SBU Inc. (evaluated as 27) is well below the norm for a "typical" specialization strategy (87), leaving a large variance (–60). Similarly, the environmental uncertainty (No. 1) recorded for SBU Inc. (71) is greater than the strategy norm (43) with a medium-size variance (27).

Strategy variance analysis contributes to the analysis of the current strategy of the business unit. Also, it indicates the direction and magnitude of changes required should the strategy-making team of this business unit decide to pursue such a strategy in the future. This analysis does not, and cannot, relate to the internal or external feasibility of such changes.

5

An Approach Map and the Ten Archetypes Strategies

The preceding chapter presented a minutely detailed analysis of the business unit's strategic profile. To understand the difference between the business unit you are evaluating and the strategy you match (or any other strategy), we used the indicator tables, examining up to ten different contributors for each variable. The necessary in-depth probing may sometimes mask the complete strategic view emphasized by our approach.

This chapter introduces an important addition to our approach, the Approach Map. The Approach Map allows you to create a two-dimensional graphical presentation of the distances among the strategies included in the approach, and between each of these strategies and the business unit you are evaluating. It is useful for understanding the position of an SBU relative to the various strategies in the approach. In this chapter, we discuss the positioning of the SBU relative to all the strategies in the approach.

THE APPROACH MAP

In previous chapters, we discussed distances among strategies and the average distance between the strategic profile of the business unit analyzed and each of the strategies in the approach. The next level of sophistication is to add a tabulation of the distances among the strategies, and then map it. This produces a graphical representation of the distances matrix. The graphical representation is called "smallest space analysis" (SSA) (Lingoes, 1973) or "multidimensional scaling" (MDS) (Davidson, 1983) in statistics and is used routinely there. The basic idea is to take the table of distances and project them on a two-dimensional graph.

Table 5.1 is an example of a symmetric matrix of distances between the strategic profile of our example business unit (SBU Inc.) and the strategic profiles of the Seven Survival Strategies, presented in the previous chapter, and *among* the Seven Survival Strategies (remember, though "generic" or "typical", each has a strategic profile).

The map presented in Figure 5.1 is a little "improved" typical output of a standard SSA or MDS statistical package (some require as an input the symmetric distances matrix, most will compute it directly from the strategic profiles). We call this figure an Approach Map. Axes are not shown on such a map, since they have no *a priori*. All positions are relative to one another. Thus, the main meaning is in the distances between points, the information that was shown in Table 5.1. In this figure, corresponding to the values in Table 5.1, specialization and diversification (for example) are 22 units apart and SBU Inc. is 18 from specialization and 19 from diversification. We have drawn a triangle to connect the points to help you see the distances.

The task of placing points in two dimensions becomes more complex as the number of strategies increases. It is always possible to create an approximate two-dimensional representation. Although in most cases a good representation is obtained, in some cases the two-dimensional representation is a poor fit to the data. A quantity called

Table 5.1 Average distances between strategies in the Seven Survival Strategies approach.

	Average distances between strategies						
Strategy	1	2	3	4	5	6	7
0. SBU Inc.	34	30	18	19	21	35	41
1. Multiplication	—	8	24	35	48	66	70
2. Monopolizing	—	—	21	31	42	61	65
3. Specialization	—	—	—	22	32	45	51
4. Diversification	—	—	—	—	20	40	47
5. Cooperation	—	—	—	—	—	23	30
6. Capitulation	—	—	—	—	—	—	8
7. Liquidation	—	—	—	—	—	—	—

the coefficient of alienation that ranges between 0 and 1 is used to measure this fit, where 0 is a perfect fit. Values of the coefficient of alienation less than 0.2 are considered acceptable. If the coefficient of alienation is near or above 0.2, you have encountered one of the rare cases in which the two-dimensional representation is inadequate for your data. If this is the case, ignore the results of the Approach Map.

Figure 5.1 shows the Approach Map for SBU Inc. and each of the Seven Survival Strategies. You will see that SBU Inc. (represented as 0 on the map) is positioned near the specialization strategy (3), the diversification strategy (4), and the cooperation strategy (5). SBU Inc. is positioned away from the other strategies in the approach. In looking at an Approach Map, remember that the map shows the relative distances of all the strategies from one another, not just their distance from SBU Inc. This will become clear as you compare Figure 5.1 with Table 5.1. Finally, the coefficient of alienation computed for this Approach Map is 0.017, well within the acceptable range.

The Approach Map is a powerful tool because it allows you to visualize the position of the SBU relative to all the strategies in the approach. You'll find this technique very useful using the Ten

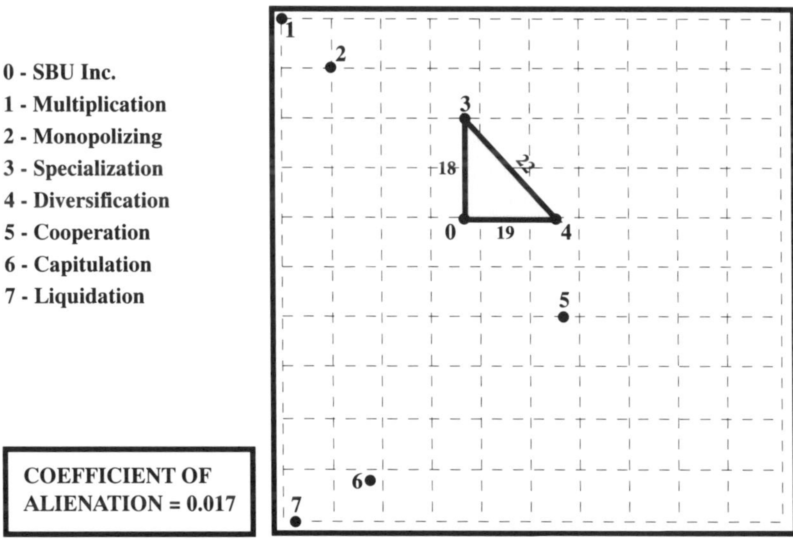

Figure 5.1 Approach map of Seven Survival Strategies.

Archetypes Strategies approach, the most comprehensive approach in this book (Miller and Friesen, 1978).

APPROACH 3: TEN ARCHETYPES STRATEGIES

In 1978, Danny Miller and Peter H. Friesen started a fruitful collaboration that resulted in important contributions to our knowledge of strategy and policy. Since his studies as a doctoral candidate at McGill University, Professor Miller has expressed deep discontent with the conventional atomistic way business strategy has been studied, claiming that this approach leads to a partial and sometimes erroneous understanding of strategic management. Instead, on the basis of previously useful research, he chose a comprehensive list of strategic variables to be studied simultaneously. This holistic approach was meticulously pursued in cooperation with Professor Friesen and has had a profound effect on the way business strategy is now studied. Indeed, our basic approach, though not the specific list of strategic variables, was greatly influenced by Miller and Friesen's Ten Archetypes approach.

The Ten Archetypes approach consists of ten strategies with different environmental, organizational, and strategy-making characteristics. Six of the strategies represent organizational success and four represent organizational failure.

Successful archetypes:

- Adaptive moderate
- Adaptive challenging
- Dominant firm
- Giant
- Entrepreneurial conglomerate
- Innovator

Failing archetypes:

- Impulsive
- Stagnant bureaucracy
- Headless giant
- Aftermath

The approach was built by Miller and Friesen by analyzing business cases. The data for the more recent cases were checked and approved by the management of the organizations studied. Following are the verbal descriptions of the ten strategies. The values of the strategic variables for these strategies are shown in Table 5.2.

Table 5.2 Variable values in the Ten Archetypes approach.

Variable	Strategy: 16	17	18	19	20	21	22	23	24	25
Metavariable: environment										
1. Environment uncertainty	45	79	27	70	65	54	86	35	70	60
2. Environment dynamism	58	95	27	79	68	74	84	47	57	61
3. Environment hostility	74	75	24	77	53	58	89	74	77	85
4. Environment complexity	42	65	38	87	85	50	87	18	63	39
Metavariable: content										
6. Product-market breadth	40	63	87	84	89	22	88	40	68	22
7. Product innovation	46	93	70	51	62	99	75	8	18	56
11. Control system level	81	78	66	86	83	53	2	13	18	36
12. Resources level	58	88	87	85	79	48	50	28	33	3
15. Professionalization	36	86	72	83	68	88	33	17	29	24
Metavariable: strategy making										
16. Internal analysis level	69	83	75	88	84	68	9	14	18	38
17. External analysis & forecast	68	91	69	84	87	53	21	8	17	32
18. Level of risk	61	75	33	68	80	52	98	34	36	71
19. Proactive management style	81	100	73	52	86	98	87	1	16	32
Metavariable: structure										
20. Size of strategy-making team	23	46	28	68	15	16	10	8	87	15
21. Degree of centralization	72	48	78	31	84	72	92	71	16	76
22. Degree of mechanism	62	22	80	28	56	55	71	87	31	58
Metavariable: performance										
23. Profitability	82	81	93	79	82	83	5	6	6	7
24. Market share	57	57	97	79	67	41	43	30	52	11
25. Rate of growth	33	78	65	43	94	74	52	2	9	4
Metavariable: characteristics										
27. Size	67	72	94	93	84	35	60	59	85	41
28. Age	79	59	88	87	79	44	27	83	85	38

Strategies:

16 = Adaptive firm under moderate challenge
17 = Adaptive firm in very challenging environment
18 = Dominant firm
19 = Impulsive
20 = Giant under fire
21 = Entrepreneurial conglomerate
22 = Innovator
23 = Stagnant bureaucracy
24 = Headless giant
25 = Swimming upstream

The adaptive firm under moderate challenge

The firm is situated in a moderately changing environment. It develops internal controls, and environmental scanning and communication mechanisms. Such firms tend to be in traditional industries, in which executives are substantially familiar with the external environment. The CEO has a major say in critical policy decisions, delegating routine functions down the line. Conflict is low. The firm has only one or two major product lines and pursues a carefully and frequently assessed product-market strategy that is in line with environmental needs. The focused orientation of the product-market scope coupled with the power of the CEO facilitates integration of strategies. Product-market innovation is usually gradual and incremental, with most changes involving modifying the product rather than changing it abruptly. Innovation, however, is more rapid and bold than that of competitors. The percentage of professionals (e.g., engineers, accountants) is low.

The adaptive firm in a very challenging environment

The SBU is geared to accommodate the challenges of changes in production technology, customer tastes, and product introduction. Its approach is proactive. It leads competitors in:

- New product and technological developments with substantial planning horizons.
- Ongoing "pure" research.
- An intelligence effort stressing product innovation.
- Change to suit its setting.
- Little adherence to past tradition.

The importance attached to tracking and analyzing information is conducive to responsiveness and adaptiveness in decision making.

The dominant firm

A dominant firm is large, its products are much in demand, and it dominates its competitors in a stable and rich environment. The firm has a formal hierarchy run by a powerful and popular CEO who has been responsible in the past for establishing the firm's now successful strategy. The CEO makes most of the critical decisions and some of the not-so-critical ones as well. Leadership and past strategies influence decision making more than intelligence efforts by lower levels in the hierarchy. An explicit, well-integrated, and established strategy is pursued. Incremental modifications of the product-market orientation to suit the changing environment are part of the unit's strategy.

The giant under fire

The giant under fire is extremely large and diversified with a successful history, but it now operates in a hostile, complex, dynamic, and challenging environment. This new situation poses tremendously complex administrative problems, including:

- The necessity for a very analytical mode of decision making.
- Decentralization.
- Delegation of all but top strategic matters to middle and lower management.
- Environmental scanning.
- Controls.
- New communication mechanisms.

Traditions impede any attempt at drastic change. The firm is reluctant to abandon its well-tested orientations. It adapts to its environment incrementally, but in the right direction.

The entrepreneurial conglomerate

The entrepreneurial conglomerate manipulates its environment instead of reacting to it. It is run by a powerful and charismatic CEO who may have a high share of ownership in the company, controls strategy making, and is interested in bold expansion via acquisition of (sometimes related) firms. Thus, the heterogeneity and complexity of the environment are increased, creating the need for intelligence activity and for the delegation of most operating functions to lower-level managers. Only major strategic changes are dealt with by the entrepreneur and his or her closest associates. The constant acquisitions require intensive planning and analysis activity.

The innovator

The innovator is guided by a successful and conscious niche strategy, developed in the past by an entrepreneur. Controls, direction, and adaptation are mostly in the hands of a strong CEO. The niche is relatively unexploited by others, and the firm consistently pre-empts competitors in revamping product-market orientations. The niche strategy is renewed by substantial product-market innovations that come from a design department or from a single creative genius, by expertise in the marketplace, and by the soundness of the original strategy.

The impulsive firm, running blind

The impulsive firm uses flamboyant and risky growth strategies. It moves boldly and without adequate precautions into complex and challenging new markets. The powerful and venturesome entrepreneur has highly concentrated strategy-making powers and relies mostly on untutored intuition to run the firm. The firm is not geared to meet these challenges. The intelligence system is inadequate. Lower levels of management have no authority or discretion. There is a lack of control and rampant ignorance of the complex and diversified nature of the operation.

The stagnant bureaucracy

The stagnant bureaucracy uses extremely rigid and conservative strategies based on traditions and antiquated concepts. The business unit lives in a dramatically changed, dynamic, and hostile environment. All major decisions are made by one or two executives who devote little effort to environmental scanning, intelligence, controls, communications, or analysis. They are unwilling to change the firm's product-market breadth or evaluate the organization's structure. Lower levels are aware of the need for change but have limited power. Information, particularly bad news, flows slowly up the hierarchy. Old ways of doing things are preserved even though they are no longer relevant.

The headless giant

The headless giant drifts without any apparent or informed sense of direction. Decisions are made in an uncoordinated manner because there is no clear leadership to deal with problems, to exploit opportunities in the environment, or to direct efforts at formulating long-term goals and product-market orientations, The result of this leaderless orientation is the absence of a well-developed strategy, a high level of conservatism, and drift that allows external factors to determine the course of the firm.

Swimming upstream: the aftermath

This is a turnaround situation. The firm has been burdened in the past with an inept management and seriously depleted resources. It now exists in an increasingly hostile setting. In an effort to correct this situation, strategy-making authority is now concentrated in the hands of an inexperienced CEO who valiantly tries, single-handed, to solve the firm's problems, down to even the lowest level of operational troubles. The attempt to modify past strategies by undertaking product-market innovations is seriously hampered by the lack of resources. Changes are usually made in desperation and involve a high element of risk. The changes produce harmful incongruities among the new and old elements of the strategy.

USES AND MISUSES OF THE TEN ARCHETYPES STRATEGIES APPROACH

The Ten Archetypes Strategies approach is comprehensive; it uses most of the strategic metavariables of our approach. The approach includes environmental variables, strategy-making variables, and organizational variables. Strategy content variables are less emphasized. The approach does not focus on an industry, and the ten strategies do not describe different strategies of competitors within the same industry. Being based on the experiences of 81 relatively large firms, this approach was not created specifically for business units. It may be applied to a wide spectrum of business organizations, from a limited product-market business unit to corporations composed of many business units. This book focuses on business units only. The approach should therefore be used with caution.

The distinction between business units and corporations (see Chapter 1) is sometimes blurred in real life. Many organizations, even those clearly identified with a single product-market, have additional interests in areas remote from their main business. These interests may be historical residues, newly developed interests for diversification, or a result of an opportunity in the market. When a business unit widens the scope of its product-markets and heavily invests in unrelated areas, our approach does not apply. What about borderline cases? Most of the other approaches included in this book were built for and analyzed only pure business units, either because the population used to develop the approach consisted only of business units or because the conceptual framework related to an industry of competing business units or a single product-market line. The Ten Archetypes approach gives us the opportunity to better understand organizations that are neither pure business units nor corporations. The original approach may be applied to full-scale corporations, but this is outside the scope of this book.

Success in this approach is achieving organizational goals. Thus, it is more general and less exact than financial success. In this approach, success/failure are not dichotomous, but rather a continuum. In ranking the ten strategies, Miller and Friesen defined less successful organizations as failures. Unlike other approaches in which a failure is a failure is a failure (this is not a typo! "A rose is a rose is a rose"), the Ten Archetypes approach suggests four failure strategies rather than one. Just as successful strategies may differ from one another, so do failures. As can be seen from the descriptions of the strategies, the reasons for failure may include:

- High risk
- Meager information
- Lack of control
- Rigidity and inability to adapt
- Lack of leadership
- Conflicting strategic decisions
- Previous failures that cannot be overcome.

As shown in Table 5.2, the only characteristics of the strategic variables values shared by all failure types are low levels of variable 16: internal analysis and variable 17: external analysis and forecasting.

Since failure profiles vary, so do possible remedies. Thus, use of this approach is highly recommended for business units that have experienced difficulties. Such units seek to find not only successful strategies but indications of how to improve their strategy to solve their specific problems. This approach is very useful for organizations that face major changes in the environment.

Miller and Friesen's definition of the approach stressed the time dimension, mainly when evaluating the environment. Thus, the current environment was evaluated as well as the environment five years hence. In this way, the approach captures the dynamic nature of the environment, in addition to its current status. The behavioral emphasis of this approach makes the marketing and operational (and financial) variables less significant. Other approaches should be used to compensate for this weakness.

ADDITIONAL VARIABLES

A strategic profile of 22 variables is needed to use this approach. Most of these variables were discussed in the previous chapters. However, three new variables appear and remain to be evaluated:

11. Control system level
15. Professionalization
28. Business unit age

We now present a detailed discussion of these additional variables. For each variable, we present:

1. The definition of the strategic variable.
2. The scale for measuring the variable.
3. Example(s) based on a real-life situation.
4. A short discussion of the place of the strategic variable in the business unit's strategy.
5. Recommended indicators for the variable.

STRATEGY CONTENT VARIABLES

Control system level

Definition. Control system level is the degree of use of mechanisms to standardize behavior and to assess performance.

Measurement. A score of 100 indicates a very strict and enforced control system, covering all activities and functional areas; zero indicates a nonexisting system; and 50 indicates the general level of control system.

Example. DuPont has a widely known system of control over the entire organization, based on profit centers ("DuPont's System of

Financial Control,'' 1987). Return on investment is computed for each product, department, or operating division. Return on investment is found by multiplying investment turnover by earnings as a percent of sales. Performance is compared by this formula to decide on the allocation of resources and incentive bonuses for managers.

DuPont is estimated to score 90 on control system level.

Example. T.J. Rodgers, CEO of Cypress Semiconductor Corp., has a reputation for detail (*Business Month*, 1987d). Cypress managers are expected to master an intricate, computerized management-by-objectives system. The system sets thousands of goals for all of Cypress's 600 employees every week and then monitors how well those goals are being met. As Rodgers explains, ''Our system forces management to stick its nose in a big book every single week and find out what is going on. We can't afford surprises.''

The system enables Rodgers to monitor both the progress of new semiconductors under development and the well-being of particular manufacturing areas. While the system doesn't actually stop mistakes, it catches them early before they evolve into expensive problems. As a result of the tight controls instituted by Rodgers, the company, in 1986, earned $14.4 million before taxes and special credits on $50.8 million in revenues, for a profit margin of 28%.

The control level at Cypress is extreme and is rated at 95.

Discussion. Here the focus is on the control system rather than the control process. Of course, any control process should focus on the firm's system. Control is sometimes further divided into management control and operational control, where management control relates to business unit resources and operational control to the specific tasks performed (Anthony, 1965).

Control systems focus on budgets; working capital and cash management; management practices and performance; production and inventory; research budgets and schedule; marketing expenses and effectiveness; and personnel. Thus, while money is an important basis of measurement in control systems, it is not the only one. Other measurements may include quantitative measurements such as output tonnage, reject percentage, yields, and turnover, as well as qualitative measures such as quality, motivation, and ability.

Indicators. A sophisticated control system level is indicated by a comprehensive management control and information system; extensive use of cost centers for cost control; extensive use of profit centers and profit targets; use of sampling and other quality control techniques; cost control by establishing standard costs and analyzing variations; and formal appraisal of personnel (Miller and Friesen, 1982).

The indicators recommended for operationalizing the control system level are:

1. Cost control
2. Profit targets
3. Quality control
4. Appraisal of personnel
5. Cash control
6. Management control
7. Production control
8. Inventory control
9. Marketing control
10.

Professionalization

Definition. The level of professionalization, sometimes denoted as technocratization, is the percentage of professionals (engineers, economists, accountants, research scientists) in the unit's workforce. It measures the level of formal education and training of employees.

Measurement. A score of 100 indicates a business unit whose employees not only have a high average number of years of education but mostly consist of professionally qualified people. A score of 50 indicates the national average of professionalization in all industries.

Example. In the late 1970s, Hospital Affiliates International Inc. (HAI) was one of the largest companies in the emerging hospital management industry ("Hospital Affiliates International Inc.," 1980). It was a leader in the management contract segment. HAI's reputation for quality was based on the group of staff specialists HAI maintained, including specialists in Accounting, Pharmacy Operations, Systems and Procedures, Community Relations, Budgeting and Finance, Radiology, and dozens of others. This group represented the widest range and highest professional level of all hospital management companies.

Clearly, HAI should be scored at or near 100.

Example. After raising $225,000 through a public issue, Merlin Microwave Inc. increased its staff from six to 21 ("Merlin-Microwave, Inc.," 1976). By 1970, the production group included four experienced tube technicians, a test engineer with an associate in engineering degree, a factory superintendent, a senior engineer with a BS degree and 12 years' experience in microwave tube development, and a physicist with an SM degree from MIT and twelve years' experience in electrical and mechanical engineering and particle physics. The selling group included a retired army procurement colonel who consulted on government procurements, a Washington representative, and a national network of 18 sales offices.

A professionalization value of 60 is suggested for Merlin Microwave.

Example. Brenda Barnes is marketing vice-president of PepsiCo Inc.'s $3 billion bottling company (*Business Month*, 1987f). She is only one of the thousands of managers who are swiftly moving up the rungs of the corporate ladder at PepsiCo. Unlike the majority of companies that prepare just a few high-potential managers for top positions, PepsiCo hires only superior talent and then gives all of them the chance to show what they are made of. The average age of the company's 500 or so senior executives is only 42, many of them reaching the position in less than ten years. Due to the company's acquisitions of Seven-Up International and Kentucky Fried Chicken, managers can look forward to even faster tracks to the top. While PepsiCo sometimes hires executives from the outside to fill special roles, it depends mostly on entry-level university graduates. In 1987, it hired about 1,000 graduates, with emphasis on marketing majors from Northwestern University and engineers from Georgia Tech.

PepsiCo values professionalization and is rated at 75.

Discussion. When job requirements entail a body of recorded knowledge, and a set of complex and nonrationalized skills that have been specified, this work is referred to as professional work. Most professionals are trained before beginning their work (Mintzberg, 1979). Thus, a specific job is either professional or not. Yet, when measuring the degree of professionalization of a business unit, generalizations are made and an average number of years of formal education are considered, although many of the workers are definitely not professionals.

Indicators. Indicators for the level of professionalization include the required level of formal technical competence of the business unit first-line supervisors (e.g., a maximum of a high school diploma or a minimum of a bachelor's degree with specialization); the percentages of professionals; and whether personnel with experience and common sense or specialized technically trained line and staff personnel are dominant within the unit.

The indicators recommended for operationalizing professionalization are:

1. Average years of formal education
2. General management education
3. First-line supervisors' education
4. Percent of professionals
5. Percent of personnel with formal technical education
6. Level of technological knowledge
7. Level of managerial knowledge
8. Percent of scientists
9. Percent of staff specialists
10. Use of external expertise

ORGANIZATIONAL CHARACTERISTICS VARIABLE

Business unit age

Measurement. The oldest business unit in the industry is given a score of 100, the newest 0. The industry median is 50.

Example. At the beginning of the 1980s, the water meter industry market leader in the North American market was a business unit within Rockwell International that had a 32% market share ("Rockwell

International (A) Municipal and Utility Division," 1982). Rockwell entered the water meter business in 1945 by acquiring Pittsburgh Equitable Meter Company, which had been formed by the amalgamation of three companies that entered the meter business between 1870 and 1900. The three other large competitors in the meter business were:

1. Neptune, which entered the meter business in 1892 and currently had a 23% market share.
2. Badger Meters (Wheelabrator-Frye), which entered the meter business in 1905 and currently had a 21% market share.
3. Hersey Meters, which entered the meter business about 1910 and currently had a 9% market share.

The water meter business changes gradually and has significant barriers to entry. Several companies tried to enter in the late 1940s but exited after a few years. No major innovations occurred between 1900 and 1957. In 1957, when Neptune was the market leader and Rockwell was second, Rockwell introduced a sealed register design that eventually had a major impact on the industry. Rockwell became the market-share leader by 1970.

Since Neptune is the oldest, it is assigned an age value of 100. The other firms are rated at 85 (Badger), 80 (Hersey) and 45 (Rockwell). These values are based on their age relative to Neptune.

Discussion. When a business unit was founded has an important effect on its initial strategy. The initial strategy reflects the situation prevalent at that time, and strategies persist over time (Brown and Schneck, 1979; Chandler, 1962; Stinchcombe, 1965).

Thus, in our approach, the unit's age relative to its competitors indicates whether the business unit took part in the creation of a particular industry, whether it is a newcomer with possibly a new competitive approach, or whether it is an average competitor. In some industries, absolute age is not the prime consideration. Rather it is the attitude of the managers relative to that of their competitors. This is particularly true if the management team keeps moving with the times.

Indicators. The following are some potential indicators operationalizing business unit age.

1. Year the SBU was founded
2. Years since SBU was founded/Years since first SBU in industry was founded
3. Attitude of SBU toward Innovation Relative to attitude of industry leader
4.
5.
6.
7.
8.
9.
10.

6

Weights for Variables and Strategy-making Modes

WEIGHTS

Normally all the variables used in an approach are assumed to be equally important; that is, they have equal weight in determining a business unit's strategy. *A priori*, there is no reason why a particular strategic variable, say, product innovation, should be more important than any other, say, the size of strategy-making team, in determining the strategic posture of a business unit. The emphasis is on the closeness of fit between the sets of strategic variables rather than on the criticality of one or another variable. Indeed, as we have just discussed, you have to determine which strategy is most closely matched on the basis of this notion.

However, this does not mean that you, as a manager, cannot assign different degrees of impact to strategic variables in defining a business unit's strategy. You can, in fact, assign a different weight to each variable in the strategic profile. Your choice would depend on your perception of the importance of these variables in your industry.

As a guide, you may want to use the following rules of thumb:

High	Twice the normal impact	Assign a weight of 2
Normal		Assign a weight of 1
Low	Half the normal impact	Assign a weight of 0.5

Be aware that when you assign different weights to variables, you can make significant changes in the strategy being matched. You should also be consistent in the weights you assign as you move from one approach to another when analyzing the same business unit. Otherwise, you run the risk of trying to make the results fit your preconceptions!

APPROACH 4: STRATEGY-MAKING MODES

Since its first publication in the *California Management Review* in 1973, Henry Mintzberg's "Strategy making in three modes" has been reprinted more than 40 times and has been included in many important management anthologies (Mintzberg, 1973b). Professor Mintzberg of McGill University in Montreal is an original and productive student of organizations, whose books and articles (such as *The Nature of Managerial Work* (Mintzberg, 1973a) *Power in and around Organizations* (Mintzberg, 1983), and *The Structuring of Organizations* (Mintzberg, 1979) to mention just a few) are beacons in our understanding of organizations. The Strategy-making Modes approach is one of his early contributions to the field.

Mintzberg(1973b) traces the origins of the study of strategy making in economics, public policy, and scientific management and sets forth their relevance for organizations. Three distinct modes of decision making are described:

- Entrepreneurial
- Adaptive
- Planning

Each mode represents a different linkage among the important decisions on which a strategy is built. Whether or not you can be successful as a business by adopting one of these modes, or a combinations of these modes, depends on the characteristics of the organization and the organizational environment. The approach thus created involves combinations of environment, organization, and strategy. Table 6.1 shows the values of the strategic variables included in the Strategy-making Modes approach.

The entrepreneurial mode

In the entrepreneurial mode, the dominant feature of strategy making is the active search for new opportunities. It is characterized by large-scale, bold, judgmental decisions made by the CEO, who holds the power in the business unit. The firm is usually young and

Table 6.1 Variable values for the strategies in the Strategy-making Modes approach.

Variable	Strategy:	26	27	28
Metavariable: environment				
1. Environmental uncertainty		91	50	18
2. Environmental dynamism		74	88	12
3. Environmental hostility		58	73	7
4. Environmental complexity		49	98	38
Metavariable: content				
5. Technological progress		93	26	63
6. Product-market breadth		14	65	78
7. Product innovation		96	15	57
10. Active marketing		94	17	70
11. Control system level		11	45	96
12. Resources level		40	65	83
Metavariable: strategy making				
16. Internal analysis level		29	36	99
17. External analysis & forecast		58	19	97
18. Level of risk		98	11	35
19. Proactive management style		98	1	50
Metavariable: structure				
20. Size of strategy-making team		1	87	57
21. Degree of centralization		94	16	44
Metavariable: performance				
24. Market share		17	60	79
25. Rate of growth		98	14	63
26. Operational efficiency		22	30	95
Metavariable: characteristics				
27. Size		4	84	81
28. Age		4	89	78

Strategies:

26 = Entrepreneurial mode 27 = Adaptive mode
28 = Planning mode

small and its primary goal is growth. The entrepreneurial mode is characterized by higher risk taking in times of crisis, rather than settling for more secure alternatives. This is counterintuitive for many students of strategy as well as for many practicing managers. Entrepreneurs, on the other hand, do not see any discrepancy.

The adaptive mode

In the adaptive mode, strategy making is characterized by reactive incremental solutions to existing problems. Power is divided among members of a complex coalition, usually leading to disjointed decision making. Feedback is a crucial part of strategy making, and decisions are made in incremental, serial steps. As a result, the strategy maker can be flexible and can adapt to the complex and dynamic environment.

The planning mode

The planning mode focuses on a systematic analysis of the cost and benefits of competing proposals. The strategy-making process depends to a large extent on analysts working closely with the CEO. This mode is characterized, moreover, by the integration of decisions and strategies. Long-term strategies are created and an explicit sense of strategic direction is developed, which influences the stable environment. The major goals of the firm are efficiency and growth.

USES AND MISUSES OF THE STRATEGY-MAKING MODES APPROACH

The Strategy-making Modes approach should be used for analyzing the strategy process in business units. Very often a specific strategy is recommended for a business unit without taking into account the way major decisions are made in the organization. This misfit between strategy content and strategy process results in the strategy's not being implemented (or being implemented in the wrong way) and, inevitably, poor performance. The major strength (and limitation) of the Strategy-making Modes approach is its emphasis on the strategy process. In applying it to your business unit, you gain substantial insight into the way strategy is made in your case.

However, the approach does not deal directly with strategy content. The major assumption of the Strategy-making Modes approach is that a strategy process compatible with the business unit's conditions will yield the required strategic content. Thus, although the approach is basically behavioral, it is related to the strategic-planning school, which views a successful strategy as a product of strategic planning (Ackoff, 1970; Ansoff, 1965). Using this approach in this book, it should be considered together with approaches that emphasize content, such as the Competing Generic approach or the Adaptation approach.

The inherent simplicity of the approach in portraying only three distinct strategy-making modes makes it easy for you to identify the major mode used in your business unit. You must, however, recognize that the real world is far more complex. In presenting this approach, Mintzberg pointed out that only a few organizations exhibit the pure modes. He gave examples of the adaptive-entrepreneur, the planning-entrepreneur, the adaptive-planner, and a mix of all three modes. That is, his examples included organizations that apply two or more modes in different units at the same time and organizations that apply different modes in the course of their life-cycle.

When using this approach you should refrain from looking for, or trying to achieve, an "ideal" match between your business unit's strategy and the approach's three strategies. You should pay attention to the relative distances of your strategy from all three strategies in this approach. There are values of environmental characteristics and of organizational characteristics, as well as of strategy-making variables, that may rightly place your business unit's strategy between two, or even between all three, reference strategies. A successful strategy should take into account the specific combination of the strategic variables, and the strategy process mix that fits the profile. In this detailed analysis, the approach of assigning different weights to the strategic variables as well as using different measures for calculating distances between strategic profiles, discussed in this chapter, is particularly useful. You should find the exact mix that currently best describes your business unit, as well as the mix you would recommend for the future.

The Strategy-making Modes approach is important for organizations in transition or in crisis; it is less useful for incremental strategic changes. The original Mintzberg paper also deals with the changes in strategy making over time. Mintzberg suggests that when organizations, environment, or leadership change, the strategy process should change to fit them. Thus, when considering a strategic change (Chapter 10), you should always use this approach as well.

Use of this approach alone will not pinpoint successful or failing strategies. The approach should be used in conjunction with other approaches. Nonetheless, when we examined a range of business units with this approach, we often found relatively low performance for business units that were identified as adapters, although this was not always the case.

AN ADDITIONAL VARIABLE

The Strategy-making Modes approach involves 21 variables (Table 6.1). Twenty of these variables were discussed in the previous chapters. One, active marketing, is new.

Active marketing

Definition. Active marketing is the amount of resource allocated by the business unit to marketing and the general awareness by management of the marketing concept.

Measurement. A score of 100 indicates the industry's most active competitor; 50 indicates the industry's average.

Example. The Taylor Wine Company, Inc., is a family enterprise whose main concern is the quality of their products ("The Taylor Wine Company, Inc.," 1977). Family members claim that their commitment to quality is one of the primary reasons for their success. The following quotation sums up the importance of quality to them: "The Taylors have their name on the bottle and to them product quality and consistency is most important."

Closely related is their marketing and distribution campaign, which is continually being strengthened. Their continuing program of advertising, sales promotion, and public relations has, according to one of the Taylor sons, remained the most consistent in the industry and has, in the judgment of Taylor's management, been largely responsible, along with product excellence, for the growth of sales and earnings.

> Taylor products have been advertised regularly in high quality national magazines; feature stories in news media, corporate publicity in trade publications, tours of thousands of visitors in the winery, distribution of millions of recipe books and the utilization of a wide variety of point-of-purchase promotion material have rounded out a thorough program of product merchandising.

Given Taylor's merchandising program, it is evaluated as 75 relative to its competitors in active marketing.

Example. Anheuser-Busch applies venerable marketing techniques more vigorously and imaginatively than the competition (*Fortune*, 1987a). The most important technique is target marketing, that is, segmenting the market with a vengeance. The company sponsors events and runs advertising aimed specifically at all sorts of consumers, including blacks, whites, blue-collar workers, computer buffs, and auto-racing fans. Anheuser-Busch even has an advertisement that salutes immigrants. The company divides the US into 210 markets, with the bulk of the budget going to Los Angeles, New York, Boston, and the 33 other markets where 75% of the beer is consumed. In target areas, the grass roots approach involves working with wholesalers to sponsor softball teams, bowling matches, rodeos, etc. Company Chairman A.A. Busch, III, takes an active role in spending the $100-million-per-year advertising budget and is responsible for the "This Bud's for you" theme chosen in 1978 from about twenty possibilities.

Anheuser-Busch's active marketing is rated 95.

Example. By the mid-1980s banks had discovered the rewards to be reaped from credit cards (*Business Month*, 1986a). Many financial institutions earned pretax profits of five percentage points on credit card lending, almost three times the margin on other lines of business. Wanting to expand their portfolios, the banks blanketed the United States with card applications. The number of accounts multiplied. Many of the aggressive banks launched massive campaigns that were just one step from actually mailing the cards out themselves. The prospect only had to return a simple application form to obtain the card.

Once the market became relatively saturated and response rates were diminishing, financial services turned to new ways of differentiating their cards from their competitors. Some competed on price, reducing financing charges or waiving the annual fee for the first year. Others "enhanced" their cards by rewarding users with bonus "dollars" applicable toward the purchase of selected brand-name merchandise. Bank of America offered a prepaid legal service in its Value America credit card program. National Westminster Visa and Mastercard customers got a chance to win prizes every time they used the card. One of the most innovative strategies was affinity group marketing in which the banks targeted groups of people with common interests. The affinity group (such as a university alumni association) would then market the card to its members, endorsing the bank's package in a solicitation on its own letterhead.

A bank engaged in such credit card marketing would be evaluated at 80.

Discussion. Marketing is defined as "the analysis, planning, implementation, and control of programs designed to bring about desired exchanges with target audiences for the purpose of personal or mutual gain. It relies heavily on the adaptation and coordination of product, price, promotion and place (programs) for achieving effective response" (Kotler, 1972). It includes well-integrated activities in which resources are directed to take advantage of market conditions and customers' needs, and to influence customers. Marketing is frequently described as the four P's:

- Product
- Price
- Promotion
- Place

Indicators. Active marketing involves identifying needs, defining the benefits the customers seek from the product or service. It includes marketing research; promotion; packaging; advertising; budget allocation; credits; relative number of marketing staff; size of the marketing function, use of marketing information system, managing marketing channels; supporting new product development; establishing market segmentation; establishing marketing communications; quality of marketing personnel; media selection; selection of distribution outlets; active reaction to competitive behavior and leading competitors' behavior; and percentage of marketing expenses from the business unit's turnover.

The indicators recommended for operationalizing active marketing are:

1. Marketing/total budget
2. Relative no. of marketing staff
3. Active promotion
4. Active advertising
5. Active packaging
6. Managing channels
7. Use of marketing information systems
8. Market surveys
9. Degree of marketing coordination
10.

7

Competitor Analysis and the Competing Generic Approach

In the previous chapters, our approach was used to analyze your own business unit. The same approach may also be used to analyze your competitors. These analyses will enable you to investigate the strategies being implemented by competing business units in your industry. Competitor analysis is an important phase in deciding your own strategy. Should you imitate a proven successful strategy (and shy away from proven failure strategies), or should you find a promising, yet unoccupied, strategic opportunity?

Competitor analysis can be performed in two ways:

- Making an in-depth analysis of a major competitor.
- Creating an industry competition map.

Conceptually, the procedures for in-depth analysis of a competitor are very simple: evaluate the variable values for the competitor and analyze these values as if they represented your own business unit. To increase accuracy, you can apply indicators. There is a major difference, however. While most data were available and known for your own business unit, in this case, many assumptions and evaluations will have to be made if you do not have complete information about your competitor (and generally, you do not!). The effort can be very fruitful. What do you really know about your competitor? Why are competing business units more successful than yours in some products and markets, but not in others? What are their competitive advantages, and how do they use them? What are the elements of their strategy, and the resultant over-all strategy?

To create an industry map, you should evaluate strategic profiles of your competitors. For this purpose, it is appropriate to use "quick and dirty" evaluation, without indicators. When the competitors' strategic profiles are created, it is possible to create graphical maps of your industry, similar to the Approach Map discussed in Chapter 5. In this case, you will create a two-dimensional representation of the distances among the strategic profiles of major competitors in your industry. This graphical presentation will help you understand the current structure of your industry. It serves as another input in determining your future strategy.

APPROACH 5: COMPETING GENERIC

The Competing Generic approach is probably the best known and most widely referred to in the business community (Porter, 1980). It was developed by Professor Michael E. Porter of the Harvard Business School, a scholar of, and consultant to, a wide range of businesses and industries. This approach is a major building block of his framework for analyzing industries and competitors. It points to three internally consistent generic strategies for taking offensive or defensive actions to cope with competitive forces and thereby yield a superior return on investment for the firm. One of the strategies included in Porter's original approach, focus, is further divided in here into focus-costs and focus-differentiation (Porter, 1983).

The successful strategies are named:

- Cost leadership
- Differentiation
- Focus-costs
- Focus-differentiation

The approach also recognizes a failure strategy, picturesquely named stuck-in-the-middle.

The four success strategies are positioned along two strategic dimensions, as shown in Figure 7.1. Each dimension is divided into two components: (1) strategic advantage: either uniqueness perceived by the customer or low-cost position; (2) strategic target: either industry-wide or particular segment only. The four elements of this matrix are:

		Strategic target	
		Industry-wide	**Segment**
Strategic advantage	**Low cost**	**Cost leadership**	**Focus-cost**
	Perceived uniqueness	**Differentiation**	**Focus-differentiation**

Figure 7.1 Porter's success strategies.

1. Low cost/industry-wide: Cost leadership.
2. Low cost/particular segment: Focus-costs.
3. Perceived uniqueness/industry-wide: Differentiation.
4. Perceived uniqueness/particular segment: Focus-differentiation.

We now present verbal descriptions of the five strategies, one of which will apply to any given business unit. The specific strategic profiles, that is, the values of the strategic variables, are shown in Table 7.1.

Over-all cost leadership

A cost leadership firm achieves its position in the industry through a high relative market share or other advantages, such as favorable access to raw materials. This strategy entails aggressive construction of efficient-scale facilities, vigorous pursuit of cost reductions that may derive from experience, tight direct and overhead cost control, avoidance of marginal customer accounts, and cost minimization in areas like R&D, service, sales force, and advertising, resulting in above average returns despite the presence of strong competitive

Table 7.1 Variable values for Competing Generic approach.

Variables	Strategy:	29	30	31	32	33
Metavariable: environment						
1. Environmental uncertainty		41	61	62	71	89
Metavariable: strategy content						
5. Technological progress		76	76	79	73	27
6. Product-market breadth		83	54	23	16	38
7. Product innovation		38	85	44	78	19
8. Quality		42	92	52	96	29
9. Price level		22	75	31	86	41
10. Active marketing		26	93	40	80	29
11. Control system level		99	41	91	44	23
12. Resources level		89	61	64	56	29
13. Investment in production		95	51	70	35	23
14. Number of technologies		38	79	33	46	49
Metavariable: strategy making						
15. Professionalization		45	87	57	87	38
16. Internal analysis level		88	61	78	62	19
17. External analysis & forecast		62	84	64	88	22
19. Proactive management style		38	84	51	82	25
Metavariable: structure						
21. Degree of centralization		86	31	62	24	30
22. Degree of mechanism		91	24	73	21	48
Metavariable: performance						
23. Profitability		75	70	77	76	8
24. Market share		98	47	33	18	26
25. Rate of growth		73	48	33	22	1
26. Operational efficiency		97	47	84	46	16
Metavariable: characteristics						
27. Size		91	44	27	18	46
28. Age		82	67	48	24	57

Strategies:
29 = Cost leadership 30 = Differentiation 31 = Focus-costs
32 = Focus-differentiation 33 = Stuck-in-the-middle

forces. The high margins are reinvested in new equipment and modern facilities to maintain cost leadership.

Differentiation

A firm follows the differentiation strategy if it offers a product or a service that is perceived industry-wide to be unique along several dimensions such as design or brand image, technology, features, customer service, and dealer network. Differentiation provides brand loyalty by customers, lower sensitivity to price, increased margins, and entry barriers. While the firm is not oblivious to costs, they are not the primary strategic target. The concept of exclusivity is incompatible with high market share and implies a trade-off with cost.

Focus-costs

A firm may focus on a particular consumer group, a segment of a product line, or a geographic market. Each functional policy is developed according to this focus. The firm is thus able to serve its chosen, narrow strategic target more effectively and efficiently than those competitors who compete more broadly. The focus-costs strategy requires capital investment in construction of efficient scale facilities, vigorous pursuit of cost reductions from experience, tight cost and overhead control, and cost minimization in areas like R&D, service, sales force, and advertising. Thus, the firm achieves a low-cost position *vis-à-vis* its narrow market target. Success derives from lower costs in serving the target market. However, the firm is limited in the overall market share achievable. The focus-costs strategy involves a trade-off between profitability and sales volume.

Focus-differentiation

Like a focus-cost strategy, in focus-differentiation a firm sees its market as a particular consumer group, a segment of a product line, or a geographic market. However, in a focus-differentiation strategy, the firm's product or service is perceived in its narrow market target as being unique along several dimensions. Focus-differentiation provides insulation against competitive rivalry because of customer brand loyalty and resulting lower sensitivity to price. It also increases margins, which avoids the need for the low-cost position. The payoff from this strategy derives from better meeting the needs of the particular target, although the firm is limited in the overall market share achievable. Like focus-cost, this strategy involves a trade-off between profitability and sales volume.

Stuck-in-the-middle

A firm "stuck-in-the-middle" lacks the market share, capital investment, and resolve to play the low-cost game, the industry-wide differentiation necessary to obviate the need for a low-cost position, or the focus to create differentiation or a low-cost position in a more limited sphere.

USES AND MISUSES OF THE COMPETING GENERIC APPROACH

The Competing Generic approach sees the world as consisting of oligopolies in every market. Each oligopoly consists of a small number of large competitors, which divide among them the major portion of the market share, and a multitude of smaller business units. In other words, the approach represents the structure of most industries. Thus, an important major assumption of this approach is the "U"-shaped relationship between market share and profitability: small (both focus types and differentiation) and large (cost leadership) business units are more profitable than medium-size units (stuck-in-the-middle). The approach does not relate to monopolies. It must be used with caution when analyzing a business unit in an unconcentrated industry composed only of very many, relatively small business units (approximating the economists' theoretical concept of "perfect competition"). Thus, if you are analyzing a business unit in an industry where the "U"-shaped relationship does not exist (e.g., in industries with distinct economies of scale such as petrochemicals or diseconomies of scale such as various craft industries), choosing this approach may lead you to erroneous conclusions.

This approach is highly recommended for analyses that focus mainly on the content of strategy and place less emphasis on the business unit's environment, its strategy-making process, or its organizational structure. When using this approach, keep in mind that the business unit's environment is not an internal part of this approach (even though environmental uncertainty may be evaluated). Also keep in mind that successful formulation and implementation of any strategy depends on (1) the process by which the strategy is formulated and implemented and (2) the organizational systems within which the strategy is pursued, particularly the unit's structure.

When using the Competing Generic approach, you implicitly assume Porter's notion that these are generic types. As a result, you must take into account the nature of the specific industry as it affects the strategy configuration, that is, the indicators used to evaluate strategic variables. For example, product-market breadth of community hospitals will be evaluated according to the range of services provided, not the geographic scope.

As with any other approach, you should be aware that you are assuming that there are only a limited number of possible strategies (in this case five, of which four are successful). However, not all industries and environments fully lend themselves to this approach. For example, not all mature capital goods industries demonstrate all these strategies (Hambrick, 1983b). Commodities inherently do not offer many opportunities for differentiation or focus.

While in his book Porter discusses industries in all stages of an industry's life-cycle (emerging industries, maturing industries, declining industries), the approach by itself does not relate to the life-cycle. Porter assumes that generic strategies are successful in every stage. However, the frequency of the generic types in a given industry is different, depending on the nature of the industry and the industry's maturity. Furthermore, adherence to the same strategy over the entire life-cycle is not always the best alternative. Thus, the business unit may switch gears, temporarily being in a transition, and identified as a stuck-in-the-middle over some time interval.

Built into this approach are the assumptions that:

1. All four successful strategies result in similar levels of profitability.
2. Profitability is the unit's dominant goal.

Is this so in your case? There are industries for which one or more of the strategies have a better fit, and their level of profitability is higher. Assuming the same rate of profitability for each strategy is the same as assuming the same rate of risk for all successful strategies. The Competing Generic approach in our system does not take the risk aspect of strategy making into account.

Because of the strategic target dimension in Porter's framework, strategy definition depends on the way the business unit defines its relevant market. This is more evident in the differences between differentiation and focus-differentiation. When the total relevant market is narrowly defined, the resultant strategy is differentiation; when top management of the business unit has high aspirations (and defines the relevant market broadly), the resultant strategy is focus-differentiation. Similar phenomena may occur with cost leadership and focus-costs.

A few words on the stuck-in-the-middle strategy. Although it may be claimed that the stuck-in-the-middle is different in each industry, indicating a mismatch with the business unit's environment, having only one failure strategy does not indicate the specific strategic mistakes, nor does it indicate the remedies. Changing a stuck-in-the-middle strategy is expensive and time consuming. The approach does not claim that these organizations are doomed, but neither does it give a very encouraging prognosis. However, stuck-in-the-middle may be a temporary situation when the business unit switches gears.

ADDITIONAL VARIABLES

The Competing Generic approach involves 23 variables (Table 7.1). Twenty of these variables were discussed in the previous chapters. Three are new:

8. Quality
9. Price level
16. Number of technologies

We now present detailed discussions of each of these additional variables. Specifically, we present:

1. The definition of the strategic variable.
2. The scale for measuring the variable.
3. Example(s) based on a real-life situation.
4. A short discussion of the place of the strategic variable in the business unit's strategy.
5. Recommended indicators for the variable.

Quality

Definition. Quality measures the customers' perception of the superiority of the business unit's products or services compared with those of the unit's competitors.

Measurement. Industry median score is 50.

Example. Throughout its history, Beech Aircraft Corporation has maintained a reputation for high-quality products ("Beech Aircraft Corporation," 1970). President Frank Hedrick claims that "Beechcraft on an aircraft is like Sterling on silver." Component quality has been kept high even for units that Beech does not produce itself (e.g., engines and instrumentation) by careful selection of quality sources. Extensive quality control has been used to ensure that raw materials are within tolerance levels specified. Its policy of constantly upgrading existing products to match or exceed the highest quality available has made Beech the price/quality leader in every segment of the market it served.

Beech, as industry leader, is rated 100 on quality.

Example. In 1981, Hewlett-Packard defined one of its basic objectives as follows: "Provide products and services of the highest quality and the greatest possible value to our customers, thereby gaining and holding their respect and loyalty" ("Hewlett-Packard Company (A): Problems of Rapid Growth,"1983). Hewlett-Packard demands total commitment to quality, a commitment that begins in the laboratory and extends to every phase of its operations. Products are designed to provide superior performance and long, trouble-free service. Careful attention to quality enables Hewlett-Packard to meet or exceed customer expectations. The company's objectives further state that once a quality product is delivered to the customer, it must be supported with prompt, efficient service of the same high quality.

Within the computer industry, Hewlett-Packard is rated 90 on quality.

Example. As discussed in the example of the Taylor Wine Company under active marketing in Chapter 6, Taylor relies on its commitment to quality as a prime way of differentiating itself in the marketplace. Taylor is rated 90 on quality.

Example. A.A. Busch, III, who runs the Anheuser-Busch Co., was quoted in *Fortune* as saying: "My father taught me the cardinal rule when I was a child: Quality is first" (*Fortune*, 1987a). Busch is fanatical about the reputation of his company and the quality of his beer. For example, the company supplements the traditional barley malt with rice instead of the cheaper corn that most rival brewers use. Even the company's major competitors agree that Busch's obsession with quality has been a major reason why Anheuser-Busch has stayed ahead. He claims his company invests more capital to produce a bottle of beer than does any competitor.

Assuming Busch's statements are correct, his company is the industry leader and rates 100 on quality.

Discussion. Although we relate to perceived quality, which is not always expressed in real superiority, higher quality is nonetheless built on less standardized production processes, and on manufacturing and management techniques above the industry's average. For example, the

Japanese method of minimizing inventories and stopping production lines when a problem is detected is a built-in pressure to minimize defects. High quality also requires the use of better components and raw materials.

Three types of factors influence consumers' perception of quality (Takeuchi and Quelch, 1983):

1. Prepurchase factors include business unit's brand name and image, previous experience, opinions of friends, store reputation, advertised price relative to performance, and published test results.
2. Point-of-purchase factors include performance specifications, comments of salespeople, warranty provisions, service and repair policies, support programs, and quoted price for performance.
3. Postpurchase factors include ease of installation and use, handling of repairs, claims warranty, spare parts availability, service effectiveness, reliability, and comparative performance.

Indicators. Indicators for quality include performance, reliability, number of defects, service, components, production technique, and manufacturing management technique.

The indicators recommended for operationalizing quality are:

1. Performance
2. Reliability
3. 1/no. of defects
4. Service & repairs
5. Components
6. Production techniques
7. Brand name & image
8. Reputation of outlets
9. Price/performance
10. Warranty

Price level

Definition. Price level is the relative price paid for the business unit's products and services, as perceived by customers, with respect to similar products and services in the market.

Measurement. The business unit perceived to offer the most expensive product or service is scored 100.

Example. Rubbermaid sells household molded-plastic products. Its market has slow growth and is fiercely competitive (*Fortune*,1987c). Rubbermaid's prices are undercut by almost all of its 150 competitors. As the head of a competing housewares company said: "For example, a–is sold by the competition for $2.50 and by Rubbermaid for $5.00."

Rubbermaid's price level is evaluated as 95.

Example. Charles River Breeding Laboratories is the price leader for every species it sells in the laboratory animal breeding business

("Charles River Breeding Laboratories",1980). Other firms in the industry follow its prices but at a 5% to 10% lower level.

As the highest-price competitor in its industry, Charles River's price level is assigned a value of 100.

Example. Merck Corporation, the world's largest prescription drug-maker, markets Mevacor, an anticholesterol (*Time*, 1988). This drug, while effective, has a major drawback for customers. A year's supply cost consumers $3,000 in 1988. Congressman Henry Waxman uses Mevacor as an example to point out that "Merck, like other big drug companies, has been raising prices dramatically and has introduced new drugs at shockingly high prices."

At the time of entry into the anticholesterol field, Merck's price level for this strategic business unit was 100.

Example. In 1986, the US airline industry was engaged in a stiff price war (*Business Month*, 1986b). The battling carriers offered discounts of 75% off regular ticket prices and $20 to $80 off super-saver fares. For example, travelers could fly from Chicago to Houston for $49 on Eastern or from Los Angeles to Denver for $79 on United. The airlines did, however, limit the number of cheap fares to protect the breakeven point on individual flights. This was done to ensure that the carriers would not sustain substantial losses, as had happened in the 1983 airline war.

In 1986, the price level was estimated at 20 for these airlines.

Discussion. When customers buy a product or receive a service, they go through a complex process of balancing the price against the perceived benefits, costs, risks, and value received (Shapiro and Jackson, 1978). The result is a standard price or an acceptable price range for many items that is regarded as fair by the customer. The price depends on a number of variables, including costs, target market and customers, and business pricing policy. Remember that the price level is the perceived price rather than the actual price.

Indicators. You can select indicators for relative price level in one of two ways:

1. Select up to ten typical products or services. Evaluate the relative weight of each product in the business unit's total product basket. Evaluate the price level of each product relative to competing products in the market.
2. Divide the price level further into advertised price, point-of-sale price (e.g., "street price" for personal computers), actual unit price, cash discounts, seasonal discounts, quantity discounts, service price, replacement price.

The indicators recommended for operationalizing price level are:

1. Advertised price
2. Point-of-sale price
3. Actual unit price
4. Cash discounts
5. Seasonal discounts
6. Quantity discounts
7. Service price
8. Replacement price
9.
10.

Number of technologies

Definition. The core technology of a business unit involves the specific use of labor and capital in transforming inputs into outputs. Technologies certainly differ among industries, and in the same industry they differ in the degree of intensity in using resources. A single business unit may operate more than one technology.

Measurement. The relative number of different core technologies employed in production processes is the number of technologies. The industry's average is scored 50. The industry's most prolific user of technologies is scored 100.

Example. Shouldice Hospital, discussed earlier, uses one basic technology in its specialized service of treating hernias. Emergency rooms at major, modern medical emergency centers such as UCLA or Cedars-Sinai Hospital in Los Angeles maintain all the latest lifesaving equipment. Shouldice would rate 10 on number of technologies, whereas the Los Angeles hospitals would rate 100.

Discussion. Technology is an important strategic variable that interacts with many other variables including organizational size, control system, degree of centralization, mechanism, and professionalization (Woodward, 1965; Thompson, 1967; Mohr, 1971; Kopp and Litschert, 1980). The wide spectrum of technologies ranges from unit or small-batch assembly or production according to customer definition (labor intensive and highly adaptive) to large batch production, mass production, and continuous process (capital intensive and highly rigid). Each technology is characterized by different equipment used in the production: manual tools, machine tools, automatic self-feeding machines, automatic-cycle machines, and computerized control machines.

Indicators. The indicators recommended for operationalizing the number of technologies are:

1. Equipment variety
2. Batch size variability
3. Process versatility
4. Raw material changeability
5. Degree of alterability
6. 1/percent of total facilities used in main core technology
7. 1/no. of subcontractors
8. No. of alternative process routes
9.
10.

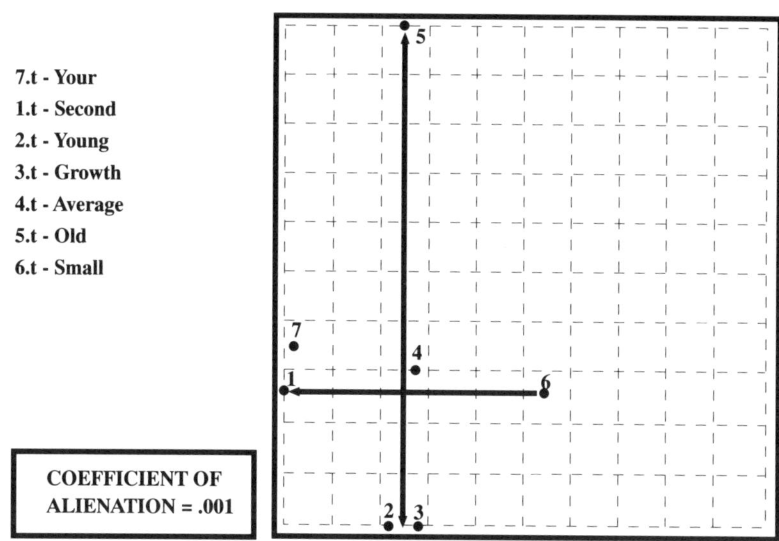

Figure 7.2 An example—an industry map.

AN INDUSTRY MAP

Figure 7.2 is a typical industry map. In this example, business unit number 7.t - Your is the focal organization ("your business unit"); 1.t - Second is the main competitor in this industry, with very similar strategy; 2.t and 3.t are young and fast-growing business units, while 5.t is the oldest business unit in the industry. 4.t represents an average competitor, and number 6.t, a small competitor. The coefficient of alienation for this example is .001, indicating a very good graphical representation of the distances matrix.

Having evaluated the strategic profiles for each competitor, the next step is to understand the axes of this map. Though each of the 28 strategic variables could be represented on this map, we show here only a few. The horizontal axis proves to represent variables No. 6 product-market breadth, No. 24 market share, and No. 27 business unit size. In this example they are highly correlated; small values on the right, high values on the left. The vertical axis represents five different variables: for No. 14 number of technologies and No. 28 business unit age, high values are at the top of the map; for No. 23 profitability, No. 25 rate of growth, and No. 26 operational efficiency, high values are at the bottom of the map.

8

Strategic Turnaround and Empiric Strategy Types

It is time to consider strategy making: the formulation of the business unit's preferred strategy. If you studied the previous chapters in sequence, you learned how:

- the business unit's current strategy was identified and analyzed
- its resources and capabilities for strategic change were checked
- environment was understood
- its competitive position, relative to its major competitors, was determined.

You are now to decide the unit's future strategic profile and to select the means to achieve it. For most business units, this means strategic change and improvement. For some business units, it may mean a strategic turnaround, a major redefinition of its strategy. In this chapter we focus mainly on strategic turnarounds. The methodology is similar to strategy modification discussed in Chapter 4. The difference is in scope and direction of analysis. While previously our starting point was the unit's current position and the changes required for improved performance, in this chapter we focus on defining normative/optimal strategies for our business unit and examining the feasibility of these strategies.

The analysis of strategic turnaround is best done in terms of the Empiric Strategies approach. This approach is, in fact, two approaches, one for consumer products and the other for industrial goods. We call these approaches Empiric Strategies—Consumer and Empiric Strategies—Industrial (Galbraith and Schendel, 1983).

APPROACHES 6 AND 7: EMPIRIC STRATEGY TYPES

This Galbraith and Schendel approach is based on an empirical analysis of the Profit Impact of Market Strategy (PIMS) database (Buzzel and Gale, 1987). Research focusing on the PIMS program and database has contributed significantly to understanding strategic management (Ramanujam and Venkatraman, 1984). PIMS, managed by the nonprofit Strategic Planning Institute, was initiated as an internal project at the General Electric Company in 1960. At the time of the Galbraith and Schendel study, the PIMS database included annual strategic information (more than 100 data items) on over 1,000 business units. The data were contributed by more than 150 companies, mostly from the *Fortune* 500 list (Abell and Hammond, 1979).

Analyzing this historical database, Professors Craig Galbraith (University of California at Irvine) and Dan Schendel (Purdue University) used a method that facilitates simultaneous cross-sectional and time-series analysis. Thus, they were able to focus on not only the current strategic posture of business units (relationships among strategic variables at a certain point of time) but also their strategic direction (the way business units change their strategic posture over time).

The result of this analysis is an approach based on a cluster analysis of different strategic posture and strategic direction components. Two approaches were identified: one composed of six strategies for consumer products, and the other composed of four strategies for industrial products.

Consumer:

- Harvest
- Builder
- Cashout
- Consumer niche
- Climber
- Continuity

Industrial:

- Low commitment
- Growth
- Maintenance
- Industrial niche

The values of the variables in the two approaches are shown in Tables 8.1 and 8.2.

Table 8.1 Variable values for Empiric Strategies—Consumer approach.

Variables	Strategy: 34	35	36	37	38	39
Metavariable: environment						
1. Environmental uncertainty	36	50	21	79	42	33
Metavariable: content						
5. Technological progress	5	68	51	54	85	30
6. Product-market breadth	74	42	55	8	21	97
7. Product innovation	3	61	59	60	83	26
8. Quality	13	57	33	27	88	92
9. Price level	11	29	43	11	83	97
10. Active marketing	12	78	45	37	29	91
12. Resources level	10	78	42	44	50	52
13. Investment in production	1	79	45	56	64	37
15. Professionalization	3	71	43	72	82	56
Metavariable: strategy making						
16. Internal analysis level	15	80	45	40	77	67
17. External analysis & forecast	13	79	51	47	90	56
18. Level of risk	27	65	27	62	44	26
19. Proactive management style	5	83	32	68	74	38
Metavariable: performance						
23. Profitability	63	37	60	41	44	88
24. Market share	41	62	56	32	49	74
25. Rate of growth	0	90	25	53	62	33
26. Operational efficiency	45	33	55	27	52	78
Metavariable: characteristics						
27. Size	67	45	61	29	12	93
28. Age	89	31	73	30	29	89

Strategies:

34 = Harvest 35 = Builder 36 = Cashout
37 = Consumer niche 38 = Climber 39 = Continuity

APPROACH 6: EMPIRIC STRATEGIES—CONSUMER

Harvest

Harvest is a strategy of disinvestment and is an indication of an inclination to go out of business. The values of the price level, promotion, quality, and new product strategy variables are low with no indication of improvement. Efforts are made to dispose of the product through discounts, and the atmosphere is one of decreasing general support for the product.

Table 8.2 Variable values for Empiric Strategies—Industrial approach.

Variable Strategy:	40	41	42	43
Metavariable: environment				
2. Environmental dynamism	8	88	63	58
4. Environmental complexity	11	89	75	40
Metavariable: content				
5. Technological progress	9	79	51	88
6. Product-market breadth	15	93	48	15
7. Product innovation	10	76	34	86
8. Quality	4	68	45	95
9. Price level	9	58	42	98
10. Active marketing	6	94	47	20
11. Control system level	21	59	83	49
12. Resources level	13	76	51	43
13. Investment in production	8	77	52	60
14. Number of technologies	19	81	50	42
15. Professionalization	14	69	43	93
Metavariable: strategy making				
16. Internal analysis level	16	76	46	73
17. External analysis & forecast	5	79	47	87
18. Level of risk	2	92	36	75
Metavariable: structure				
20. Size of strategy-making team	83	17	54	46
22. Degree of mechanism	16	73	86	53
Metavariable: performance				
24. Market share	32	71	41	47
25. Rate of growth	7	86	24	75
26. Operational efficiency	52	15	87	36
Metavariable: characteristics				
27. Size	46	76	77	17
28. Age	90	30	83	25

Strategies:

40 = Low commitment 41 = Growth
42 = Maintenance 43 = Industrial niche

Builder

A builder strategy represents a strong commitment to the product. Promotion and R&D are priorities. The high general level of investment indicates an attempt to expand sales and/or market share position rapidly by using low pricing behavior. This strategy requires high levels of product visibility, product differentiation and development, and investment support that is higher than that of competing firms.

Cashout

The cashout strategy is characterized by high price levels, quality, and product-market breadth. Profitability is high while both old and new product development are low. Little effort is devoted to product improvement. Promotion (i.e., active marketing) is high in this strategy. Promotion helps maximize profits by raising price levels and extending the life of the product.

Consumer niche

The salient features of the consumer niche or specialization strategy are high quality and price of products and services. Efforts are concentrated on maintaining the old and introducing new products, with little emphasis on advertising. Some effort is directed at lowering costs.

Climber

A climber currently has narrow product bases, low prices, inferior quality and a significant disadvantage in margins. The firm tries to improve its strategic posture through increased investment in promotion, price, R&D and new product development.

Continuity

Continuity is a status quo strategy which mainly involves following industrial norms. Investment and other strategy components are set according to industry norms. Future strategic behavior is not expected to change very much.

APPROACH 7: EMPIRIC STRATEGIES—INDUSTRIAL

Low commitment

The business unit is not willing to commit significant funds to its product, but no effort is made to improve its already deficient strategic posture. Efforts at vertical integration are limited, and the trend to high-cost structures appears to be increasing. In short, the firm is unwilling to invest an additional effort in the product.

Growth

Growth involves commitment to the product. Investment is quite high, and market position is expanded by promotion. Quality and cost structures are close to the industry norm, although the price level is slightly above the industry norm.

Maintenance

Maintenance emphasizes cost reduction in manufacturing and distributing the product while maintaining the business unit's position in the market place. Very often, strategic posture components such as price, promotion effort and quality are close to industrial norms. Cost reductions are perceived, however, to be quite important, and considerable efforts are directed to this end.

Industrial niche

An industrial niche is a specialization strategy involving superior quality, high price levels, and a narrow product line. There is only slight emphasis on promotional activities while cost structures are quite high.

USES AND MISUSES OF THE EMPIRIC STRATEGY TYPES APPROACH

The Empiric Strategy Types approach is the only approach included in the book which makes the important distinction between business units focusing on consumer products and those focusing on industrial products. The approach is best for manufacturing businesses, but it can be applied to any business unit by choosing the consumer or industrial approach as appropriate.

This approach derives from the marketing school of thought, and its database is oriented accordingly. In using the Empiric Strategies approach you should be aware of its marketing orientation, and you should compensate for it by using other approaches as well.

This approach does not account for the size of the business unit. Since the PIMS database includes information on businesses that are parts of very large companies (*Fortune* 500), this approach should be used for relatively small businesses with extreme caution. Although many of the business units in the database are themselves not necessarily large, being an integral part of a large corporation may affect strategy.

By emphasizing both strategic posture and strategic direction, this approach is important in considering strategic change over time. Most strategic moves should evolve over time, and only in special cases should change be revolutionary. Use of this approach points out the business unit's strategic actions that will affect its future strategic position.

On the basis of this approach alone, successful businesses may not be clearly distinguished from failing businesses. It should be used together with other approaches (such as the Competing Generic approach or the Ten Archetypes approach), which are more exact on this point.

This approach to business unit performance deserves elaboration. Rather than focusing on one performance measure, say return on investment, Galbraith and Schendel checked the effect of the business unit's strategy on three different performance measures: profitability, cash flow; and change in market share. They clearly found trade-offs among these three performance measures: some strategies result in higher return on investment, with relatively negative cash flow, others increase their market share at the expense of profits. Thus, business units may pursue success by different strategies, depending on their specific goals. The kind of success to be pursued should be defined in advance, and the appropriate strategy sought. This approach to performance was adapted in our approach. Performance is a metavariable in our framework composed of four strategic variables (profitability, market share, rate of growth and operational efficiency). The combination of variable values is unique for each of the 53 strategies.

Because it is based on the PIMS database, this approach focuses on strategy content. The use of this approach should be complemented by approaches emphasizing the environment, strategy making and structure (for example, the Strategy-making Modes approach and the Adaptation approach). When using this approach for analyzing an organization focusing on both industrial and consumer products, the best approach is to define two separate business units and analyze each according to its relevant approach.

STRATEGIC TURNAROUND

To analyze the strategic profile of SBU Inc., the example we used in Chapter 3, we chose the Consumer approach (assume SBU is producing are consumer products). The Empiric Strategy that currently matches most closely SBU's strategic profile is the consumer niche strategy (average distance 16). Assume that when the strategy-making team of SBU Inc. read both the short statements of the consumer niche strategy and the climber strategy, they liked the second better, and decided to consider the climber strategy as a basis for strategic turnaround. A comparison of SBU's strategic profile with the climber's reveals the following variances:

An example: variances (Var.) between the strategic profiles of SBU Inc. and the climber strategy (Clim.)

Strategic variable*	SBU	Clim.	Var.
1. Environmental uncertainty	71	42	29
5. Technological progress	55	85	−30
6. Product-market breadth	16	21	−5
7. Product innovation	53	83	−30
8. Quality	80	88	−8
9. Price level	50	83	−33
10. Active marketing	54	29	25
12. Resources level	59	50	9
13. Investment in production	51	64	−13
15. Professionalization	64	82	−14
16. Internal analysis level	63	77	−14
17. External analysis & forecasting	62	90	−28
18. Level of risk	43	44	−1
19. Proactive management style	52	74	−22
23. Profitability	68	44	24
24. Market share	50	49	1
25. Rate of growth	26	62	−36

26. Operational efficiency	27	52	−25
27. Size	29	12	17
28. Age	40	29	11

* Only the strategic variables included in the Empiric approach.

Both current technological progress (variable No. 5) and product innovation (No. 7) for SBU are low for a "typical" climber strategy. If the decision is to pursue this strategy changes should be made (this analysis does not, and cannot, answer the question if SBU can make these changes). Each variance should be analyzed. Can this change be made? How much should it cost? Analysis of variable 23, profitability, points out that the typical profitability of a climber strategy is somewhat below the industry average, much below current profitability (variance is 24). Should this strategy be considered at all?

9

Strategic Team and the Adaptation Approach

STRATEGIC TEAM

In organizations, be they public or private, Japanese, European, or American, most decisions are taken only after extensive deliberation. Although it is sometimes possible for decision makers to go counter to the consensus of their organization, this is not a viable long-term position for them. Decision makers out of tune with the people in their organization either depart from the organization or the organization undergoes massive personnel turnover. The concept of group involvement in decisions applies to strategy making, since the outcome of the strategy-making process is a major decision taken by the organization.

Although most business organizations are hierarchical, strategy making in an environment involving choices among alternatives and assessment of risks is usually a shared process. Face-to-face meetings among members of the strategy-making team are an essential element of reaching a consensus. The team may be involved in deciding on a strategy or in a strategy-related task such as creating a short list of acceptable alternatives or creating a recommendation for approval at a higher level. The group meetings are characterized by the following activities and processes:

- The meetings are a joint activity, engaged in by a group of people of equal or near equal status.

- The activity, as well as its outputs, is intellectual in nature.
- The product depends in an essential way on the knowledge, opinions, and judgments of its participants.
- Differences in opinion are settled either by fiat by the ranking person present or, more often, by negotiation or arbitration. The results lead to a strategy for the organization.

Another way of looking at strategy-making meetings is in terms of what groups do. Specifically, groups:

- Retrieve (or generate) information.
- Share information among members.
- Use information to reach consensus or decision.

Our approach may be used to establish common language and terms among strategic teams. First, you can aggregate group inputs to assess the values of a strategic variable. In a typical case, you would gather a group and ask each member for his or her assessment of the value of a variable, for example, product-market breadth. Each group member would state his or her value. At the simplest level, you would average the responses, weighting each input equally. At the next level of sophistication, you would recognize that some opinions deserve greater weight than others (e.g., based on knowledge of that variable) and compute the weighted average of the group opinion and use that average as the value of the strategic variable. Or, you might just discuss each variable with the strategic team. Based on our experience, these discussions are highly informative for some members of the team, bring into the open different perceptions, and create mutual evaluations.

Second, the strategic team may use the 53 strategies included here to compare the SBU's current strategy, and to describe their preferred future strategy. Use of this approach by hundreds of graduate student teams, tens of executive teams, and more than fifty strategic teams of real-life business units always resulted in:

- Focused discussions.
- High level of participation.
- Common language.
- Efforts to reach consensus.

APPROACH 8: ADAPTATION

Vying with Porter's Competing Generic approach for wide acceptance is Raymond E. Miles and Charles C. Snow's Adaptation approach (Miles and Snow, 1978). Miles, then a professor at the University of California at Berkeley, and Snow, a professor at Pennsylvania State University, developed their approach in 1978 by interpreting existing findings in the strategic literature. They studied:

- 16 firms in the college textbook publishing industry.
- 49 organizations in electronics and food processing industries.
- 19 voluntary hospitals.

Their framework emphasizes the business unit's rational selection of and purposive decision in changing its products/markets to fit its environment. Later this approach was used extensively in the study of industries and populations of business units (Hambrick, MacMillan, and Barbosa, 1983; Snow and Hrebiniak, 1980; Adam, 1983).

In this approach, a successful business unit is one that finds, defines, and maintains an existing market for its products or services; and constantly changes and improves the organizational structure and management processes (mechanisms) that enable adaptation of the market strategy.

An unsuccessful business unit, on the other hand, is one that:

- fails in maintaining its market
- fights its own organizational structure and processes.

In Miles and Snow's framework, the organization is analyzed as an integral and dynamic whole, taking into account the interrelationships among the environment, the strategy, the process, and the structure. Since this framework is based on the way an organization adapts to its environment, the environment becomes the departure point for this approach. Linkages among the environment, the strategy content, the strategy process, the organizational structure, and processes are identified and defined.

The Adaptation approach assumes that every firm has to make strategic choices based on three broad problems:

- The entrepreneurial
- The engineering
- The administrative.

Together these strategic choices form an adaptive cycle. On the basis of this adaptive cycle an approach of four strategic types is described, three successful and one failure strategy:

Successful strategies:	*Unsuccessful strategies*:
• Defenders	• Reactors
• Prospectors	
• Analyzers	

We now present verbal descriptions of these four strategies. The specific strategic profiles, that is, the values of the strategic variables are shown in Table 9.1.

Defenders

Defenders define their entrepreneurial problem as how to create a stable domain by cornering a portion of the total market. To this end, they produce only a limited set of products directed at a narrow segment of the total potential market. They grow through market penetration and perhaps some limited product development. Over time, a true defender is able to carve out and maintain a small niche within the industry which competitors are able to penetrate only with difficulty. The defender develops a single core technology that is highly cost efficient. The administrative system also aims at maintaining efficiency. There is little scanning of the environment for new opportunities. Management is concerned mainly with intensive planning, cost efficiency, centralized control, and maintaining stability through a functional structure.

Prospectors

Prospectors are mainly concerned with the location and exploitation of new product and market opportunities. A prospector maintains a broad and continuously developing domain of interest while monitoring a wide range of environmental conditions and events.

Table 9.1 Variable values for an Adaptation approach.

Variable	Strategy:	44	45	46	47
Metavariable: environment					
1.	Environmental uncertainty	10	42	79	79
2.	Environmental dynamism	7	59	99	53
4.	Environmental complexity	9	68	91	49
Metavariable: content					
5.	Technological progress	64	64	77	20
6.	Product-market breadth	10	70	78	32
7.	Product innovation	11	61	99	17
8.	Quality	81	72	75	20
9.	Price level	5	57	94	55
10.	Active marketing	36	74	92	18
11.	Control system level	100	58	24	18
12.	Resources level	55	70	64	28
13.	Investment in production	86	60	32	43
14.	Number of technologies	1	46	96	37
15.	Professionalization	22	62	95	20
Metavariable: strategy making					
16.	Internal analysis level	97	77	45	12
17.	External analysis & forecast	18	71	99	6
18.	Level of risk	28	27	83	90
19.	Proactive management style	31	65	96	16
Metavariable: structure					
20.	Size of strategy-making team	5	60	92	42
21.	Degree of centralization	99	47	2	47
22.	Degree of mechanism	95	52	2	49
Metavariable: performance					
23.	Profitability	85	91	57	3
24.	Market share	33	74	75	19
25.	Rate of growth	16	56	89	8
26.	Operational efficiency	96	67	21	14
Metavariable: characteristics					
27.	Size	37	86	50	50
28.	Age	81	81	19	63

Strategies:

44 = Defender 45 = Analyzer
46 = Prospector 47 = Reactor

The prospector creates changes in the industry through product and market development, although these developments may come at sporadic intervals. Flexible, prototypical, multiple technologies are used with a low degree of routinization. To stay flexible, the firm tends toward decentralized control and low reliance on formal procedures.

Analyzers

The analyzer moves toward new products and customers, mainly through imitation and only after viability has been demonstrated. The firm is interested in locating and exploiting new product and market opportunities on the one hand while maintaining a firm base of traditional products and customers on the other. As a result, the firm has a dual technological core—one stable and the other exploratory. In this type of firm, marketing, engineering, and production play an important role. Because the domain is hybrid, the organizational structure is a matrix combining both functional divisions and product-market divisions.

Reactors

The reactor can be characterized by its lack of a consistent strategy and by its inconsistent, random reactions to environmental changes. Because of its inability to respond appropriately to its environment, a reactor firm is perpetually unstable and, as a result, exhibits poor performance. The reactor, lacking a consistent strategy, cannot act proactively upon its environment. Instead, it reacts to clues it receives from its environment in an arbitrary way. This situation may be the result of unclear definition of the firm's strategy, or of an inability to shape the firm's structure and processes to fit the strategy chosen, or of maintaining a strategy inappropriate to a changing environment.

USES AND MISUSES OF THE ADAPTATION APPROACH

When choosing the Adaptation approach for use you are focusing on the dynamics of the business unit's decision to modify its products and markets. The objective is the unit's ability to meet suitable, steady levels of achievement. Thus, you are intentionally emphasizing product-market innovation. This approach is effective in expressing how organizations design alternative methods with which to pursue strategies involving their product-market domains.

The Adaptation approach relates to the business unit's:

- Environment
- Strategy
- Structure

Although the approach is concerned with the interrelationships between the management method and strategy, its focus is on the strategy, not on the process used to create and implement strategies (Snow and Hambrick, 1980). If you use this approach, you should also use at least one approach that emphasizes strategy making (such as the Strategy-making Modes approach or the Deliberate and Emergent Strategies approach).

Use of the Adaptation approach reminds us again that any business unit's behavior is only partially determined by the environment. Decisions made by top management are major factors in determining the pattern by which the business unit adapts to environmental conditions. Although it is complicated and time consuming, by identifying this pattern it is possible to describe and even to forecast the way the unit will adapt to the environment in the future. This is an important stage in understanding your business unit and your competitors' actions. The approach assumes an industry composed of many business units, not one firm, or even a few firms, dominating the industry. Thus, this approach is highly recommended for analyzing business units in unconcentrated industries. The approach will also yield many insights when analyzing other kinds of industries (for example, oligopolies). However, in evaluating the results, you should take into account the industry's specific structure. The approach's "pure" world is composed of only four strategies.

In each industry, there are three success strategies, which occur with about the same frequency. Each strategy is pursued by more than 25% and less than 33% of the business units in the industry. The rest of the business units are reactors whose return on investment is lower than the other three types. Empirical studies using Miles and Snow's Adaptation approach resulted in some observations that managers using this approach should be aware of (Hambrick, 1983b; Meyer, 1982; Segev, 1987):

1. The analyzer is a hybrid of the prospector and the defender. Sometimes analyzers are distinctly composed of two related business units; in such cases, each business unit should be analyzed separately, one as a defender, the other as a prospector. On the other hand, a business unit will often have two or more different product-markets, each at a different stage of maturity, such as an established line of personal computers and

a new generation that will eventually replace the old line. In these cases, application of the analyzer model is particularly illuminating.

2. Not all industries have the same number of defenders, analyzers, and prospectors. Old industries may be dominated by defenders, while new high-tech industries are not.
3. Level of performance is not necessarily the same for the three successful strategies. Well-established industries with low rates of technological innovation favor defenders. Innovative industries tend to be prospectors. Some process industries are predominantly analyzers. You should investigate the situation in your industry before drawing conclusions.
4. The reactor strategy is claimed to have low levels of performance and not to exist for a long period. In at least one industry (airlines), it was found that because of excessive government intervention and frequent changes in regulations, reactors demonstrated higher performance than their competitors. Thus, finding yourself a reactor should turn on a warning light. Before panicking, you should first examine the fit between your business unit's performance levels and the reactor's performance levels. If your business unit exhibits high performance (profitability, growth, market share, operational efficiency), you should examine the strategic profile of some of your successful competitors. You may find that in your industry a reactor strategy is a success strategy. However, be aware that these peculiarities of your industry may change suddenly, since they are caused by external, intervening forces.

10

Future Strategic Position and the Product-market Strategies Approach

In the previous chapters, when a new approach was introduced, it was first used to identify the current strategic position of the business unit. In this chapter, we present an approach, the Product-market Strategies approach, that focuses on the SBU's strategic position in the future assuming that the current strategy is continued.

APPROACH 9: PRODUCT-MARKET STRATEGIES

The Product-market Strategies approach, developed by J.G. Wissema, H.W. Van der Pol, and H.M. Messer, management consultants in Amsterdam, is based on the business unit's market and its relative potential in this market (Wissema, Van der Pol, and Messer, 1980). The point of departure for this approach is the Boston Consulting Group (BCG) matrix, which describes the industry's current stage along the product-market life-cycle (Boston Consulting Group Staff, 1968).

The Boston Consulting Group matrix and its market stages are shown in Figure 10.1. This approach takes a two-dimensional view of how a product behaves in the market over time. The dimensions are market share and the industry's growth rate. To read this diagram, you start in the upper-left corner, where the product is introduced, and it is a question mark as to whether it will be a success or not. Such products have high growth potential but initially low market penetration. They require large net cash outflows if their market

		Relative Market Share (Cash Generation)	
		Low	**High**
Industry growth rate (Cash use)	**High**	**Question mark-Introduction**	**Stars-Growth stage**
	Low	**Dogs-Declining stage**	**Cash cows-Maturity stage**

Figure 10.1 The Boston Consulting Group matrix.

penetration is to be maintained or increased. You then proceed clockwise to the growth stage. Here the product has both high growth and high market share. It is truly a "star." These products usually have the highest profit margins but require investment to keep their market share. As the product becomes established, the need for investment to maintain market share diminishes and the product is in its mature stage. It produces profit and requires relatively little managerial attention. Eventually, the product declines as it is replaced by new technology or affected by changing tastes. It is kept on the market as long as it remains profitable.

The product-market life-cycle is used only as a surrogate for the business environment. Four distinct stages along the life-cycle are defined:

- Introduction
- Growth
- Saturation (or maturity)
- Decline

Each market is at one of these stages. Depending on the industry, the third stage, saturation, may continue for relatively long periods.

Its life-cycle stage and its internal potential define the business unit's strategic situation. This internal potential, which is categorized as high, moderate, or low, is defined primarily by the business unit's market share. Internal potential also takes into account such factors as the business unit's power over distribution, its reputation, its exclusivity of know-how, and its service quality. In summary, each business unit is at one of the four stages of the product-market life-cycle and at one of the three levels of competitive potential.

The strategic question is not its present position but its position in the future. The approach consists of the strategies for reaching the desired strategic position. A product-market combination is defined as one of the six routes from the current to the desired strategic position. (In their original paper, Wissema, Van der Pol, and Messer also suggested an approach for managers, which is based on managerial behavior and the compatibility of each type of manager with the six product-market strategies. In this book, we adopt the strategic approach only.) Table 10.1 shows the variables used in this approach and their values for each of the six product-market strategies.

SIX PRODUCT-MARKET ROUTES

The following are the six product-market routes:

- Explosion
- Expansion
- Continuous Growth
- Slip
- Consolidation
- Contraction

Explosion

An explosion firm is determined to improve its competitive position within a short period of time. For new products, this goal is achieved by creating the market. For existing products, takeovers or dumping may be the chosen course of action.

Expansion

An expansion firm aims at consolidating its position in a growing market over a longer period by creating temporary overcapacity,

Table 10.1 Variable values for Product-market Strategies approach.

Variables	Strategy: 48	49	50	51	52	53
Metavariable: environment						
2. Environmental dynamism	95	79	57	56	24	48
4. Environmental complexity	93	71	69	52	50	46
Metavariable: content						
5. Technological progress	93	79	59	8	30	1
6. Product-market breadth	48	71	74	32	56	21
7. Product innovation	97	82	53	5	37	1
8. Quality	86	92	64	1	75	1
9. Price level	64	74	62	19	31	1
10. Active marketing	93	85	62	10	44	1
12. Resources level	92	85	76	18	32	1
13. Investment in production	82	92	74	8	24	2
14. Number of technologies	23	63	87	21	43	13
Metavariable: strategy making						
16. Internal analysis level	44	82	92	47	54	56
17. External analysis & forecast	73	85	92	21	51	9
18. Level of Risk	95	79	56	29	43	18
19. Proactive management style	98	85	64	9	27	1
Metavariable: structure						
20. Size of strategy-making team	1	40	66	29	36	65
21. Degree of mechanism	23	43	58	94	78	35
Metavariable: performance						
23. Profitability	81	78	61	25	45	2
24. Market share	79	86	58	23	49	2
25. Rate of growth	98	83	56	11	24	3
26. Operational efficiency	57	76	86	38	57	1
Metavariable: characteristics						
27. Size	15	48	73	44	62	36
28. Age	9	48	53	73	78	88

Strategies:

48 = Explosion 49 = Expansion 50 = Continuous growth
51 = Slip 52 = Consolidation 53 = Contraction

purchasing a foreign license, or acting in other ways that require good planning and involve considerable risk.

Continuous growth

A continuous growth firm seeks to maintain its competitive position through growth. This strategy requires making additional investments in a growing market, avoiding the creation of substantial overcapacity, and applying accurate judgment and timing.

Slip

A slip firm follows a "no-growth in a growing market" strategy. Although the market is growing, the firm deliberately gives up part of its existing market share. It does not expand capacity, or engage in promotional activities, or make further investment. However, price campaigns may be launched and continued as long as they are profitable. The art in the slip strategy lies in stretching out activities for as long as possible with as little investment as possible.

Consolidation

In a saturated or diminishing market, a consolidation firm may use a "no-growth in a stabilized market" strategy. The firm does respond to growth in population or prosperity. Consolidation requires dexterity, adaptability over the short term, and artistry in continually appearing in the market with cost-saving initiatives achieved with limited resources. The risk in the consolidation strategy is that the right changes may be discerned too late.

Contraction

A contraction firm experiences negative growth. Activity is considerably reduced or ended by closure or sale.

USES AND MISUSES OF THE PRODUCT-MARKET STRATEGIES APPROACH

The Product-market Strategies approach is essentially future oriented. The dynamic nature of the current strategy is identified and is used to indicate the future strategic position if the current strategy is maintained. The current life-cycle stage should be identified independently of the six product-market routes. The business unit's relative competitive potential is embedded in its strategic profile. Together they define future strategic position. Even without considering an intentional strategic change, a business unit has to be aware of its product-market strategy. All SBUs move along the product-market life-cycle. Their strategic positions are altered over time whether they want them changed or not. Market expansion or contraction affects the business unit's position. As the Red Queen explained to Alice in Wonderland: If you stand still you are retreating, if you progress you stay at the same place, and to advance you have to run.

An important limitation of the Product-market Strategies approach is the implicit assumption that the product-market life-cycle is external and independent of the firm's actions. That is, the life-cycle is immutable and cannot be affected by what the business unit does. This assumption is sometimes correct for highly unconcentrated markets with many competitors. In practice, businesses are known to affect the speed of the life-cycle (and even their progress from one stage to another) by aggressive marketing projects and by introducing (or withholding) technological innovations.

Any business unit considering its future strategic position should use this approach. It is particularly useful for business units competing in product-markets in the early stages of their life-cycle and those with a relatively short expected saturation (i.e., maturity) stage. A business competing in a mature static product-market may find this approach less useful.

The approach is useful to any industry or business unit, independent of technology, size, or other characteristics. However, since the strategic route is dependent on the business unit's strategic intentions and the progress of the product-market life-cycle, not all strategies are possible for a given point of departure. For example, a consolidation strategy is not feasible in the early stages of the product-market life-cycle: introduction and growth. The industry will probably advance along its life-cycle, rendering consolidation impossible. The result may be slip or contraction. Similarly, expansion or continuous growth strategies are not feasible in the saturation stage of the industry's life-cycle. Here either explosion or consolidation is an appropriate strategy. Infeasible strategies are clearly failing strategies. If the strategy you match most closely is infeasible for your SBU because of your industry's life-cycle stage, then yours is a failure strategy.

This approach is concerned with survival rather than level of performance. Except for mismatch between product-market route strategy and industry life-cycle stage, the approach does not differentiate between success and failure strategies. Each of the strategies, even contraction, may be successful. In such a case, the business unit would take the strategic resources it divests from its current product-market and invest them in another, more promising, product-market.

When the business unit's product-market is composed of two or three distinguishable product-market combinations, each should be analyzed as a separate business unit. Organizations with many product-market combinations are not business units and cannot be analyzed using this approach; such organizations should use portfolio models.

11

Other Approaches

For the last ten years, each semester a few teams of students preferred to investigate new approaches, rather than using the "classic" ones. In developing our approach, we used only universal approaches that apply to all or most industries. Because of scope, and their limited general relevance, specific approaches, for example, for mature capital goods industries (Hambrick, 1983) or the banking industry (Jemison, 1987), were not included in this book.

Skeptical (and good) students usually find a new approach, published in one of the scientific journals, which may cater better to "their" business unit. Like some of them, on reviewing the 53 strategies included in this book, you may feel that they do not represent your situation exactly. For example, you may feel that the approaches here do not reflect your industry, the cultures or political systems in your organization or in the countries in which you operate. Or, you just reread Porter's book and you have some reservations about the way we operationalized his strategies. This chapter is dedicated to all these cases: other approaches not included in this book.

The opportunities are numerous. The strategic literature indulges us with new approaches. Some are refinements of previously suggested approaches, some are new approaches to categorize business unit's strategies. It is very tempting to "update" the approaches every time a new one captures our attention, mainly when the author is a well-known authority in the field, the methodology is rooted, and the database used in developing the approach is sound. On the other hand, good approaches are those which are studied, debated, used, and being taught in business schools. This chapter discusses what should you do to integrate our approach with other approaches not included in this book.

APPROACH 10: YOUR APPROACH

In developing your approach you can use all or a subset of the 28 strategic variables we used here. If you decide that a specific strategic variable is irrelevant in your case, or if you do not have enough information to evaluate it, omit it from the approach. We believe the 28 variables are comprehensive. Should you find an approach in which other variables are required, you can always add them when using your approach (but not when using the original approaches). We never used more than ten strategies, but if required by the approach, you may define as many as needed.

Your approach can be a revision of one of the approaches included in this book, an approach based on a scientific journal article (or book), or a unique approach which applies to the industry in which you compete. The specific industry structure, the technology being used, the nature of the raw materials, the historical development of the industry, and unique regulation and public interests are a few of the factors that may create special types of strategic success and failure in your industry. On the basis of your accumulated experience in the industry, you may formulate successful and less-successful strategic profiles.

CREATING YOUR APPROACH

You can create your own approach in three ways:

1. By modifying the strategies in an existing approach.
2. By choosing an entirely new set of strategies: new approach.
3. By using the strategies of representative competitors in your industry.

Modifying an existing approach

You may believe that the expert data included in this book, which define each of the strategies are either inadequate for your industry or unrepresentative of it. You can create new strategic profiles, or change the value of some strategic variables if you wish. These changes might include:

- Adding or deleting one or more variables.
- Adding or deleting one or more strategies.
- Changing individual values within strategies.

Creating a new set of strategies

If you wish to operationalize a new approach or believe that your industry is governed by a unique approach that differs considerably from the nine provided in this book, you can define your own approach in terms of a completely new set of strategies. To do so, you:

1. Decide which variables are included in your approach (you can choose any subset of the 28 variables defined here, or add variables, if required).
2. Decide how many strategies are included in your approach and assign them names.
3. Assign values to the variables in each strategy.

This procedure can be time consuming, particularly if you define ten or more strategies.

Using representative competitors

Another systematic way of creating your approach is to evaluate the strategic profiles of the main competitors in the industry and use these strategic profiles as the approach. This can easily be done by the methods described in Chapter 7 for competitor analysis. That is, having evaluated the strategic profiles of each competitor, you display a Competitive Map on your computer screen. You may decide that you want to include all of your competitors, or you may feel that your industry can be adequately represented by only a few of them. Having selected which ones you want to use as the basis for your approach, you assign the values of the strategic profiles into your approach.

MAXIMUM NUMBER OF STRATEGIES

The maximum number of strategies we encountered, for one approach, was ten strategies. Even with ten strategies, strategic profiles tend to come close to each other, and on the Approach Map the strategies group together. We doubt you may encounter a new approach with more than ten strategies. However, you may face this situation when creating a unique industry approach (we did).

If you have more than ten competitors, you can follow two approaches: (1) select specific competitors (typically the most important ones in the industry or the ones with whom you compete most closely), or (2) use the Competitive Map (Chapter 7) to help you decide whether there are as many different strategies as competitors or whether, and this should typically be the case, there are several competitors who share the same basic strategy with minor differences. To reduce the number of strategies, you might pick one of a cluster as representative or you might average the values of the variables of the strategies in the cluster. Because the clusters and the general structure of the Competitive Map depend very much on the strategies included, you should try a number of combinations before deciding on the strategies to include in your approach.

You can follow a similar procedure, using the Approach Map, if you have already defined ten strategies in your approach and want to add a new one. Examine the Approach Map for your approach. See whether any strategies cluster. If they do, pick one to delete and add the new strategy.

A word of caution: when creating the tenth approach in this book, you can use it the same way you used other approaches; but keep in mind that you yourself assigned the strategic profiles, and a bias or preconception might have crept in. Use it with caution, and compare results with the results obtained using other approaches. Also, when creating an approach for a specific industry, you should use your approach only for business units in the industry for which you built it. If you are responsible for several business units in different industries, you should create a new approach for each industry.

12
Conclusions

SUMMARY OF OUR APPROACH

In this book, you have learned nine different approaches and the ways they can be used to analyze the strategy of your business unit. In chapter 1 we stated that after studying this book, you will be able to decompose a strategy systematically into identifiable components and subsequently reconstruct a recognizable comprehensive strategic profile. Once you have identified your strategic profile, you will be able to:

1. Evaluate it and analyze the opportunities and limitations in your business environment.
2. Investigate the feasibility of potential strategic changes.
3. Construct viable strategic alternatives.

To help you recapture what you have learned while reading this book, we will now highlight the major components of our approach, and summarize and describe the different ways the approaches can be used in analyzing your business unit.

Strategy

Strategy is created at the topmost level of the organization. This level, intentionally or not, sets the organization's goals and decides on its investments and the deployment of resources. Although many other forces have an impact on strategy, it is the mandate of top management to make strategy. In this book, we have divided strategy into:

- Corporate strategy (includes many business units).
- Business-level strategy (one business unit).
- Functional strategy (e.g., finance, information systems, or marketing).

Many organizations are single business units, and thus their highest level of strategy is business level. On the other hand, many large organizations are corporations, composed of multi-industry or multi-product-market units. For these firms, corporate strategy is the highest level of strategy. This book focuses on the business unit level, implying that it is appropriate for single-product firms, as well as for business units within corporations.

Success and failure of a business strategy

The success of a business unit's strategy is indicated by the unit's profitability. Although different measures of profitability exist, it is possible to divide business units into two nonoverlapping groups:

- Businesses whose performance is above the industry average.
- Businesses whose performance is below the industry average.

Strategies applied by the first group have proved successful, whereas those used by the second group are defined as failure strategies. The strategies described in this book use this definition of success.

To achieve a successful strategy, it is important to realize that strategies do not happen, they are made. Top management plays an essential role in the making of business strategies. Although constraints exist, it is the strategy-making team that selects the business unit strategy and implements it.

A comprehensive integrative approach to business strategy

Our approach is based on an internally consistent framework of strategic variables. A business unit is a complex system that is composed of subsystems and conducts multiple transactions with its environment. A business unit's strategy is the composite pattern in which the unit conducts its multifunctional activities. Its success, therefore, does not depend on just one strategic variable, but rather on the internal consistency of a group of variables which together form the business unit's strategy. In other words, we adopted the holistic approach, viewing strategy as a framework of a number of variables joined together in a particular configuration to achieve higher performance.

The approaches are classifications of clusters of organizations that share a common strategy. The common strategy is identified and defined, based on an extensive list of strategic characteristics. In other words, it is possible to subdivide a population of organizations into groups, each pursuing a similar generic strategy. In this book, nine such approaches are described.

The strategic business unit profile

A strategy is identified by a particular business unit according to four levels:

- Strategy
- Metavariable
- Variable
- Indicator

The highest level in the hierarchy is a concise verbal description of the strategy. This description captures the essence of the unit's business approach at a specific point of time; we present 53 such business unit strategies.

The second level describes the different metavariables. We use the following metavariables: (1) the business unit's environment, (2) the content of the strategy, (3) the strategy-making process, (4) the business unit's organizational structure, (5) performance, and (6) the basic characteristics of the business unit.

The six metavariables are described in terms of 28 strategic variables. Table 2.1 in Chapter 2 lists the 28 variables in our approach and gives a short definition of each. Indicators are discussed later in this chapter.

The concept of integrative approach

Our total integrative approach is built around approaches. The term approach is used to describe classifications of strategies. If we start with the universe of all firms, we can subdivide the universe into categories that contain clusters of firms following similar strategies. Thus, each approach tries to categorize strategic business units in terms of typical strategies that the business units follow. Each approach has a different set of strategies associated with it. Furthermore, each approach defines these strategies in terms of a subset of the 28 variables. The nine approaches chosen for this book are listed in Table 2.2 in Chapter 2. These approaches were chosen from the existing professional literature, based on criteria described throughout the book. In addition we have included space for a tenth approach, termed your approach, discussed in Chapter 11. The approaches reinforce one another by emphasizing different aspects of a business unit's strategy. Each uses a different subset of variables, taken from the group of 28 variables.

The subsections that follow summarize the approaches and their uses and misuses. Discussions of the variables used in our approach were presented in earlier chapters.

Approach 1: deliberate vs. emergent strategies

The Deliberate vs. Emergent Strategies approach (Chapter 3) focuses on the strategy development process and distinguishes between "deliberate" and "emergent" strategies. Eight strategies, lying on a continuum that ranges from completely planned strategies (called deliberate) to strategies created with no prior specific intent (called emergent), are described. Each strategy in this approach represents a unique pattern of decision making used in organizations.

This approach should be used to study the relation between the business unit and its environment, so as to assess environmental turbulence and the organization's ability to control and forecast environmental conditions. The approach should be used before an in-depth analysis of the business unit is made, as it immediately places the business unit's strategy on the deliberate—emergent continuum and thus supplies you with a starting point from which the content of the strategy can be analyzed. It is important to realize that you may fall between two adjacent benchmark strategies, indicating a hybrid strategy. The approach is universal and as such can be used to analyze different types of organizations, including nonprofit organizations.

Approach 2: seven survival strategies

The Seven Survival Strategies approach (Chapter 4) describes the optimal behavior of a strategic business unit for a spectrum of strategic postures. The strategies are based on the firm's superiority and flexibility in adapting to its environment. The strategies range from a superior position in a market with weak competition and high purchasing power to liquidation when it is the only viable option left. The different strategies described follow the product life-cycle and, as such, are dependent on it.

This approach focuses only on survival and is not concerned with maximum performance once survival is ensured. Although managers may view some of the strategies described as failure strategies (capitulation, cooperation, and liquidation), they are not presented as such. Still, the use of this approach places the business unit, albeit crudely, on a success—failure scale. Other approaches introduced later in the book refine this initial placement. Thus, this approach is recommended for the initial stages of business unit analysis. This approach is appropriate only for business units focusing on one product-market.

Approach 3: ten archetypes

The Ten Archetypes approach (Chapter 5) is the largest approach discussed in this book. The approach presents a group of ten strategic archetypes with different environmental, organizational, and strategy-making characteristics. Six of the strategies represent organizational success, and four represent organizational failure. This approach is based on the analysis of case studies, and as a result the different strategies are appropriate for a corporation as well as a single business unit. Therefore, this approach should be used with caution because in this book we focus on business units only. The Ten Archetypes approach also gives you the opportunity to analyze organizations that are neither pure business units nor corporations, but rather lie somewhere in between. In this approach, success is defined as achieving organizational goals. Although achieving corporate goals is more general than financial success, it is also less precise.

The approach is especially appropriate for business units that face major changes in the environment, as well as for business units that have experienced difficulties. This approach recognizes that different types of failure exist, that different remedies exist, and that there are alternative ways of improving the strategy to solve specific problems.

Approach 4: strategy-making modes

The Strategy-making Modes approach (Chapter 6) emphasizes decision making and describes three distinct modes. Each mode represents a different linkage among the important decisions on which a strategy is built. Whether or not you can be successful as a business by adopting one of these modes, or a combination of them, depends on the characteristics of the organization and the organizational environment. The approach thus created involves combinations of environment, organization, and strategy.

The approach should be used for analyzing the strategy process in business units. Strategy process is an inseparable part of strategy; without taking into account the way decisions are made, no strategy can be implemented. The inherent simplicity of this approach lies in its use of only three distinct Strategy-making Modes, which makes it easy for you to identify the major mode employed by your business unit. However, it is important to keep in mind that only a few organizations exhibit pure modes. Usually a combination of two, or even all three, modes is found.

The approach is important for organizations in transition or crisis; it is less useful for incremental strategic changes. Thus, when considering a strategic change, you should always use this approach in addition to others described in this book.

Approach 5: competing generic

The Competing Generic approach (Chapter 7), due to Porter, is probably the best known and most widely referred to in the business community. Developed as an instrument to analyze industries and competitors, it presents an additional way to analyze your business unit. Four internally consistent generic strategies for taking offensive or defensive actions to cope with competitive forces, and thereby yield a superior return on investment for the firm, are presented. Of these four strategies, two are industry-wide strategies and two are appropriate for business units situated in market niches. In addition, one failure strategy is described. The four success strategies are positioned along two strategic dimensions: strategic advantage and strategic target.

The approach assumes that each industry is an oligopoly, implying that both small and large business units are more profitable than medium-sized ones. It must be used with caution in relatively unconcentrated or monopolistic industries because this approach could lead to erroneous conclusions in these industries. It is highly recommended for analyses that focus primarily on the content of strategy and place less emphasis on the business unit's environment, its strategy-making process, or its organizational structure.

Approaches 6 and 7: empiric strategies—consumer and empiric strategies—industrial

Both the six Empiric Strategies—Consumer and the four Empiric Strategies—Industrial approaches discussed in Chapter 8 are based on an empirical analysis of the PIMS database. These approaches focus both on the current strategic posture of a business unit and on its strategic direction (i.e., the way business units change over time). For strategic posture and strategic direction, different components were identified and incorporated in our approach.

These two approaches are the only ones included in this book that make a distinction between business units focusing on consumer products and those focusing on industrial products. They are most appropriate for manufacturing businesses. However, they can be applied to any business unit for which it is possible to identify the market as consumer or industrial.

Although the approaches are strongly market oriented, they provide for an important addition to the other approaches, as they emphasize both strategic posture and direction and consider change over time. Use of these approaches points out the business unit's strategic actions that will affect its future strategic position. However, it is important to keep in mind that these approaches do not distinguish clearly between success and failure strategies. Therefore, they should be used in combination with other approaches. Because they are based on the PIMS database, these approaches focus on strategy content. Their use should be complemented by others emphasizing environment, strategy making, and structure.

Approach 8: adaptation approach

The Adaptation approach framework (Chapter 9) emphasizes the business unit's rational selection of and purposive decision in changing its products/markets to fit its environment. According to this approach, a successful business unit is one that:

1. Finds, defines, and maintains an existing market for its products and services:
2. Constantly changes and improves the organizational structure and management processes that enable adaptation of the market strategy:

In this approach, the organization is analyzed as an integral and dynamic whole, taking into account the interrelationships among the environment, the strategy, the process, and the structure. The environment is the departure point for this approach. Based on these assumptions, three successful strategies and one failure strategy are defined.

The emphasis of this approach lies with the innovation of the product-market. Therefore, it is effective in expressing how organizations design alternative methods with which to pursue strategies involving their product-market domains. Although the approach is concerned with the interrelationships between management and strategy, its focus is on the strategy, not on the process used to create and implement strategies. Therefore, this approach should be used together with at least one other that emphasizes strategy making. Because the approach assumes an industry composed of many business units, it is highly recommended for use in unconcentrated industries.

Approach 9: product-market strategies

This last approach, Product-market Strategies (Chapter 10), focuses on the business unit's market and its relative potential in the market. Based on the Boston Consulting Group (BCG) matrix, which describes the industry's current stage along the product life-cycle, it analyzes the behavior of a business unit over time. Four distinct stages along the life-cycle are identified:

1. Introduction
2. Growth
3. Saturation (or maturity)
4. Decline

Each market is at one of these stages. Depending on the industry, the third stage, saturation, may continue for a relatively long period. The life-cycle stage and the internal potential of the business unit together define its strategic situation. The internal potential, categorized as high, moderate, or low, is defined primarily by the business unit's market share. Together, the two dimensions, internal and external potential, form a grid on which the business unit is placed. The strategic question, however, does not concern the business unit's posture but rather its direction. This approach consists of the strategies for reaching the desired strategic position. Six possible routes are described to reach a desired position from the existing posture.

This approach is essentially future oriented and should be used as such. It is important to realize that every business unit goes through a product-market life-cycle, which influences its posture and direction. However, a salient assumption of this approach is that the product-market life-cycle is external and independent of the firm's actions. This assumption is often not true. Businesses are known to be able to affect the speed as well as other aspects of the life-cycle. If your business is considering its future strategic position, you should use this approach. However, you are advised, as you were previously, to use additional approaches that emphasize other aspects of the business unit's strategy.

WHAT YOU CAN DO WITH THIS APPROACH

Throughout the book you learned how to employ the different approaches presented. In addition, we have tried to show you that different types of analyses, highlighting the various aspects of your business unit strategy, can be executed using our approach. This section summarizes these different types of analyses.

Indicators

Although you can assign a value to each of the 28 variables directly based on your subjective judgment, you will often find it helpful to analyze a variable in terms of factors that influence it. Indicators provide you with a way of defining the components that make up a variable and aggregating the influences of these components on variable value. We suggest you use up to ten indicators to define each variable. In this book, we propose indicators that we believe are appropriate in defining the different variables. You are free to add or delete some or all of the indicators, according to your judgment about which are relevant to your own business unit. After choosing the indicators relevant to your business unit, you can assign values to them. Because indicators are not equally important, you can also assign weights to each indicator.

Weights

Sometimes you may feel that certain variables have more (or less) impact than others on your business strategy. If this is the case, you are free to assign different weights to the variables; you can, in fact, assign a different weight to each variable in the strategic profile. The choice would depend on your perception of the importance of these variables in your industry. Values less than 1 imply lower impact; values greater than 1 imply higher than average impact. Be aware that when you assign different weights to variables, you can make significant changes in the strategy being matched.

Norms

You can compare the strategy of a business unit against standard strategies within an approach. This comparison is multivariate in that it is based on the difference between the values of the variables for the business unit's strategy and the values of the variables for the standard strategy. The term norm is used to refer to the value of a variable in the standard strategy against which you are making your comparison.

You are able to use any of the following as the standard strategy:

1. The strategy in the approach that is closest to the business unit you are evaluating.
2. A specific strategy in the approach.
3. The strategy of a competitor.

Strategic variance analysis

Strategic variance analysis tells you the relative distance between your business unit's strategy and each of the strategies in an approach. To analyze a business unit's strategic profile, the differences (variances) between the values of the variables in the business unit's strategy and the standard strategy should be reviewed and understood. The difference between the value of each variable in the approach is compared with the value of the variable of your business unit. Because these comparisons are multidimensional, it is desirable to have a single number that aggregates the observed differences. In this book we suggest three such single number measures: average distance, RMS distance, and SMR distance. The average distance represents the average absolute difference observed. The other two measures weight outliers either more or less heavily than the average distance which weights all distances equally.

Approach map

The Approach Map allows you to create a two-dimensional graphical presentation of the distances among the strategies included in the approach, and between each of these strategies and the business unit you are evaluating. The Approach Map is based on a technique called multivariate scaling. For this purpose, you have to calculate the distances of the strategic profile of the business unit from all strategies composing the approach. It is important to keep in mind that the Approach Map is only an approximation made for supporting managerial decision making and should not be seen as an exact representation of distances.

Competitor analysis

The same approach may be used to analyze your competitors as well as your own business unit. These analyses enable you to examine the strategies being implemented by competing business units in your industry. Competitor analysis is an important aspect of deciding your own future strategy. For example, should you imitate a proven successful strategy or should you find a promising, yet unoccupied, strategic opportunity? Competitor analysis can be performed in two ways:

1. By making an in-depth analysis of a major competitor.
2. By creating an industry competition map.

Conceptually, the procedures for in-depth analysis of a competitor are very simple: evaluate and analyze the variable values for your competitor's business unit as you did with your own. You can estimate the competitor's variable values directly or, if you want to increase accuracy, employ indicators. The major difference is that you usually have less information available for your competitor than you have for your own business unit. Although you will have to make assumptions and perform evaluations, the analysis process may well enhance your understanding of your competitor, as well as point out to you how much you really know about the competing business unit.

To create an industry map, you should evaluate strategic profiles of up to ten of your competitors. As you probably do not have much detailed information about their strategies, we advise you not to use the indicators, but rather base your analysis on your subjective evaluation of the different variables. After creating the strategic profiles of your competitors, you may produce a strategic map of your industry, similar to the Approach Map described before. The graphic display will help you to understand the current structure of your industry, as well as to determine your future strategy.

Strategic turnaround

After identifying and analyzing your business unit's current strategy, checking its resources and capabilities for strategic change, and understanding its environment and its competitive position relative to its major competitors, it is time to consider strategy making. Strategy making involves the formulation of the business unit's preferred strategy, deciding on its future strategic profile, and selecting the means to achieve it. For some business units, this may imply the need for strategic turnaround. For others, it merely involves a redefinition of current strategy. This type of analysis is based on defining normative/optimal strategies for your business unit and examining the feasibility of these potential strategies. Strategic turnaround analysis is appropriate when your current strategy is a failure strategy or is not the one the business unit's strategy-making team wants to follow. Otherwise, strategy modification, as described in Chapter 4, is usually sufficient.

In strategic turnaround analysis, you choose one of the strategies presented in this book as defining the strategic profile you want for the unit. By calculating strategic distances, you can measure the gap between the strategic profile you want and your existing strategy. You then undertake a "what if" analysis by changing different strategic variables in the direction of your desired strategic profile. As you make changes in your strategic variables, you can see how much closer you would align your strategy to your desired strategy by repeating the strategic distance measurement.

Strategic team

Strategy making is one of the most important and central processes taking place in organizations. It usually involves making choices among alternatives and assessing different risks. As such, it involves many members of the organization. A strategy-making team may be involved in deciding on a strategy or in strategy-related tasks, generating and sharing information and reaching joint decisions. The team members can help assess the values of strategic variables. A consensus value can be obtained for each variable by averaging the assessments of the team members. If desired, different weights can be assigned to the inputs from different team members. The consensus values, then, represent the strategic profile for the business unit.

Future strategic positions

All SBUs move forward along their product-market's life-cycle. Therefore, even without implementing a deliberate strategic change, the strategic position of a business unit changes over time. Units in the early stages of their life-cycle or in life-cycles with short saturation stages are particularly advised to consider their future strategic position. To study your future strategic position, you are provided with the Product-market Strategies approach. By measuring the strategic distance between your current position and the product-market strategies, you can identify the dynamic nature of the current strategy and can indicate your future strategic position if you continue to follow your current strategy. This feature of our approach also facilitates analyzing the implications of strategic turnaround options for your unit's future strategic position.

WHAT YOU HAVE LEARNED

This volume is not a textbook on business strategy and policy. Yet, if you have read to this point, you now know a lot about the practicalities of business-level strategies. You have been introduced to the main concepts and variables, the important schools of thought, the theories and the findings, all mixed with a generous number of real-life examples. But the most important thing this approach teaches you is how to use this knowledge systematically.

Defining a business unit, you learned how to:

- Identify its past and current strategies.
- Analyze its potentials and limitations relative to its competitors in the industry.
- Formulate a preferred strategy for the business unit.
- Plan to implement the preferred strategy over time.

Our approach is rich in detail: six metavariables, 28 strategic variables, up to 280 indicators, nine different approaches, 53 strategies each with a unique strategic profile, and over 90 examples. Our approach is comprehensive and integrative, allowing you to deal with this richness in a systematic way. We taught you the importance of strategic fit, of a pattern to which the multitude of business variables must adhere. In short, it has introduced you to the systems approach to business-level strategy.

WHAT YOU CAN'T LEARN

This book is devoid of financial information. As Alice, before going down into Wonderland, doubted the value of books without dialog or pictures, a manager may doubt the value of a book on strategy without financial considerations in it. However, we found that financial data do not distinguish among the strategies, at least in the approaches we used. This is not to say that financial variables are not important in identifying and formulating a strategy. Rather, since their values are highly dependent on the specific industry, they are specific rather than universal and were therefore not included here.

Our variables are more subjective than financial ratios. Even when a variable is based on quantitative measures (for example, market share or age), its inclusion in here calls for subjective management evaluation. For some readers, it may seem a little vague and imprecise. Well, that's the way strategies are made. At the beginning of every elaborate and detailed ten-year plan, complete with pro forma yearly balance sheets and income statements, there is a subjective strategy for the next ten years. Since we focus on strategy making rather than on strategic planning, the result is a strategy, not detailed five-year pro forma financial statements.

This book relates to some important aspects of functional strategies but does not elaborate on each functional area and its strategy. This book is intended for managers involved in business-unit-level strategy making. It takes the chief executive officer's point of view. Many such managers also assume the responsibility for making strategies in specific functional areas such as finance, marketing, production, research and development, manpower, or information systems. They will find our approach insufficient for their needs in the functional area, and are advised to complement it with books that focus on the strategy of the specific functional areas such as marketing (Day, 1986), finance (Higgins, 1988), information systems (Cash et al, 1988), and operations (Wheelright, 1979).

In this book we relate indirectly to some important aspects of corporate-level strategy. Some of the strategies included in here (e.g., the entrepreneurial conglomerate in the Ten Strategic Archetypes approach or diversification in the Seven Survival Strategies approach) are useful in analyzing corporate-level strategy and provide insights for business-unit-level analysis. These strategies are included in the original approaches and are therefore included here for completeness and because they capture the original author's view of the world.

This book does not deal with corporate-level strategy if the corporation is involved in multiple businesses. How should you perform analysis if you are dealing with many business units in different industries? What are, what might be, what should be, the relationships among these units? These important topics are outside the scope of the current book. If you are interested in corporate strategy, you should investigate the portfolio approach to corporate level strategy (Weiss and Tallett, 1986; Robinson, Hichens, and Wade, 1978; Walker, 1984). Corporate portfolio approaches were developed in the 1970s and 1980s by large corporations (such as General Electric and Shell Oil) and their consultants (such as the Boston Consulting Group). These approaches differ because each starts from a particular point of view about corporate-level strategy. The next stage, therefore, is to synthesize these different approaches (Segev, 1995a,b). That, of course, is the subject of my books *Corporate Strategy: Portfolio Models* (Segev, 1995a), and *Navigating by COMPASS* (Segev, 1995b).

WHAT YOU CAN ADD FOR A BETTER APPROACH

After reviewing the nine approaches and the 53 strategies included in this book, you may feel that they do not represent your situation exactly. Your approach can be used to personalize evaluations in terms of the nine approaches described in this book. The tables in Chapters 3 through 10 show the values that were derived from this process. You (or your staff) may want to review the original papers that describe the approaches. If you agree with our methods and our data, fine. If you perceive the world differently and would like to change some or all of the numbers in our database, you are welcome to do so. The "your approach", discussed in Chapter 11, shows you how to make these changes as you see fit.

"Your approach" can also be used to create an approach based on a published material, or an original approach, one specifically adapted to your industry. Again, you may use our methodology or you may evaluate the main competitors in your industry. You can use their strategic profiles as the strategies that make up the approach. An easy way to do so is to use the method described in Chapter 11. You create a Competitor Map and select representative competitor strategies, choosing those that differ most from one another.

When you add the tenth approach, you may do it by:

1. Modifying the strategies in an existing approach.
2. Creating an entirely new set of strategies: new approach.
3. Using the strategies of representative competitors in your industry.

CONCLUSION: APPLYING THE APPROACHES TO YOUR BUSINESS UNIT

The nine approaches presented here offer a rich set of alternatives. They allow you to view your business through different eyes. They are tools that help you in long-range planning for your business unit. Each approach has a different view of the world because it is based on different assumptions and emphasizes different aspects of strategy.

Having understood the various approaches, the natural question is how to apply them to your own business unit. Your first step is to sharpen your mental model of your business and your own approach to the world. You may want to begin with focus. Are you worried about survival? performance? the way you make strategy? Next you may want to consider which functions are critical to your firm. Is your firm production oriented? marketing oriented? people oriented? planning oriented? With which theoretical approaches are you comfortable and with which uncomfortable? Which combination of metavariables is important to your industry and your firm? Are you driven by your environment? Are you concerned about strategy content? process? organizational structure? Are you judged on the basis of specific performance variables?

Once you have your mental model, you are ready to compare it with the models implicit in the nine approaches. Remember, the creators of these approaches considered generic situations. They did not tailor them specifically to your firm or industry. Thus, you cannot expect that one of their approaches will match your situation exactly. More likely, you will find that several of the approaches come close to emphasizing some of your concerns. If this is the case, we recommend that you evaluate your business unit in terms of these approaches.

Each approach will provide you with different insights about your business and each will lead you to new ideas about your competitive strategy. You should however, synthesize these ideas and insights into a unique strategy for your firm. Be innovative and creative. Don't follow the generic strategies slavishly. Fit them to your firm and your situation. Having done so, you are ready to explore the changes you need to make in your business to achieve your new strategy.

Is it possible to create a meta-approach, a synthesis of all the approaches presented here (and others)? This is much beyond the goals and scope of this book. However, for those of you who would like to pursue further this possibility, and for those who would use this approach on many business different business units and would observe some repeating patterns, Appendix 12.1, at the end of this chapter, presents such a synthesis.

APPENDIX 12.1

STRATEGIC ARCHETYPES AT THE BUSINESS LEVEL: A SYNTHESIS OF EIGHT TYPOLOGIES[1]

Tamar Almor-Ellemers and Eli Segev

Theoretical framework

This appendix presents a collection of eight different typologies that have been published over the last 15 years and encompass the different aspects of organizational gestalts, including strategy content and process, posture and direction. The following typologies were included: Galbraith and Schendel (1983), Miles et al (1978), Miller and Friesen (1978), Mintzberg (1973b), Mintzberg and Waters (1985), Porter (1980), Vesper (1979), Wissema et al (1980). These specific typologies were chosen according to the following criteria.

Our first criterion was nonspecifity. Therefore, taxonomies and typologies which dealt with certain industrial segments only (e.g., Jemison, 1987; Lenz, 1980) or certain stages of the product life-cycle (e.g., Hambrick, 1983b; Hambrick and Schecter, 1983; Harrigan, 1980; Harrigan and Porter, 1983; Zeithaml and Fry, 1984) were not included.

As one of the major topics of discussion in the literature is concerned with process vs. content (Bourgeois, 1980; Burgelman, 1983b; Camillus, 1981; Jemison, 1987; Venkatraman and Camillus, 1984), we were interested to include typologies that relate to either of these two dimensions. Two typologies which concentrate on analyzing the process of strategy making are those of Mintzberg (1973b) and Mintzberg and Waters (1985). As each stresses different facets of the process of strategy making, it was decided to include both. The process of strategy making, how strategies are formed and interrelated, can, according to Mintzberg (1973b) be divided into three generic decision-making modes. Mintzberg and Waters (1985), developing this concept further, proposed that the underlying dimension of the process of strategy making is the degree of intention/emergence of the planned and realized strategies.

Strategy content refers to the output of the strategy-making process, i.e., the realized strategy (Mintzberg and Waters, 1985). Emphasis on the content of strategy can be found in Porter's (1980)

[1]Almor-Ellemers, T. and E. Segev, 1988. "Strategic archetypes at the business level: a synthesis of eight typologies," Working Paper 979/88, The Israel Institute of Business Research, Faculty of Management, Tel Aviv University.

study, which has a non-empirical basis, in the work by Galbraith and Schendel (1983), which developed a framework based on the analysis of PIMS data, and in Miles et al (1978), which proposes a typology based on a theoretical framework and is supported by an in-depth analysis of case studies. Miller and Friesen's (1978) research, which employed the largest set of variables of all eight typologies, is viewed here as a study combining elements of content and process, while emphasizing the latter.

In addition two typologies were included which employ the product life-cycle approach (Vesper, 1979; Wissema et al, 1980), the first emphasizing strategic posture, the second strategic direction. Strategic posture refers to the environment in which the business unit is situated at present and the strategy employed by the SBU to cope with this environment, while strategic direction refers to the options open to the SBU to shift to a desired position. Using the eight different typologies also gave us the opportunity to employ studies based on empirical, or empirically derived, variables (Galbraith and Schendel, 1983; Miller and Friesen, 1978), as well as research based on case studies (Miles et al, 1978; Mintzberg, 1973b; Mintzberg and Waters, 1985; Vesper, 1979) and otherwise developed frameworks (Porter, 1980; Wissema et al, 1980). Table A12.1 presents the various aspects emphasized by the typologies discussed.

Several of the typologies are based upon assessment of the attractiveness of the industry, or competitive environment, the relative competitive position of the business and the resulting content of its strategies.

One of the best-known conceptual frameworks of strategy content, which takes into account the competitive environment, is that developed by Porter (1980). Porter suggested three generic strategies which may lead a business to a success ("cost leadership", "differentiation" and "focus") as well as a failure strategy ("stuck-in-the-middle"). According to Porter, the employment of any one of the three abovementioned success strategies will result in a competitive advantage to the firm and above-average returns. As pointed out by Miller (1986), Porter's work received the attention that it did because he focused on variables that are relevant to industrial economists, have been shown to influence performance, and can often be manipulated by management.

Galbraith and Schendel's (1983) study is similar to Porter's in that they concentrated upon variables controllable by management which influence strategy posture, strategy change and performance of the

Table A12.1 Aspects Emphasized by the Various Approaches.

	Porter	Galbraith & Schendel	Wissema et al	Vesper	Miles & Snow	Miller & Friesen	Mintzberg	Mintzberg & Waters
Analytical basis for development of archetypes	Theoretical	Empirical PIMS/ SPIYR	Theoretical	Theoretical/ case studies	Theoretical/ case studies	Empirical/ case studies	Theoretical/ case studies	Case studies
Theoretical approach	Competitive environment	Portfolio models	Portfolio models	Portfolio models	Contingency theory	Decision making	Decision making	Decision making
Focus	Optimization of performance	Performance	Optimization of performance	Survival	Performance	Performance	Strategy making	Strategy making
Number and type of strategies	3 success strategies 1 failure strategy	6 consumer goods strategies, 4 industrial product strategies	6 strategies	7 strategies	3 success strategies 1 failure strategy	6 success strategies 4 failure strategies	3 strategies	8 strategies
Content:								
a: Posture	—	X	X	X	X	X	X	X
b: Direction	X	X	X	—	—	X	—	—
Process:								
a: Formulation	—	—	—	—	—	X	X	X
b: Implementation	X	—	X	—	X	X	X	X

firm. However, in contrast to Porter's (1980) conceptual typology, their taxonomy is based on an empirical analysis of the PIMS/SPIYR database for consumer goods and industrial products. For consumer goods Galbraith and Schendel reported a taxonomy of six strategies (harvest, builder, cashout, niche, climber, and continuity), while for industrial products they named four strategy types: low commitment, growth, maintenance, and niche.

Other typologies which have emphasized the competitive environment are those derived from the Boston Consulting Group portfolio models. Wissema et al (1980) developed a set of strategic-management archetypes on the basis of the product life-cycle approach and the competitive position of the firm, employing variables such as market share, reputation, exclusivity of know-how, product quality, etc. Together the variables create an existing product-market combination and a desired state; the archetypes proposed are the possible route firms can take to achieve the desired state.

Vesper (1979) employed similar variables based on product-market evolution and competition. However, the emphasis of his typology is on survival strategies for business firms and optimal behavior within a strategic posture. This typology differs from that of Wissema et al (1980) in that, while Wissema et al proposed ways to reach a desired state, Vesper emphasized optimal survival within a strategic posture.

Other researchers have approached the development of typologies in a different way and have emphasized the strategy—structure relationship. Miles et al (1978) suggested four strategic types ("defender", "analyzer", "prospector", and "reactor"), each employing its own unique market-based strategy to adapt to the environment, resulting in a particular configuration of technology, structure and process.

The typologies discussed so far have in common that they view strategy making in light of content rather than process. Strategies are thus seen as the intentional or unintentional content or product (Mintzberg, 1978) of strategy making. The first to emphasize the process whereby strategies emerge was Mintzberg (1973b), who identified three modes: the entrepreneurial, the adaptive, and planning modes. These modes, according to Mintzberg, represent, either in pure or combined form, a description of the strategy-making processes, taking into account environment and organizational characteristics.

Strategy as "a pattern in a stream of decisions" (Mintzberg, 1978; Mintzberg and Waters, 1982, 1984) has since been studied extensively in a broad range of organizations. On the basis of these studies, Mintzberg and Waters (1985) identified eight types of strategy-formation processes lying on a continuum which ranges from pure deliberate (i.e., strategies which originate in formal, well-defined plans and can be implemented as such) to pure emergent strategies (i.e., strategies which originate in the environment).

A typology which incorporated aspects of process as well as content is that developed by Miller and Friesen (1978). Miller and Friesen employed variables which were extracted from 81 existing case studies, measuring strategy content and process, organization and environment. Ten archetypes, six successful and four failing types, are described.

Other researchers have studied the relationship among the previous mentioned metavariables as well (e.g., Anderson and Zeithaml, 1984; Lenz, 1980; Miller, 1987; Thietart and Vivas, 1984; Zeithaml and Fry, 1984). However, these studies did not propose a set of strategic archetypes, nor did they suggest a rational framework for the relationships reported. In addition a number of attempts have been made to validate existing theoretical typologies through empirical testing (e.g., Anderson and Zeithaml, 1984; Dess and Davis, 1984; Hambrick, 1983b). Although these studies are interesting and useful, they do not offer additional strategy archetypes and are therefore not included in this study.

Eight typologies : a synthesis

At the beginning of this appendix, it was stated that the objective was to develop an encompassing, holistic framework which integrates the eight previously described typologies presented in Table A12.1. White and Hamermesh (1981) proposed an integrative model of performance, incorporating business position, environment, structure and strategy. The advantage of their framework lies in the fact that it incorporates in a single scheme concepts from different areas of research, enabling a comprehensive analysis of variables

Table A12.2 A Framework of Strategic Archetypes.

SBU life-cycle phase	Startup		Rat race						
Archetype	Innovative niche	Crib death	Explosion			Development			
			Market share expansion	Conglomerate building	Running blind	Posture improvement	Consolidation	Posture decline	Swimming upstream
Sources	— Niche ind. (G&S) — Niche con. (G&S) — Innovators (M&F)	—	— Builder G&S — Multi-plication (V) — Explosion (W) — Prospec-tors (M et al)	— Entrepre-neurial conglo-merate (M&F)	— The impulsive firm (M&F)	— Expansion (W) — Contin-uous growth (W) — Climber (G&S) — SB (M&F)	— Monopo-lizing (W) — Growth (G&S) — Analyzers (M et al)	— Slip (W)	— Swimming upstream — The aftermath (M&F)
Environment	Uncertain dynamic	Uncertain dynamic, hostile	Dynamic friendly	Uncertain, complex	Hostile complex	Dynamic, complex	Dynamic complex	Dynamic, hostile, complex	Dynamic, hostile, complex
Structure	Entrepre-neurial	Entrepre-neurial	Entrepre-neurial organic	Entrepre-neurial, flexible, centralized	Differentiated, centralized, lack of controls	Functional, organic	Functional, mechanistic	Functional, mechanistic	Functional low integration
Content	Focus-differ-entiation (P)	No strategy	Invest in R&D, promotion; average/low price	Invest in financial projects	High-risk investments	Invest in R&D, promotion; innovation, differenti-ation (P)	Economy of scale, efficiency + some product innovations	Divest	Modifying past strategies of low success, risk-taking
Process	Entrepre-neurial mode (M)	Imposed (M&W)	Entrepreneurial (M&W); enrepreneurial/planned (M)		Intuition of leader	Umbrella (M&W) planning (M)	Planned (M&W)	Imposed (M&W)	Reactive, adaptive (M) centralized
Performance	Successful	Failure	Successful	Successful	Failure	Successful	Successful	Failure	Failure

SBU life-cycle phase	Settling down					Retrenchment	
		Continuity		Survival		Harvest	Contraction
Archetype	Conservative niche	Maintenance	Stagnation	Staying alive	Drifting		
Sources	— Defenders (M et al) — Specialization (V) — SIA (M&F)	— Continuity (G&S) — Maintenance (G&S) — Dominant firm (M&F)	— Stagnant bureaucracy (M&F) — Reactor (M et al) — Stuck-in-the-middle (P)	— Diversification — Cooperation (V) — The giant under fire (M&F) — Consolidation (W)	— Headless giant (M&F)	— Harvest (G&S) — Cashout (G&S) — Low commitment (G&S)	— Capitulation (V) — Liquidation (V) — Contraction (W)
Environment	Certain, stable	Certain, stable, friendly	Dynamic, hostile	Dynamic, hostile complex	Dynamic, hostile, complex	Dynamic, complex	Hostile
Structure	Functional, mechanistic	Large, functional, centralized	Large, bureaucratic, rigid, very centralized	Large, decentralized	Large, decentralized, no leadership	Functional	Functional, simple
Content	Cost-focus (P)	Overall cost leadership (P)	According to tradition, past strategies	Cost efficiency, incremental change	No strategy	Profit maximization without additional investment	Acitivity is reduced/ended
Process	Planned (M&W); planned/adaptive (M)	Planning (M&W); planning mode (M)	Imposed (M&W)	Umbrella mode (M&W)	Imposed (M&W)	Process (M&W)	Imposed (M&W)
Performance	Successful	Successful	Failure	Successful	Failure	Successful	Failure

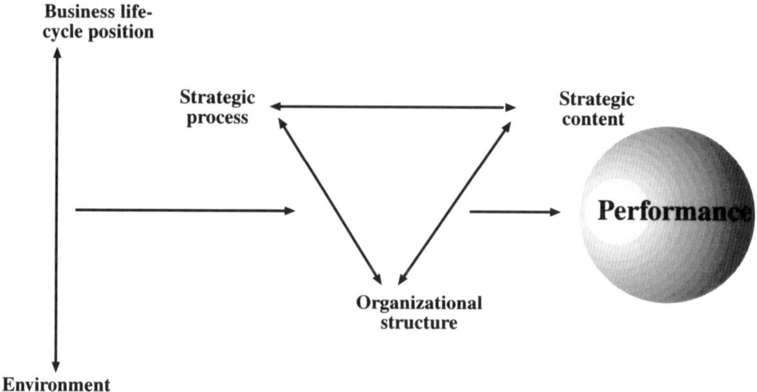

Figure A12.1 Classification scheme.

affecting strategy and performance. On the basis of their framework, the scheme presented in Figure A12.1 is proposed. The scheme presented in Figure A12.1 is based on the assumption that performance is the result of the interaction of variables external to and inherent in the business unit. The environment of the business unit, as well as the business position within the environment, affect the process of strategy making, the strategy content and the organizational structure, while these three aspects are interrelated as well; the result of these interactions is the business unit performance. We propose that a finite number of combinations of the variables exist at the business level, which are presented in Table A12.2, and which we will subsequently call archetypes. Following, we will briefly discuss the definitions of the metavariables contained in the scheme which is presented in Figure A12.1.

Business life-cycle position

Organizations develop and grow as a result of the need to survive. Business position is largely dependent upon the life-cycle stage of the organization.

Most typologies inherently relate to some extent to the different stages of the organization's life-cycle, as described in a number of studies (Adizes, 1979; Greiner, 1972; Miller and Friesen, 1984;

Quinn and Cameron, 1983). Although none of the typologies employed in this analysis refers explicitly to the organizational life-cycle stages, it seems that the various strategic archetypes are especially appropriate to specific stages in the organizational life-cycle. As a result a framework was developed, encompassing the strategic gestalts described by the typologies included in this paper, which uses organizational life-cycle stages to distinguish among groups of strategic archetypes.

In the present study, we are interested in integrating typologies which are appropriate for the strategic business unit (SBU). While few typologies explicitly address the strategic business level, they do for the most part refer either to single SBU organizations or SBUs of a conglomerate. However, the three typologies emphasizing strategy process (Miller and Friesen, 1978; Mintzberg, 1973b; Mintzberg and Waters, 1985) do not distinguish between the corporate and the SBU level. We argue that strategy processes take place at both levels and have therefore included them, even though they do not pertain specifically to the SBU level.

SBU development, in contrast to corporate development as described by Miller and Friesen (1984), is very closely linked to the industry life-cycle. The reason for this is that the SBU is usually built around a number of specific products or a specific product line, which is homogeneous and situated in one industry. As a result, the development stage of the industry greatly influences the SBU development stage; for instance, an entrepreneurial SBU will usually not start its development in a market which has reached maturity or saturation, and much less so in one that has reached decline. On the other hand, an SBU with a large, formalized structure will not easily compete in a market which is in its developmental stage and which requires flexibility and niche-searching behavior.

We propose an SBU life-cycle model which encompasses four phases: startup, rat race, settling down, and retrenchment. The startup phase is characterized by the birth of the SBU, the creation of a product, and close involvement of the entrepreneurs. The second phase, the rat race, emphasizes survival in a competitive market, a more formalized structure and the search for a fitting survival strategy. The settling down phase includes SBUs which are well established and seek to maintain their share. The last, retrenchment phase, is characterized by shrinkage, employee layoffs and divestments.

As pointed out in previous studies (Day, 1986; Miller and Friesen, 1984; Quinn and Cameron, 1983), life-cycle modes are viewed as evolutionary. However, this does not imply that all stages are necessarily followed by each SBU, nor does it imply that it is impossible for SBUs to return to a previous stage, as do industries which de-mature (Dowdy and Nikolchev, 1984).

Table A12.2 presents the proposed grouping of the different archetypes according to the four phases of the SBU life-cycle. Each phase encompasses a number of strategic archetypes which fit the specific phase.

Environment

The concept of environment has been discussed exhaustively since the sixties (e.g., Burns and Stalker, 1961; Duncan, 1972; Lawrence and Lorsch, 1967; Milliken, 1987; Shortell, 1977) and so far no consensus has been reached on how to define and operationalize environment. However, a number of environmental dimensions recur in many studies and have become accepted measures of environment. They include: uncertainty, dynamism, complexity, and hostility. Uncertainty pertains to the lack of information decision makers have concerning the environment, dynamism to the degree of stability of the environmental elements, complexity to the heterogeneity of these elements, and hostility to the prevalence of elements which are negative to the interests of the SBU. These four dimensions are used to typify the environments of the archetypes.

Structure

The organizational structure of a business unit is usually limited to the simpler forms typical of small organizations. The most prevalent structure is probably the functional one, which enables us to use the dimension developed by Burns and Stalker (1961): the degree to which the structure is organic/mechanistic.

Strategy content and process

These two concepts have already been discussed, and therefore it is sufficient simply to reiterate that process pertains to the decision-making process, while content pertains to the output of this process: the realized strategy.

Performance

Performance is defined as a dichotomy: the archetype is either successful or not.

Startup strategies

The startup phase includes two archetypes, a successful type named the innovative niche and a failure type named crib death.

The innovative niche

This archetype is characteristic of a newly established SBU. The SBU, being young and small, is trying to establish itself by pursuing a niche strategy. It has only a few products, which are still in the developmental, basic stage. The salient goal of the SBU is to differentiate its products from others in the industry, in order to create a niche for itself. The environment, although uncertain and dynamic, is not very hostile or complex, as the competition is not yet very strong. The organizational structure is an entrepreneurial one, small, simple and centralized.

The content of this archetype is based on Porter's (1980) focus strategy, which we have further classified as "focus-differentiation", emphasizing innovativeness, which recurs periodically, and high product quality. The strategic process has the features of Mintzberg's (1973b) entrepreneurial mode and is based on intuition, risk-taking and proactiveness of the entrepreneur. According to this description three strategic gestalts fit this category: Galbraith and Schendel's (1983) "industrial niche" and "consumer niche", and Miller and

Friesen's (1978) "innovators". These strategic gestalts have in common the pursuit of a niche strategy, emphasizing innovativeness and high product quality, while concentrating upon a limited number of products.

Crib death

This failure archetype is not described by any of the typologies included in this paper, even though, as pointed out by Quinn and Cameron (1983), 54% of all newly established firms fail within their first one and a half years. It seemed opportune, therefore, to add this archetype. This failure type is probably not included in the various typologies because the firms did not survive long enough to be included in the databases. The entrepreneurial SBU which fits the archetypes is newly established and tries to capture part of the market share with its line of products, which is still narrow and basic. However, in contrast to the innovative niche, this archetype is characterized by a failure to capture a niche within the market, and therefore has to compete in a very hostile environment already dominated by SBUs which have entered the market at an earlier stage. There is no consistent strategy and, as a result, the decision processes are characterized by features of Mintzberg and Waters' (1985) imposed mode, resulting in a reactive decision-making process and an inability of the entrepreneur to act in a proactive, innovative way.

Rat race strategies

This second category is well represented in most typologies. Apparently the strategies belonging to this category appeal to researchers and managers alike, as they represent the best opportunity to grow and capture a sizable part of the market.

We decided to divide the strategic gestalts proposed by the various typologies into two broad groups: the explosion strategies, representing fast growth, and the development strategies, representing the slower-growth strategic gestalts. Within the first (explosion) category a subdivision of two success types and one failure type can be found. The second (development) category is subdivided into two success and two failure types.

Explosion

The salient feature of the explosion strategies is their rapid expansion, which is indeed their foremost goal. SBUs which employ these strategic archetypes are young, but have developed a solid basis. This basis can sustain and finance their rapid growth. SBUs which have started out with successful niche strategies, for instance, might at a later stage in their organizational life opt for the rapid expansion. A prerequisite for such rapid expansion is an entrepreneur with strong central vision who can steer the SBU in the direction desired. Within this category we have distinguished two success strategies, one based on rapid market-share expansion, the other on rapid acquisition.

Market-share expansion

Rapid market-share expansion is possible if the environment is not too cluttered with competitors, but still dynamic enough to accommodate changes in market share. This situation exists mainly in the developmental product stages, when only a few competitors have entered the market (Hofer and Schendel, 1978). It furthermore requires an entrepreneur in personal control of the SBU, who is prepared to invest in rapid expansion. A flexible, centralized structure is therefore needed in order to accommodate rapid changes. In order to achieve and hold on to the market-share expansion, investments in R&D and product promotion are required, while average/low prices are frequently employed to gain market share. This implies either a strong corporate backing or a sound financial basis which can carry the requisite heavy financial investments. Strategic gestalts which fit this archetype are: "builder" (Galbraith and Schendel, 1983), "multiplication" (Vesper, 1979), "explosion" (Wissema et al, 1980) and "prospectors" (Miles et al, 1978).

Conglomerate building

This second successful explosion archetype is described by Miller and Friesen (1978) in their entrepreneurial conglomerate and is frequently found with firms which so far have been single SBU organizations and are interested in diversification. Though the subject of conglomerates is outside the scope of this appendix, since they come into existence through diversification strategies of the single business firm, the archetype describing the development of the SBU into a conglomerate is included in this appendix.

The emphasis in this archetype is on rapid expansion, too, though here it is achieved through acquisition rather than market-share expansion for a narrow line of products. Because of the acquisition strategy, the environment becomes more uncertain, complex and less friendly and stable. The structure of the firm in this instance is similar to the previously described category in that it is entrepreneurial and centralized but flexible. An entrepreneur who actively searches for new opportunities, and has the power to exploit them, is the central force of the firm. It is clear that, in order to use this strategic gestalt, the firm needs strong financial backing either from outside sources or from financial resources previously acquired.

Running blind

The third archetype in this group is an unsuccessful one, typified by a lack of alignment of the various facets, as described in Miller and Friesen's (1978) impulsive firm. Although this SBU is interested in rapid expansion, it does not have the requisite means. Though the environment is very hostile and complex, and the organizational structure lacks controls and is too big for a centralized management, the entrepreneur continues to invest in risky ventures.

Development

This category emphasizes market-share expansion, too, but the pace is slower, and the organizational structure has already been consolidated into a more formal one. A number of archetypes can be detected in this category as well.

Posture improvement

This successful archetype emphasizes growth, though at a slower pace than in the previously described expansion category. SBUs employing this strategy frequently have products which are in their growth or shake-out phase (Hofer and Schendel, 1978), implying that the environment is dynamic, complex, and somewhat hostile and competitive. The SBU has an organic structure capable of dealing with this type of environment. Growth is the result of investments in R&D, product promotion, and innovations. Decision-making processes are of an umbrella type, as described by Mintzberg and Waters (1985). Because the environment is complex and somewhat uncontrollable, general organizational actions are planned (Mintzberg, 1973), but organization members are free to decide upon actions, as long as they are concurrent with the planned direction. Strategic gestalts which were categorized into this archetype are: "expansion", "continuous growth" (Wissema et al, 1980), "the adaptive firm in a very challenging environment" (Miller and Friesen, 1978), and "climber" (Galbraith and Schendel, 1983).

Consolidation

The second successful archetype of this group emphasizes consolidation of position, implying that a certain amount of growth exists, which is linked to the overall market growth. The main difference between this archetype and the posture improvement described previously is that, instead of emphasizing additional market-share expansion, economies of scale and efficiency are considered to be most important. Although some product innovation takes place, the SBU is mainly interested in internal efficiency. The environment is similar to the environment of the posture improvement archetype; however, the structure is more mechanistic, and the strategy process is a planned type. Strategic gestalts classified as belonging to this archetype are those of "monopolizing" (Vesper, 1979), "growth" (Galbraith and Schendel, 1983), and "analyzers" (Miles et al, 1978).

Posture decline

This unsuccessful archetype is described by Wissema et al (1980) as a slip strategy. The products of the SBU still have growth potential, but the SBU's posture is not very strong, and it has been decided that resources would be better invested elsewhere. As a result, a conscious decision to divest has been taken. This implies that decision processes from this point onward are imposed (Mintzberg and Waters, 1985). Management plays it by ear in order to continue as long as possible without investing additional resources.

Swimming upstream

The second failing archetype in this category is described by Miller and Friesen (1978) as the "aftermath." As with the posture decline, the SBU's posture has not been very strong, but instead of deciding to divest, an attempt is made to modify past strategies which have never been really successful. Risks are taken, but in a reactive, adaptive way (Mintzberg, 1973b) by an inexperienced manager trying to turn the company around single-handedly.

Settling-down strategies

The third phase of the organizational life-cycle is named settling down. With this phase a number of archetypes are classified. They have in common that the organizational structure of the SBUs have expanded over time and have become more formal and less flexible, while production and marketing have become routinized, and product lines have become more complete. As for the previously described phases, both successful and failure types are included.

The conservative niche

This archetype is similar to the innovative niche of the birth phase insofar as both pursue a niche strategy. The SBU is able to employ this strategy because of the stable environment in which it is situated. The product market in which it operates is not very dynamic, and competitive forces have been stabilized which might be the result of reaching product-market maturity. Emphasis is on elements of Porter's (1980) "focus" strategy, which we have further classified as "focus costs," i.e., a narrow product line within a stable niche, internal efficiency, and incremental innovations when necessary. The organizational structure is a simple, functional one and decision processes are planned as described by Mintzberg and Waters (1985). The strategic gestalts categorized as belonging to this archetype are "defenders" (Miles et al, 1978), the "adaptive firm under moderate challenge" (Miller and Friesen, 1978), and "specialization" (Vesper, 1979).

Continuity

These archetypes are characterized by the maintenance of a large market share. Over time the SBU has grown, its product lines have become wide and its organizational structure is quite large. Within this category two different archetypes can be detected: a successful one and a failing type.

Maintenance

This successful archetype can be employed when the SBU has a large market share in a relatively certain and stable environment which has reached maturity or saturation. The SBU structure has grown over time and, though large, is still functional and rather mechanistic. Because of its size, the SBU can employ Porter's (1980) overall cost leadership strategy in order to remain a dominant force in the market. Decision-making processes are planned (Mintzberg, 1973; Mintzberg and Waters, 1985), which is necessary if overall cost leadership is to be retained. The strategic gestalts categorized as belonging to this archetype are "consolidation" (Wissema et al, 1980), "continuity" and "maintenance" (Galbraith and Schendel, 1983), and the "dominant firm" (Miller and Friesen, 1978).

Stagnation

This failure archetype is also a continuity type. However, in contrast to the maintenance type, this one is characterized by incongruity between the SBU structure, environment, and strategy content. The SBU has grown large, bureaucratic and rigid while the environment has become hostile and dynamic. Decision-making processes are routine and, like strategy content, is based on past experience and tradition. Therefore, we call the strategic process imposed; it is imposed upon the SBU as a result of historic forces. The main problem is that this type of strategy making does not fit the changing environment and does not provide tools to adapt to the changes in the environment. The strategic gestalts categorized as belonging to this archetype are the "stagnant bureaucracy" (Miller and Friesen, 1978), the "reactor" (Miles et al, 1978) and "stuck-in-the-middle" (Porter, 1980).

Survival

This is the last category within the phase of settling down and includes two archetypes; a success and a failure type. SBUs which employ these strategies have large decentralized structures and exist in hostile, complex, and dynamic environments.

Staying alive

This successful archetype fits large, decentralized SBUs existing in environments which have become hostile, complex and dynamic, as for instance can be the case with industries which have reached the stage of late maturity or saturation. The SBU emphasizes cost-efficient methods in order to stay competitive, but at the same time, being aware of the changes in the environment, accommodates for incremental change as well. Enough discretion is left to the various departments to adjust to environmental changes in their domains, by employing an umbrella mode of decision making (Mintzberg and Waters, 1985). Strategic gestalts categorized within this archetype are "diversification" and "cooperation" (Vesper, 1979), "the giant under fire" (Miller and Friesen, 1978), and "consolidation" (Wissema et al, 1980). Although Miller and Friesen (1978) described large firms as belonging to this type, rather than SBUs, we propose that similar strategic behavior can be found among SBUs in environments and structures as described above.

Drifting

This archetype is described by Miller and Friesen as the "headless giant." The argumentation to categorize this type is similar to the "giant under fire." The SBU employing this archetype is large and decentralized and is situated in a hostile, dynamic, and complex environment. However, in contrast to the above-described archetype, this one is typified by a lack of leadership and lack of strategic content. Decision-making processes are imposed (Mintzberg and Waters, 1985) by the environment, and the SBU, lacking leadership and a consistent strategic content, only knows how to react to the environment.

Retrenchment strategies

The last stage of the SBU's life-cycle is one of retrenchment and decline and includes two archetypes.

Harvest

This archetype is appropriate to a SBU which is situated in a saturated or declining industry. At this stage, some of the competitors leave the industry, while others try to extend profitability for as long as possible. As a result, the environment experiences a change in competitive forces which creates a dynamic and complex situation.

The SBU in this environment has a functional structure and emphasizes profit maximization without having to invest additional resources; i.e., the firm is harvesting its products. A process type (Mintzberg and Waters, 1985) of decision making is used in order to enable the marketing and sales departments to adjust to changes in the environment. Strategic gestalts categorized in this archetype are "harvest," "cashout," and "low commitment," all three being taken from Galbraith and Schendel's (1983) taxonomy.

Contraction

This last archetype suits a SBU situated in a petrifying industry which is turning increasingly hostile. The only option left is to get out, and activity is therefore reduced and eventually ended. Any decisions that remain to be made are imposed by the environment. Strategic gestalts included in this category are "capitulation," "liquidation" (Vesper, 1979), and "contraction" (Wissema et al, 1980).

Discussion

In this paper we have presented a framework which encompasses and synthesizes eight different typologies developed over the last 15 years. This framework integrates the various aspects emphasized by each typology through the use of 16 archetypes which incorporate environment, organization life-cycle stages, structure, strategy process, and content.

Comparison of the 16 strategic archetypes included in the meta-analysis with the comprehensive list of the eight typologies provided in the appendix clearly shows that all 53 original strategic gestalts were included, except for three from the Mintzberg and Waters (1985) typology. In addition, some of the strategic gestalts from this typology were used in more than one archetype. The Mintzberg and Waters typology is unique in that it provides a theoretical framework, based on the analysis of case studies, along one dimension, namely, that of deliberateness of the strategic process. As such, the degree of deliberateness of a strategic process can lead to different strategic archetypes, as is shown in this appendix. Moreover, not all the strategic gestalts described by Mintzberg and Waters are based on cases of businesses. The ideological strategy, for instance, was not found by them, but, they say, might be found in Israeli kibbutzim. The unconnected and consensus strategies were both found in one and the same organization, which was a public one. As a result, we were unable to include these three strategies in the present framework.

Except for one archetype, the failing birth strategy, all are based on existing typologies and their strategic gestalts. This archetype was added because it has not been found in any other typology. There seem to be two reasons for its absence. First, as the firms cease to exist within a year, they are not recorded in databases or case studies, and second, the entrepreneurial stage as a whole has received little attention in the various typologies. However, since, as pointed out by Quinn and Cameron (1983), more than half of all startups fail within a short period, it seemed appropriate to add this archetype.

The framework developed and discussed is a theoretical one, based on the scheme developed by White and Hamermesh (1981), and as such, presents a holistic encompassing framework of strategic archetypes at the business level. While most of the typologies employed in this paper are theoretical or based on case studies, some are empirical. We have been able to encompass both types of typologies in our holistic framework, employing nearly all strategic gestalts found in the eight typologies. The fact that nearly all the strategic gestalts fit into the framework encompassing multidimensional archetypes shows its viability and justifies empirical testing in order to enhance its further development.

It is, of course, possible to criticize the underlying basis of most of the typologies employed here. Typologies which are based on case studies can be criticized as lacking an empirical basis, and on the grounds that the choice of cases included in a study can greatly influence the typology developed. While the typology developed by Galbraith and Schendel (1983), which is an empirically developed typology, can be criticized for the fact that the PIMS database was used, other types of studies on the subject, not included in this paper, can be criticized as well. For instance, a number of the typologies which were developed for a specific industry or product life-cycle stage are based on empirical data, but these data were taken from the PIMS database (Zeithaml, 1984; Anderson and Hambrick, 1983b; Hambrick and Schecter, 1983; White, 1986; Zeithaml and Fry, 1984). One of the problems with the PIMS database is that it does not provide information concerning the organizational structure or the process of strategy making, limiting both the development of additional typologies as well as the empirical verification of existing typologies to those which center around strategy content. This is probably one of the reasons why Porter's (1980) typology has been studied more frequently than any other typology with PIMS data (e.g., Hambrick, 1983b; White, 1986).

In addition, it is important to realize that some of the typologies employed in this framework were not reported as having been tested empirically, either by the researchers who originally developed them, or by other researchers.

Although some recent studies employ empirical data generated through means other than PIMS (Dess and Davis, 1984; Herbert and Deresky, 1987; Jemison, 1987; Robinson and Pearce, 1988; Segev,

1987) not all have tested existing typologies, and some have even added typologies. However, it seems that the time has come to test the existing typologies, instead of continually adding new ones to the existing list. A synthesis of existing typologies as presented here will enable researchers to study empirically an archetype and all its facets at once, instead of developing yet another, very similar typology which employs only part of the metavariables.

References

Aaker, D.A. and G.S. Day, 1986. "The perils of high growth markets," *Strategic Management Journal*, Vol. 7, pp. 409–421.

Abell, D.F. and J.S. Hammond, 1979. *Strategic Management Planning*. Englewood Cliffs, N.J: Prentice Hall.

Abernathy, W.J. and K.B. Clark, 1985. "Innovation: mapping the winds of creative destruction," *Research Policy*, Vol. 14, pp. 3–22.

Ackoff, R.L., 1970. *A Concept of Corporate Planning*. New York: John Wiley.

Adam, E.E., Jr., 1983. "Toward a typology of production and operations management systems," *Academy of Management Review*, Vol. 8, pp. 365–375.

Adizes, I., 1979."Diagnosing and treating life cycle problems in organizations," *Organizational Dynamics*, Summer, pp. 2–24.

"Aerosol Techniques, Inc.," 1984. In C.W. Hofer, E.A. Murray, Jr., R. Charan, and R.A. Pitts, *Strategic Management*. St. Paul, MN: West Publishing (2nd edn), p. 222.

Aguilar, F.J., 1970. *Scanning the Business Environment*. New York: John Wiley.

Aharoni, Y., 1966. *The Foreign Investment Decisions Process*. Boston: Division of Research, Graduate School of Business Administration, Harvard University.

"Albertson's Inc.," 1984. In W.F. Glueck and L.R. Jauch, *Business Policy and Strategic Management*. New York: McGraw-Hill, pp. 745–774.

Aldrich, H.E., 1979. *Organizations and Environments*, Englewood Cliffs, NJ: Prentice Hall.

Allison, G.T., 1971. *Essence of Decision: Explaining the Cuban Missile Crisis*. Boston: Little, Brown.

Almor-Ellemers, T. and E. Segev, 1988. "Strategic archetypes at the business level: a synthesis of eight typologies", The Israel Institute of Business Research, Faculty of Management, Tel Aviv University, Working Paper 979/88.

Anderson, C.R. and F.T. Paine, 1975. "Managerial perceptions and strategic behavior," *Academy of Management Journal*, Vol. 18, No. 4, pp. 811–823.

Anderson, C.R. and C.P. Zeithaml, 1984. "Stage of the product life cycle, business strategy, and business performance," *Academy of Management Journal*, Vol. 27, No. 1, pp. 5–24.

Andrews, K.R., 1971. *The Concept of Corporate Strategy*. Homewood, IL: Richard D. Irwin.
"Anheuser-Busch Companies, Inc.," 1983. In T.L. Wheelen and J.D. Hunger, *Strategic Management and Business Policy*. Reading: Addison-Wesley, pp. 451-481.
Ansoff, H.I., 1965. *Corporate Strategy*. New York: McGraw-Hill.
Anthony, R.N., 1965. *Planning and Control Systems: A Framework for Analysis*. Boston: Harvard University Press.
Ashby, W.R., 1961. *An Introduction to Cybernetics*. London: Chapman and Hall.
"AT&T Longlines Department National Account Selling," 1980. Harvard Business School Case Services Order Number 9-582-085.
Barnes, F.C., 1977. "Artisan Industries (R)." Charlotte, NC: University of North Carolina.
"BASF Corporation versus the Hilton Head Island Developers," 1983. In T.L. Wheelen and J.D. Hunger, *Strategic Management and Business Policy*. Reading: Addison-Wesley, pp. 356-370.
Beard, D.W. and G.G. Dess, 1981. "Corporate-level strategy, business-level strategy, and firm performance," *Academy of Management Journal*, No. 4, pp. 588-663.
"Beech Aircraft Corporation," 1970. Harvard Business School Case Services Order Number 0-369-008, Rev. 1970.
"Black Hills Bottling Company," 1982. In LaRue T. Hosmer, *Strategic Management: Text and Cases on Business Policy*. Englewood Cliffs, NJ: Prentice Hall, pp. 70-91.
"Blakeston and Wilson," 1947. Harvard Business School Case Services Order Number 9-347-003.
"Blow-Mold Packers, Inc.," 1976. In C.R. Christensen, N.A. Berg, and M.S. Salter, *Policy Formulation and Administration*. Homewood, IL: Richard D. Irwin (7th edn), pp. 487-519.
"Borden Inc.," 1974. Harvard Business School Case Services Order Number 1-374-013, Rev. 8/74.
Boston Consulting Group Staff, 1968. *Perspectives on Experience*. Boston: Boston Consulting Group.
Bourgeois, L.J., III, 1980. "Strategy and environment: a conceptual integration," *Academy of Management Review*, Vol. 5, No. 1, pp. 25-39.
Bower, J., 1970. *Managing the Resource Allocation Process*. Boston: Division of Research, Graduate School of Business Administration, Harvard University.
Brown, J.L. and R. Schneck, 1979. "A structural comparison between Canadian and American industrial organization," *Administrative Science Quarterly*, Vol. 24, No. 1, March, pp. 24-47.
Burgelman, R.A., 1983a. "A process model of internal corporate venturing in the diversified major firm," *Administrative Science Quarterly*, Vol. 28, pp. 223-244.
Burgelman, R.A., 1983b. "Corporate entrepreneurship and strategic management: insights from a process study," *Management Science*, Vol. 29, No. 12, pp. 1349-1364.
Burns, T. and G. Stalker, 1961. *The Management of Innovation*. London: Tavistock.
Business Month, 1986a. "A Hot New Strategy for Credit Cards," February, pp. 46-47.
Business Month, 1986b. "Airfares: Oh, What a Lovely War!" February, p. 19.
Business Month, 1986c. "Jury Clears R.J. Reynolds," February, p. 15.
Business Month, 1987a. "Compaq Computer—Take That, Goliath," December, p. 25.

Business Month, 1987b. "Fuel Ruling Hurts GM and Ford," January, p. 26.
Business Month, 1987c. "FDA Moves against Skin Creams," June, p. 9.
Business Month, 1987d. "The Goals System That Drives Cypress," July, pp. 30-32.
Business Month, 1987e. "GF Tries the Old Restructuring Ploy," November, pp. 37-39.
Business Month, 1987f. "PepsiCo's Fast Track," June, pp. 50-52.
Business Month, 1987g. "Reebok: In for the Distance," August, pp. 22-25.
Business Week, 1984. "Apple's New Crusade," November 26, pp. 405-407.
Business Week, 1986a. "A Crystal-Clear View of the World's Tiny Wonders," November 3, pp. 42-43.
Business Week, 1986b. "A French Upstart's Computer-aided Pattern Success," December 15, p. 38.
Business Week, 1986c. "Can High Tech Put Milacron Back on the Cutting Edge," November 17, pp. 75-76.
Business Week, 1986d. "Can Sir Eric Sharp Ring the Earth with Glass Cable?" November 3, pp. 82-84.
Business Week, 1986e. "Ford and VW: A Marriage of Convenience," December 8, p. 21.
Business Week, 1986f. "Is Serge Crasnianski's Instant Empire Headed for a Fall?" December 22, pp. 16-18.
Business Week, 1986g. "Spectra's Instant Success Gives Polaroid a Shot in the Arm," November 3, pp. 38-39.
Business Week, 1986h. "Thinking Ahead Got Deere in Big Trouble," December 8, p. 83.
Business Week, 1986i. "This Takeover Artist Wants to Be a Makeover Artist, Too," December 1, pp. 69-70.
Business Week, 1986j. "Watch Out, File Cabinets—Here Comes FileNet," December 1, pp. 78-79.
Business Week, 1987a. "Canon Finally Challenges Minolta's Mighty Maxxum," March 2, p. 54.
Business Week, 1987b. "For Bally, Dumping Trump Raises the Ante," March 9, p. 45.
Business Week, 1987c. "Heileman's Russel Cleary: Brawling for Breweries," March 2, pp. 61-62.
Business Week, 1987d. "High Drama from the Folks Who Brought You Godzilla '85," September 7, p. 30.
Business Week, 1987e. "Just How High Can Digital Equipment Climb?" July 20, pp. 78-80.
Business Week, 1987f. "Mellon's Turnaround Man Is Racing the Clock," September 14, p. 53.
Buzzel, R.D., and B.T. Gale, 1987. *The PIMS Principles*. New York: Free Press.
Camillus, J.C., 1981. "Corporate strategy and executive action: transition stages and linkage dimension," *Academy of Management Review*, Vol. 6, No. 2, pp. 253-259.
Cash, J.I., Jr., F.W. McFarlan, J.L. McKenney, and M.R. Vitale, 1988. *Corporate Information Systems Management: Text and Cases*. Homewood, IL: Richard D. Irwin (2nd edn).
"The Chain Saw Industry 1978," 1981. Harvard Business School Case Services Order Number 9-379-176, Rev. 8/81.
Chandler, A.D., 1962. *Strategy and Structure*. Cambridge: MIT Press.

Channon, D.F., 1973. *The Strategy and Structure of British Enterprise*. Boston: Division of Research, Graduate School of Business Administration, Harvard University.

"Charles River Breeding Laboratories," 1980. In C.R. Christensen, N.A. Berg, and M.S. Salter, *Policy Formulation and Administration*. Homewood, IL: Richard D. Irwin (8th edn), pp. 446-485.

Child, J., 1972. "Organizational structure, environment, and performance: the role of strategic choice," *Sociology*, Vol. 6, pp. 1-22.

Christensen, R.C., K.R. Andrews, J.L. Bower, R. Hamermesh, and M.E. Porter, 1982. *Business Policy*. Homewood, IL: Richard D. Irwin (5th edn).

"Club Mediterranee (A)," 1984. In C.W. Hofer, E.A. Murray, Jr., R. Charan, and R.A. Pitts, *Strategic Management*. St. Paul, MN: West (2nd edn), pp. 628-647.

"Coca Cola Company," 1986. In L. Rue and P. Holland, *Strategic Management*. New York: McGraw-Hill, pp. 238-240.

"Crown Cork and Seal Company and the Metal Container Industry," 1972. Harvard Business School Case Services Order Number 373-077.

Cyert, R.M. and J.G. March, 1963. *A Behavioral Theory of the Firm*. Englewood Cliffs, NJ: Prentice Hall.

Davidson, H.L., 1983. *Multidimensional Scaling*. New York: John Wiley.

Day, G.S., 1986. *Analysis for Strategic Market Decisions*. St. Paul, MN: West.

Dess, G.G. and P.S. Davis, 1984. "Porter's generic strategies empirically studied," *Academy of Management Journal*, Vol. 27, No. 3, pp. 467-488.

Dowdy, W.L. and J. Nikolchev, 1986. " Can industries de-mature?—Applying new technologies to mature industries," *Long-Range Planning*, Vol. 19, No. 2, pp. 38-49.

Downey, H.K., D. Hellreigel, and J. Slocum, 1975. "Environmental uncertainty: the construct and its application," *Administrative Science Quarterly*, 20, December, pp. 613-629.

Duncan, R.B., 1972. "Characteristics of organizational environments and perceived environmental uncertainty," *Administrative Science Quarterly*, Vol. 17, No. 2, pp. 313-327.

Duncan, R.B., 1979. "Qualitative research methods in strategic management," in D.E. Schendel and C.W. Hofer (eds), *Strategic Management*. Boston: Little, Brown and Company, pp. 424-447.

"DuPont's System of Financial Control," 1987. In L.L. Byars, *Strategic Management Planning and Implementation, Concepts and Cases*. New York: Harper & Row, p. 177.

Emery, F.E. and E.L. Trist, 1965. "The causal texture of organizational environments," *Human Relations*, Vol. 18, pp. 21-32.

"Federal Express Corporation (A)," 1984. In W.F. Glueck and L.R. Jauch, *Business Policy and Strategic Management*. New York: McGraw-Hill, pp. 536-546.

Fortune, 1985. "Behind the Fall of Steve Jobs," August 5, pp. 20-24.

Fortune, 1987a. "How Busch Wins in a Doggy Market," June 22, pp. 67-77.

Fortune, 1987b. "Merck Has Made Biotech Work," January 19, pp. 45-49.

Fortune, 1987c. "Why the Bounce at Rubbermaid?" April 13, pp. 49-50.

Galbraith, J.R. and D.A. Nathanson, 1978. *Strategy Implementation: The Role of Structure and Process*. St. Paul, MN: West.

Galbraith, C. and D. Schendel, 1983. "An empirical analysis of strategy types," *Strategic Management Journal*, Vol. 4, pp. 153-173.

"G.E.", 1970. Harvard Business School Case Services Order Number 9-381-174, Rev. 1970.

Glaser, B.G. and A.L. Strauss, 1967. *The Discovery of Grounded Theory: Strategies for Qualitative Research*. Chicago, IL: Aldine Publishing Company.

Glueck, W.F., 1976. *Business Policy: Strategy Formation and Management Action*. New York: McGraw-Hill.

Glueck, W.F. and L.R. Jauch, 1984. *Business Policy and Strategic Management*. New York: McGraw-Hill (4th edn).

"Gould, Inc.," 1977. Harvard Business School Case Services Order Number 9-678-184.

Govindarajan, V., 1986. "Decentralization, strategy and effectiveness of strategic business units in multi-business organizations," *Academy of Management Review*, Vol. 11, pp. 884-856.

Greiner, L., 1972. "Evolution and revolution as organizations grow," *Harvard Business Review*, July/Aug., pp. 37-46.

Grinyer, P.H. and M. Yasai-Ardekani, 1981. "Strategy, structure, size, and bureaucracy," *Academy of Management Journal*, Vol. 24, No. 3, pp. 471-486.

Hambrick, D.C., 1981. "Environment, strategy, and power within top management teams," *Administrative Science Quarterly*, Vol. 26, pp. 253-276.

Hambrick, D.C., 1983a. "An empirical typology of mature industrial-product environments," *Academy of Management Journal*, Vol. 26, No. 2, pp. 213-230.

Hambrick, D.C., 1983b. "High profit strategies in mature capital-goods industries: a contingency approach," *Academy of Management Journal*, Vol. 26, pp. 687-707.

Hambrick, D.C., 1984. "Taxonomic approaches to studying strategy: some conceptual and methodological issues," *Journal of Management*, Vol. 10, pp. 27-41.

Hambrick, D.C. and S.M. Schecter, 1983. "Turnaround strategies for mature industrial product business units," *Academy of Management Journal*, Vol. 26, No. 2, pp. 231-248.

Hambrick, D.C., I.C. MacMillan, and R.R. Barbosa, 1983. "Business unit strategy and changes in the product R&D budget," *Management Science*, Vol. 29, pp. 757-769.

"Hamlin Machinery Company, Inc.," 1982. In LaRue T. Hosmer, *Strategic Management: Text and Cases on Business Policy*. Englewood Cliffs, NJ: Prentice Hall, pp. 478-491.

Harrigan, R.K., 1980. "Strategy formulation in declining industries," *Academy of Management Review*, Vol. 5, No. 4, pp. 599-604.

Harrigan, K.R. and M.E. Porter, 1983. "End-game strategies for declining industries," *Harvard Business Review*, July/Aug., pp. 111-120.

Herbert, T.T. and H. Deresky, 1987. "Generic strategies: an empirical investigation of typology validity and strategy content," *Strategic Management Journal*, Vol. 8, pp. 135-147.

"Hershey Foods Corporation," 1983. In T.L. Wheelen and J.D. Hunger, *Strategic Management and Business Policy*. Reading, MA: Addison-Wesley, pp. 838-853.

"Hewlett-Packard Company (A): Problems of Rapid Growth," 1983. In T.L. Wheele and J.D. Hunger, *Strategic Management and Business Policy*. Reading, MA: Addison-Wesley, pp. 636-652.

Higgins, R.C., 1988. *Analysis for Financial Management*. Homewood, IL: Richard D. Irwin (2nd edn).

Hofer, C.W., 1975. "Toward a contingency theory of business strategy," *Academy of Management Journal*, Vol. 18, No. 4, p. 784.

Hofer, C.W. and D. Schendel, 1978. *Strategy Formulation: Analytical Concepts*. St. Paul, MN: West, p. 4.

Hofer, C.W., E.A. Murray, Jr., R. Charan, and R.A. Pitts, 1984. *Strategic Management*. St. Paul, MN: West (2nd edn).

Horovitz J.H. and R.A. Thitart, 1982. "Strategy, management design and firm performance," *Strategic Management Journal*, Vol. 3, No. 1, pp. 67–76.

"Hospital Affiliates International Inc.," 1980. Harvard Business School Case Services Order Number 9-377-170, Rev. 5/80.

"Hudepohl Brewing Company," 1980. Harvard Business School Case Services Order Number 381-092.

Jauch, L.R. and R.N. Osborn, 1981. "Toward an integrated theory of strategy," *Academy of Management Review*, Vol. 6, No. 3, pp. 491–498.

Jemison, D.B., 1981a. "The importance of an integrative approach to strategic management research," *Academy of Management Review*, Vol. 6, No. 4, pp. 601–608.

Jemison, D.B., 1981b. "The contribution of administrative behavior to strategic management," *Academy of Management Review*, Vol. 6, No. 4, pp. 633–642.

Jemison, D.B., 1987. "Risk and the relationship among strategy, organizational processes and performance," *Management Science*, Vol. 33, No. 9, pp. 1087–1101.

"Joseph Schlitz Brewing Company", 1984. In C.W. Hofer, E.A. Murray, Jr., R. Charan, and R.A. Pitts, *Strategic Management*. St. Paul, MN: West (2nd edn), pp. 266–302.

Jurkovitch, R., 1974. "A core typology of organizational environments," Administrative Science Quarterly, Vol. 18, pp. 380–394.

Keys, J.B. and T.R. Miller, 1984. "The Japanese management theory jungle," *Academy of Management Review*, Vol. 9, pp. 342–352.

Khadwalla, P.N., 1972. "Environment and its impact on the organization," *International Studies in Management and Organization*, Vol. 11, No. 3, pp. 297–313.

Kopp, D.G. and R.J. Litschert, 1980. "A buffering response in light of variation in core technology, perceived environmental uncertainty and size," *Academy of Management Journal*, Vol. 32, No. 2, pp. 252–266.

Kotler, P., 1972. *Marketing Management*. Englewood Cliffs, NJ: Prentice Hall, p. 13.

Kuhn, T.H., 1972. "The structure of scientific revolutions," *International Encyclopedia of United Science*, Vol. 2, No. 2, University of Chicago Press, Chicago, IL.

Lawrence, P. and J. Lorsch, 1967. *Organization and Environment*. Boston: Division of Research, Harvard Business School.

Lenz, R.T., 1980. "Environment, strategy, organization structure and performance: patterns in one industry," *Strategic Management Journal*, Vol. 1, pp. 209–226.

Lenz, R.T., 1981. "Determinants of organizational performance: an interdisciplinary review," *Strategic Management Journal*, Vol. 2, No. 2, pp. 131–154.

Lingoes, J.C., 1973. *The Guttman-Lingoes Nonmetric Program Series*. Ann Arbor, MI: Mathesis Press.

Lyles, M.A. and I.I. Mitroff, 1980. "Organizational problem formulation: an empirical study," *Administrative Science Quarterly*, Vol. 25, No. 1, pp. 102–119.

"McDonald's Corporation," 1987. In L.L. Byars, *Strategic Management Planning and Implementation, Concepts and Cases*. New York: Harper & Row, pp. 511–528.

McGlashan, R. and T. Singleton, 1978. Exxon Office Systems, Case Research Association.

Mansfield, R., D. Todd, and J. Wheeler, 1978. "Company structure and market strategy," *OMEGA*, Vol. 6, No. 2, pp. 133–138.

"Marion Laboratories, Inc.," 1984. In C.W. Hofer, E.A. Murray, R. Charan and R.A. Pitts, *Strategic Management: A Casebook in Policy and Planning*. St. Paul, MN: West, pp. 408-433.
"Mary Kay Cosmetics, Inc.," 1981. Harvard Business School Case Services Order Number 9-481-126.
"Merlin-Microwave, Inc.," 1976. In C.R. Christensen, N.A. Berg, and M.S. Salter, *Policy Formulation and Administration*. Homewood, IL: Richard D. Irwin (7th edn), pp. 50-80.
"Methocel Product Division at the Dow Chemical Company," 1982. In LaRue T. Hosmer, *Strategic Management: Text and Cases on Business Policy*. Englewood Cliffs, NJ: Prentice Hall, pp. 137-164.
Meyer, A.D., 1982. "Adapting to environmental jolts," *Administrative Science Quarterly*, Vol. 27, pp. 515-537.
Miles, R.E. and C.C. Snow, 1978. *Organizational Strategy, Structure, and Process*. New York: McGraw-Hill.
Miles, R.E. and C.C. Snow, A.D. Meyer and H.J. Coleman, 1978. "Organizational strategy, structure and process," *Academy of Management Review*, Vol. 3, No. 3, pp. 546-562.
Miller, D.M., 1981. "Toward a new contingency approach: the search for organizational gestalts," *Journal of Management Studies*, Vol. 18, pp. 1-26.
Miller, D.M., 1984. "Profitability = Productivity + Price Recovery," *Harvard Business Review*, May-June, pp. 145-153.
Miller, D., 1986. "Configurations of strategy and structure: towards a synthesis," *Strategic Management Journal*, Vol. 7, pp. 233-249.
Miller, D., 1987. "Strategy-making and structure: analysis and implications for performance," *Academy of Management Journal*, Vol. 30, No. 1, pp. 7-32.
Miller, D. and P.H. Friesen, 1978. "Archetypes of strategy formulation," *Management Science*, Vol. 24, No. 9, pp. 921-933.
Miller, D.M. and P.H. Friesen, 1980. "Archetypes of organizational transition," *Administrative Science Quarterly*, Vol. 25, pp. 268-299.
Miller, D.M. and P.H. Friesen, 1982a. "Innovation in conservative and entrepreneurial firms: two models of strategic momentum," *Strategic Management Journal*, Vol. 3, No. 1, pp. 1-25.
Miller, D.M. and P.H. Friesen, 1982b. "Structural change and performance: quantum versus piecemeal incremental approaches," *Academy of Management Journal*, Vol. 25, No. 2, pp. 237-253.
Miller, D. and P.H. Friesen, 1984. "A longitudinal study of the corporate life cycle," *Management Science*, Vol. 30, No. 10, pp. 1161-1183.
Miller, D.M., F.R. Kets de Vries, and J.H. Toulouse, 1982. "Top executive locus of control and its relationship to strategy making, structure and environment," *Academy of Management Journal*, Vol. 25, No. 2, pp. 237-253.
Milliken, F.J., 1987. "Three types of perceived uncertainty about the environment: state, effect, and response uncertainty," *Academy of Management Review*, Vol. 12, No. 1, pp. 133-143.
Mintzberg, H., 1973a. *The Nature of Managerial Work*. Englewood Cliffs, NJ: Prentice Hall.
Mintzberg, H., 1973b. "Strategy making in three modes," *California Management Review*, Vol. 16, No. 2, pp. 44-53.
Mintzberg, H., 1978. "Patterns in strategy formation," *Management Science*, Vol. 24, pp. 934-948.

Mintzberg, H., 1979. *The Structuring of Organizations*. Englewood Cliffs, NJ: Prentice Hall.

Mintzberg, H., 1983. *Power in and around Organizations*. Englewood Cliffs, NJ: Prentice Hall.

Mintzberg, H and J.A. Waters, 1982. "Tracking strategy in an entrepreneurial firm," *Academy of Management Journal*, Vol. 25, No. 3, pp. 465–499.

Mintzberg, H and J.A. Waters, 1984. "Researching the formation of strategies: the history of Canadian Lady." In R. Lamb (ed.), *Competitive Strategic Management*. Englewood Cliffs, NJ: Prentice Hall.

Mintzberg, H. and J.A. Waters, 1985. "Of strategies, deliberate and emergent," *Strategic Management Journal*, Vol. 66, pp. 257–273.

Mohr, L.B., 1971. "Organizational technology and organizational structure," *Administrative Science Quarterly*, Vol. 18, No. 4, pp. 444–459.

"Montedison, S.p.A.," 1985. Harvard Business School Case Services Order Number 4-385-065, Rev. 3/85.

Murray, A.I., 1988. "A contingency view of Porter's 'Generic Strategies'," *Academy of Management Review*, Vol. 13, No. 3, pp. 390–400.

Newsweek, 1984, "Raiders of the Lost Art: Dominance," February 6, p. 59.

Olson, R.P., 1983. "Lavalle Steel Company, Ltd." Still River, MA: Still River Press.

Perrow, C., 1970. *Organizational Analysis: A Sociological View*. Monterey, CA: Brooks/Cole.

Pfeffer, J. and G.R. Salancik, 1978. *The External Control of Organization: A Resource Dependence Perspective*. New York: Harper & Row.

Phillips, L.W., D.R. Chang, and R.D. Bussel, 1983. "Product quality, cost positions and business performance: a test of some key hypotheses," *Journal of Marketing*, Vol. 47, pp. 26–43.

Porter, M.E., 1980. *Competitive Strategy: Techniques for Analysing Industries and Competitors*. New York: Free Press.

Porter, M.E., 1983. *Competitive Advantage*. New York: Free Press.

Quinn, R.E. and K. Cameron, 1983. "Organizational life cycles and shifting criteria of effectiveness: some preliminary evidence," *Management Science*, Vol. 29, No. 1, pp. 33–51.

Ramanujam, V. and N. Venkatraman, 1984. "An inventory and critique of strategy research using the PIMS database," *Academy of Management Review*, Vol. 9, No. 1, pp. 138–151.

Robinson, R.B. and J.A. Pearce, 1988. "Planned patterns of strategic behavior and their relationship to business-unit performance," *Strategic Management Journal*, Vol. 9, pp. 43–60.

Robinson, S.J.Q., R.E. Hichens, and D.P. Wade, 1978. "The directional policy matrix-tool for strategic planning," *Long Range Planning*, Vol. 11, No. 3, pp. 8–15.

"Rockwell International (A) Municipal and Utility Division," 1982. Harvard Business School Case Services Order Number 383-019.

Rumelt, R.P., 1974. *Strategy and Economic Performance*. Boston: Harvard University Press.

Scully, J., with J.A. Byrne, 1987. *Odyssey*. New York: Harper & Row, pp. 183–188.

Segev, E., 1987. "Strategy, strategy making and performance—an empirical investigation," *Management Science*, Vol. 33, pp. 258–268.

Segev, E., 1988a. "A framework for a grounded theory of corporate policy," *Interfaces*, Vol. 18, No. 5, pp. 42–54.

Segev, E., 1988b. "A systematic comparative analysis and synthesis of two business-level strategic typologies." Unpublished manuscript.

Segev, E., 1995a. *Corporate Strategy: Portfolio Models*. London: International Thompson; Danvers, MA: Boyd and Fraser.

Segev, E., 1995b. *Navigating by COMPASS: Corporate Matrix Analysis Support System*. London: International Thompson; Danvers, MA: Boyd and Fraser.

Shapiro, B.P. and B.B. Jackson, 1978. "Industrial Pricing to Meet Customer Needs," *Harvard Business Review*, November-December, pp. 119-127.

Sharplin, A., 1984. "The Lincoln Electric Company." Monroe, LA: Northeast Louisiana University.

Shortell, S.M., 1977. "The role of environment in a configurational theory of organizations," *Human Relations*, Vol. 30, No. 3, pp. 275-302.

"Shouldice Hospital," 1983. Harvard Business School Case Services Order Number 9-683-068.

Slovacek, R., 1978. "Kroehler Manufacturing Company." Naperville, IL: North Central College.

Snow, C.C. and D.C. Hambrick, 1980. "Measuring organizational strategies: some theoretical and methodological problems," *Academy of Management Review*, Vol. 5, No. 4, pp. 527-538.

Snow, C.C. and L.G. Hrebiniak, 1980. "Strategy, distinctive competence, and organizational performance," *Administrative Science Quarterly*, Vol. 25, pp. 317-336.

Stinchcombe, A.L., 1965. "Social structure and organizations." In J.G. March (ed.), *Handbook of Organizations*. Chicago: Rand McNally, pp. 142-193.

Takeuchi, H. and J.A. Quelch, 1983. "Quality is more than making good product," *Harvard Business Review*, July-August, pp. 139-145.

"The Taylor Wine Company, Inc.," 1977. In H.R. Uyterhoeven, R.W. Ackerman, and J.W. Rosenblum, *Strategy and Organization: Text and Cases in General Management*. Homewood, IL: Richard D. Irwin, pp. 483-526.

"Texas Instruments Incorporated Management Systems," 1972. Harvard Business School Case Services Order Number 172-054.

Thietart, R.A. and R. Vivas, 1984. "An empirical investigation of success strategies for businesses along the product life cycle," *Management Science*, Vol. 30, No. 12, pp. 1405-1423.

Thompson, J.D., 1967. *Organizations in Action*. New York: McGraw-Hill.

Time, 1984. "A Tangy Super Bowl for Tampa—Redskins and Raiders: The Juiciest Possible Match," January 23, pp. 38-40.

Time, 1988. "Merck's Medicine Man," February 22, pp. 44-45.

"Tom McGuire," 1978. Harvard Business School Case Services Order Number 179-068.

Tosi, H., R. Aldag, and R. Storey, 1973. "On the measurement of the environment: an assessment of the Lawrence and Lorsch Environmental Subscale," *Administrative Science Quarterly*, Vol. 18, March, pp. 27-36.

Venkatraman, N. and J.C. Camillus, 1984. "Exploring the concept of 'fit' in strategic management," *Academy of Management Review*, Vol. 9, pp. 513-525.

Vesper, V.D., 1979. "Strategic mapping—a tool for corporate planners," *Long Range Planning*, Vol. 12, No. 6, pp. 75-92.

"Vlasic Foods Inc.," 1977. In H.R. Uyterhoeven, R.W. Ackerman, and J.W. Rosenblum, *Strategy and Organization: Text and Cases in General Management*. Homewood, IL: Richard D. Irwin, pp. 607-627.

Walker, R.F., 1984. "Portfolio analysis in practice," *Long Range Planning*, Vol. 17, No. 3, pp. 63-71.

Wall Street Journal, 1982. "Life at IBM: Rules and Discipline, Goals and Praise Shape IBMer's Taut World," April 8, p. 1.

Weiss, F.G and E.E. Tallett, 1986. "Corporate portfolio analysis," in J.R. Gardner, R. Rachlin, and H.W. Allen Sweeny, *Handbook of Strategic Planning*. New York: John Wiley.

"The Westinghouse Electric Corporation," 1976. In C.R. Christensen, N.A. Berg, and M.S. Salter, *Policy Formulation and Administration*. Homewood, IL: Richard D. Irwin (7th edn), pp. 328-342.

Wheelright, S.C. (ed.), 1979. *Manufacturing Strategy*. Boston: Harvard College.

White, R.E., 1986. "Generic business strategies, organizational context and performance: an empirical investigation," *Strategic Management Journal*, Vol. 7, pp. 217-231.

White, R.E. and R.G. Hamermesh, 1981. "Toward a model of business unit performance: an integrative approach," *Academy of Management Review*, Vol. 6, pp. 213-223.

Wissema, J.G., H.W. Van der Pol, and H.M. Messer, 1980. "Strategic management archetypes," *Strategic Management Journal*, Vol. 1, pp. 37-47.

Woodward, J., 1958. *Management and Technology*. London: Her Majesty's Stationery Office.

Woodward, J., 1965. *Industrial Organization*. London: Oxford University Press.

Yuchtman, E. and S.E. Seashore, 1967. "A system resource approach to organizational effectiveness," *American Sociological Review*, Vol. 32, pp. 891-903.

Zeithaml, C.P. and L.W. Fry, 1984. "Contextual and strategic differences among mature business in four dynamic performance situations," *Academy of Management Journal*, Vol. 27, No. 4, pp. 841-860.

Index

C

D

E

T

U

V

W

Y